WORSHIP AS EXPERIENCE:
An Inquiry into John Dewey's Aesthetics, the Community, and the Local Church

BY
PAUL R. SHOCKLEY

STEPHEN F. AUSTIN STATE UNIVERSITY PRESS

Copyright ©2018 by Paul R. Shockley

All rights reserved. Printed in the United States of America. No part of this book may be used or reproduced in any manner whatsoever without writer permission except in the case of brief quotations in critical articles or reviews.

For more information:
Stephen F. Austin State University Press
P.O. Box 13007 SFA Station
Nacogdoches, Texas 75962
sfapress@sfasu.edu
www.sfasu.edu/sfapress

Book design: Thomas Sims
Cover design: Thomas Sims
Distributed by Texas A&M Consortium
www.tamupress.com

ISBN: 978-1-62288-185-7

I dedicate this work to my mom:
Patricia Cora Smith Shockley

Even in the midst of my mother's plight with dementia,
I've experienced the power of her love.

AKNOWLEDGMENTS

Deepest appreciation is given to SFASU Academic Press for being enthusiastic of publishing a work that integrates John Dewey's philosophy within the greater framework of John Dewey's aesthetics. Many thanks to the editing work of Thomas Sims.

Special word of appreciation for the investment made into me by both the College of Biblical Studies and Stephen F. Austin State University's Division of Multidisciplinary Studies Program. I'm most appreciative of all the scholars, students, friends, and benefactors who have supported me along the way.

Words are inadequate to express my appreciation to the late Dr. Scott Austin, Dr. John J. McDermott, Dr. Gregory Fernando Pappas, and Dr. Ben Welch. Dr. Austin undergirded my efforts with qualitative friendship, strength, and philosophical support. His untimely death remains painful. Dr. McDermott is an exemplar of the live art of pedagogy. Dr. Pappas worked with me offering brilliant insight, critical feedback, and nurturing support. Their love for students and openness to engage with people like me models the type of teacher I would like to be. Dr. Welch, a kindred spirit, offered incredible encouragement.

I'm also indebted to Dr. Mike Ayers, Dr. Kim Diaz, Dr. Kent Dunnington, Matias Perez, Samuel Palacios, Dr. John Tyler, Pastor Wayne Smith, Julian Solis, Dr. Timothy Demy, Dr. Jogvan Zachariassen and Dr. Raul F. Prezas. Also, I greatly appreciate the support of dear friends, namely, Chris and Mary Gianakos, Tim and Nancy Lorensen, Patsey Crews, Dee Schmidt, and Dr. Jim Towns.

Lastly, this project would be impossible without the undergirding care, love, and support of my family: my wife Jill, and my children Schaeffer Wesley, Spencer Paul, Seth Michael, and Julianna Grace. They enlarge my vision of what it means to experience the extraordinary in the ordinary details of daily living.

TABLE OF CONTENTS

CHAPTERS

    Introduction ♦ 7

    Art as Experience ♦ 16

    Aesthetic Problems in Traditional Evangelical Churches ♦ 53

    Reengineering the Local Church:
    Seeker Sensitive & Emerging/Emergent Churches ♦ 88

    Aesthetic Problems in Seeker Sensitive & Emerging/
    Emergent Churches ♦ 131

    The Live Church ♦ 173

    Appendix One: The Aesthetic Value Of Nature In Everyday
    Living ♦ 193

    Appendix Two: Can You Tell Me How
    To Get *Out* Of Sesame Street? ♦ 211

NAME INDEX ♦ 218

BIBLIOGRAPHY ♦ 225

    Books ♦ 225
    Online Resources ♦ 232
    Periodicals ♦ 232
    Secondary Sources ♦ 234
    Unpublished Sources ♦ 243

INTRODUCTION

"Without worship, we go about miserable."
~ A. W. Tozer

Many years ago I was considering the privilege of pastoring a local church in a fast-growing and busy community. As I learned about this wonderful church, I discovered that it had once been visited by certain men who were in the business of putting a "struggling church" back on its feet. These "church medics" had been asked by the local church leadership to examine their church, just as one in the medical profession would examine the ailing body, looking at the different aspects of it to determine where damage has occurred and bring new insights in hopes that their ideas might serve as an instrument, a defibrillator of a different sort, to revive the heartbeat of the church that was losing its vitality and impact. I found their diagnoses and prescriptions both beneficial and enlightening as a scholar, pastor, and member. Their processes and results generated for me a new inquiry into what it means to have a healthy local church, one that makes a life-giving difference to their members and their the local community. This new intellectual and spiritual journey led me into a variety of situations, hundreds of conversations, pastor conferences, and large stacks of contemporary books on how to and how not to "do church," to reveal that a wide variety of churches are struggling indeed. Local churches that have a doctrinal statement that would make even the apostles and early church fathers smile, are unsure why congregational members are anemic, discontent, frustrated, and unhappy. Not only have I shared some of those particular sentiments, but I have also felt this certain restlessness, a longing for something more in corporate worship that I have experienced in other facets of daily living. In sum, I have walked out of a more than one local church service in a state of dissatisfaction, frustration, and incompleteness. Yet in my comings and goings in every day living, where I work, play and have my being and becoming, I have experienced fulfillment, peace, and even indescribable joy in the toil of my work, my responsibilities to my family and friends, the pursuit of certain goals, unexpected encounters, and even certain sufferings-given the frail and vaporous conditions of our physical lives. Those moments were not only qualitatively enriching to my personhood and particular context, they also pointed me to something or someone beyond myself. The aesthetic activity gave way to a religious experience that pointed me to God. For example, simply working in my vegetable garden has aesthetic experience qualities, a rich interplay, a dynamic cultivation between the soil and my soul.

The opposite has also been true. There have been moments in corporate activities of worship whereby the worship not only became an aesthetic experience, but also a religious one whereby affections for God were not only stirred holistically (e.g., mind, heart, and will), but also unabated. In that moment of authentic worship, God's excellences and our lowliness, His presence, and our worship converge, resulting in the Giver of divine grace receiving sincere praise, thankfulness, and holy love in an experiential union. The Scripture is animated, the proclamations are earnest and received, spiritual conviction runs deep, and religious affections for Him become satisfying. Indeed, the experience is a foretaste of what will follow for all eternity when we are in His heavenly presence (Revelation 4-5). Yet what lies beyond the walls of the local church is a monotonous grind, "a Monday" that repeats itself every remaining day of the week. The only thing that seems to get us through the dull experience of mechanical oppression and alienation is coffee, trivial diversions, the anticipation of sleep, the possibility of a future vacation, and more coffee. Thus, against the flat backdrop of gray dull colors, wearisome patterns of repetitiveness, and the ever-present fog that accompanies slow days, no breeze, and humid nights, the worship experience is a moment of catharsis, a recalibration of our humanity, a restoration of our commitments, a rebirth of our dreams, and a welcoming rescue from the poisonous vice of apathy.

While we may contend that the contrariety of our experiences are part and parcel of the human condition, especially given the empirical fact of our personal depravity and existential Godward longings, I have continued to investigate common denominators that help explain the consequential shortcomings of corporate church worship. One particular malady I have discovered seems to emerge wherever I go, namely, the failure to rightly do aesthetics. What I discovered not only changes the way I perceive and engage activities of corporate expressions of worship, but also affects deeply the way I go about a wide array of ordinary daily activities such as teaching and mentoring students, fulfilling my obligations, and caring for those in my spheres of influence.

THE PROBLEM OF AESTHETIC EXPERIENCE

In particular, my inquiry revolves primarily around the nature of aesthetic experience and how churches relate to the community in which they are embedded. All too often I have experienced a worship service that is either conducted in a manner that is mechanical and routine or indulgent and sensational. In either case the worship experience falls short of what it could be. The worship service is either forgettable or disconnected. But in both cases it is not qualitatively nutritious, that is, it fails to feed me. Thus, I leave the worship service anemic because the practical aesthetic problems (horizontal level) became roadblocks to worshipping God (vertical level). The service did not rouse, stir, or awaken my mind, heart, and will, prove to be existentially relevant, or enrich my situational setting in a meaningful way. While it is certainly true there is a certain disposition, mindset, and responsibility that I am to bring to the corporate worship whereby my personhood and contribution affects the conditions and qualities of aesthetic experiences, my concerns here are the anemic practices evidenced in corporate worship that can hinder one's worship of the one and only Triune God. These contrasting experiences found in the local church vs. God's creation reminds me of Vincent van Gogh's 1889 Post-Impressionistic painting, "Starry Night." The night sky reflects God's creative glory, power, and presence while many of the homes in this nameless village softly aglow with light from within. Yet while the impressive church stands out in the center of the community with its steeple pointing upward to the starry sky (like the cypress tree), there is no light coming from within the church. The church stands large but isolated, shrouded in darkness. Why?

THE CHURCH'S RELATIONSHIP TO COMMUNITY

When it comes to the local church's relationship to the community I also find myself perplexed in many ways. Some churches disregard community altogether whereas others seek to serve community, but strictly on the pastors' terms. Others attempt to attract community to their location by using entertainment. While entertainment may be memorable, the question becomes did it qualitatively "feed" the soul. Still there are those who contextualize their message in a manner that they compromise faithfulness to the timeless truths of biblical orthodoxy (Jude 3). The anemia continues.

If I am in a particular leadership position in academic and pastoral ministry, where should my inquiry begin if I want to address these two related problems? As one whose worldview is clearly indebted to philosophers and theologians like St. Augustine, St. Thomas Aquinas, Blaise Pascal, Thomas Reid, Jonathan Edwards, C. S. Lewis, Francis A. Schaeffer, John F. Walvoord, and Charles C. Ryrie, I found myself greatly surprised when I discovered valuable answers from an unlikely source, namely, the aesthetics of John Dewey (1859-1952).

Perhaps no other philosopher of the American philosophical tradition (with the possible exception of Jonathan Edwards) has more fully and broadly addressed the aesthetics of experience than John Dewey. This elusive philosopher explored the nature of aesthetic experience in everyday living incorporating rich terms such as the doing and the undergoing, tension, consummation, inner harmony, and the unaesthetic. He broke the museum windows and purged the rich man's vaults of art-products in order that we all might experience intensified works of art in everyday events, doings, and sufferings.[1] He offered a new way of looking at our encounters, difficulties, successes, disappointments, and delights. This was very surprising since I too was quick to dismiss the philosophy of John Dewey given his naturalistic worldview and the consequences that flowed from his writings in American thought and life. In essence, I found Dewey's aesthetic insights to be commonsensical and valuable in addressing aesthetic problems in society and the local church. The sources of and remedy for aesthetic anemia in experience are similar. [2]

---

[1] John Dewey, *Art as Experience* (New York: Penguin Press, 1934, 2005), 2.

[2] *Four Views on Christianity and Philosophy*, edited by Paul Gould and Richard Brian Davis, four major views of Christianity's relationship to philosophy are debated: (1) Conflict view—philosophy is superior to Christianity in both truth and as a way of life; (2) Covenant view—Christianity is superior to philosophy in both truth and as a way of life; (3) Convergence view—Christianity is not only confirmed by philosophy, but also completes philosophy;

Therefore, the central question pursued in this inquiry is what beneficial insights can be gleaned for the local church from the philosophy of John Dewey.[3] More specifically, we will examine the aesthetics of four problem churches and two recent movements within the evangelical tradition. We will use John Dewey's aesthetics in order to help us understand why worship services in local churches drift toward the non-aesthetic. I define "non-aesthetic" in this setting as being conducted in a manner that is humdrum, mechanical, and routine or in a manner that is aimless, incoherent, and indulgent. Both extremes are enemies to aesthetic experience, for they are out of balance. We will also use Dewey to investigate whether and how churches use art-products in relation to certain activities to bridge the disparity between themselves and community.[4] In sum, when we apply Dewey's philosophy to a worship service in a local church, evaluate its aesthetic strengths and weaknesses, and explore how the church can better relate to community, his acute insights will bring important issues to light and perhaps revitalize or create aesthetic activities local churches need to consistently practice for internal health, organic growth, and significant presence and contribution to community.

Our inquiry will involve five sequential areas of thought. In order to better understand how Dewey's aesthetics may benefit the local church, we must first examine his major ideas in *Art as Experience* (1934). Thus, Chapter 2 will be an exposition of Dewey's aesthetics whereby we will consider four questions that summarize his contribution to philosophical aesthetics. The questions are: What is Dewey's starting point for aesthetics? What distinguishes aesthetic experiences or activities from

---

(4) Conformation view—re-conceiving philosophy in Christ-shaped terms [Grand Rapids: Zondervan, 2016, 19]. The position assumed in this work is a convergence view.

[3] Unless other wise stated, citations of John Dewey's works are from the thirty-seven volume critical edition published by Southern Illinois University Press under the editorship of Jo Ann Boydston. Citations give text abbreviation, series abbreviation, followed by volume number and page number. Series abbreviations for *The Collected Works*:

EW   *The Early Works* (1882-98)
MW   *The Middle Works* (1899-1924)
LW   *The Later Works* (1925-53)

[4] Unless otherwise stated, when I refer to "church" I'm referring to the local assembly, not the church universal. While this information is readily available in numerous sources, Earl D. Radmacher, *The Nature of the Church: A Biblical and Historical Study,* offers an excellent summary of the usage of *ekklesia* in classical Greek, the Septuagint, and New Testament Greek (Chicago: Moody Press, 1972).

others? What is his criticism of the "museum conception of art"? Lastly, what is the significance for Dewey of our activities having or not having aesthetic quality?

In Chapter 3 I will offer an aesthetic philosophical and theological diagnosis of the local church by investigating four types of unhealthy churches. All four churches are real. The first type, the "elite" church, promotes an aesthetic that is exclusively reserved for certain members of community. The second type, the "broken" church, has separated or divorced itself from community. The third type, the "humdrum" church, ignores the aesthetic, for its members are preoccupied with the routine and afraid of change. This church not only glorifies the past, but is also unwilling to embrace change. The fourth type, the "sensational" church, promotes a non-nutritious aesthetic, one that is characterized by indulgence.

In Chapter 4 our attention will be directed to two recent and pervasive critiques of the traditional church: "seeker-sensitive" critique and the "emerging" critique. Both movements recognize a gap, that is, a cultural discontinuity (e.g., art-products, behavior, practices) between traditional churches and community. Thus, these two movements offer a way that the local church may bridge this gap in order to proclaim the gospel message and make a life-giving difference in community. The seeker-sensitive paradigm seeks to correct this culture gaps by appealing to business paradigms or marketing theories and practices to restructure the local church. In essence, the seeker church strives to be "culturally inviting." Traditional aesthetics of historical and liturgical elements are stripped and replaced with contemporary forms of entertainment. This church targets felt-needs through mass marketing. The latest technology is used to aesthetically enhance the worship experience. The second critique is identified by the term "emerging." Though emerging churches vary according to their particular context, they argue that the traditional local church and the seeker-sensitive church are aligned with the Enlightenment, namely, a late eighteenth-century scientific, social, and political revolution that advanced human rationality, personal autonomy, and the scientific method to create better people and better societies.[5] Through various means emerging

---

[5] *Cambridge Dictionary of Philosophy*, ed. Robert Audi. 2nd ed. (Cambridge, UK: Cambridge University Press, 1995, 1999), 266. Paul R. Shockley, "Postmodernism as a Basis for Society?" in *God of the Bible and Other Gods* by Robert P. Lightner (Grand Rapids, MI: Kregel, 1998), 198.

churches seek to dismantle the relationship between church thought and practice from modernism. For example, emerging churches seek to reconstruct religious worship in terms that are creative, pluralistic, experiential, and sensory, and advocate an ecclesiology that is more concerned with the church's mission than with its form or authority.

My argument in Chapter 5 will attempt to show that the "seeker-sensitive" critique and "emerging" critique misunderstand the nature of a changing culture as well as undervalue the process of aesthetic experience. While their proposals are well meaning, their applications are inadequate because these two movements do not adequately handle the environment and our relationship to it.[6] The gap between the local church and culture will inevitably reappear or remain and their solutions may cultivate non-aesthetic activities, habits, and rituals. Moreover, by breaking away from the past in an effort to become relevant, these churches neglect the theological, biblical, and philosophical heritage received from past generations. But if the local church will continually aesthetically adjust itself to culture in appropriate ways, recognizing that the community itself changes, then it will be in a better position to interact with its particular setting and promote an aesthetic that is consistently relevant and worthwhile to the community. Though a church's aesthetics (e.g., architecture; art products; music) can adapt to its community without biblical compromise, it may still promote non-aesthetic experiences. Therefore, both adaptability and qualitative aesthetic experience within the contours of biblical orthodoxy need to be stressed.

Finally, in Chapter 6, I will offer three major lessons from our examination of these four problem churches and recent church movements. The first lesson teaches that churches fail to adequately understand the nature of aesthetic experience. Therefore, we must consider, emphasize, and value aesthetic experience, realizing that it is crucial in bridging the gap and generating a meaningful experience in the lives of people. We must focus on process and not merely end-results. The second lesson will be built on the strengths of these churches examined as we discover seven truths, that if applied, will place local churches in a better position to "take in" the moments and enjoy immediate delight, a heightened vitality, and be free of non-

---

[6] John Dewey, "From Absolutism to Experimentalism" in *On Experience, Nature, and Freedom*, ed. Richard Bernstein (Indianapolis, IN: Bobbs-Merrill, 1960), 145; xiii.

aesthetic hindrances that can hinder our worship to God. The third lesson instructs churches to contribute to society, as they once did in generations past, by seeking to produce art-products and participate in activities that will benefit both the church and the greater community.

Two last comments before we examine John Dewey's aesthetics. First, the tendency among philosophers and theologians to focus on one idea to the neglect of other related ideas lingers and often impedes growth.[7] Too many of us fail to take seriously the insights of those with whom we may disagree. Like C. S. Lewis once stated, "An open mind, in questions that are not ultimate, is useful." As one who pursues truth, goodness, and beauty in ordinary living unto the glory of God, I am open to wherever the evidence leads. I want to want be a lover of truth. Said differently, our reflective glory can be great (Genesis 1:26-27) and I am open to insights discovered by those who differ from me; they too are made in God's image. A person who is merely assimilated, processed, stripped, and indoctrinated into that which is static, closed, weak, and unforgiving has precious little to offer struggling churches or society. Like an adventurer in a foreign land or unexplored territories, I inquire into the potentialities that such an exploration might yield, no matter how preposterous it may seem to those who see no merit in the philosophy of John Dewey or Judeo-Christian thought and practice. While we may not be able to eliminate our fixed biases, moldable fluid-like influences, and noetic effects of sin, I hope to better identify with others, learn to understand, discover why we do what we do, and love others with truth and truth in love (2 John). G. K. Chesterton put it this way, "Merely having an open mind is nothing. The object of opening the mind, as of opening the mouth, is to shut it again on something solid."

And second, this work is concerned about the practical aspects of worship services and how aesthetic problems abound. These problems, at least in my own experience, have hindered me from beholding God in corporate worship. For example, when a sermon is delivered without inflexion, creative intelligence, and structured anticipation, the message falls short of what it could have been. While some people might be able to worship God in a non-aesthetic setting, it will prove fruitful to examine how worship services are done, and consequently, minimize the

---

[7] Gregory Fernando Pappas, *John Dewey's Ethics: Democracy As Experience* (Bloomington, IN: Indiana University Press, 2008), 68.

non-aesthetic activities, and cultivate aesthetic ones that will qualitative contribute to transformative corporate worship, spiritual formation, and church unity (Colossians 1:18b). Therefore, it is beyond the scope of this book to deal with the vertical level of worship.[8] Rather, this inquiry focuses on aesthetic problems practiced in the local church.

> *The only thing that consoles us for our miseries is diversion, and yet this is our greatest of miseries. For it is mainly what prevents us from thinking about ourselves, leading us imperceptibly to our ruin. Without it we would be bored, and this boredom would drive us to seek a more solid means of escape. But diversion amuses us and guides us imperceptibly to death.*
>
> ~ Blaise Pascal

---

[8] For those interested in the vertical dimensions of worship, namely, considering the pursuit, characteristics, and private and corporate worship of the God of the Bible, I recommend A. W. Tozer's two classic works, *The Pursuit of God* and *Knowledge of the Holy*. See also J. I. Packer, *Knowing God*, 20th Anniversary ed (Downers Grove, IL: InterVarsity, 1973, 1993) and John Piper's *Desiring God, Meditations of a Christian Hedonist*, revised ed. (Colorado Springs, CO: Multnomah Press, 1986, 2014). For those interested in a biblical study of worship, *Recalling the Hope of Glory: Biblical Worship from the Garden to the New Creation* by Allen P. Ross (Grand Rapids: Kregel, 2006). Lastly, Ronald B. Allen's *Wonder of Worship* (Nashville: Thomas Nelson Publishers, 2001) examines how vertical and horizontal aspects of worship can harmonize together.

ART AS EXPERIENCE

> "One of the grand defects, as I humbly conceive is this, that children are habituated to learning without understanding."
> ~ Jonathan Edwards

In order to see how John Dewey's aesthetics can be used to analyze aesthetic problems and provide beneficial solutions in the local church, we must first understand what his philosophical aesthetic insights are. Our exposition of John Dewey's aesthetics will entail answering four questions. First, what is Dewey's starting point for doing aesthetics? Second, what distinguishes aesthetic experiences or activities from others? Third, what is his criticism of the "museum conception of art?" And last, what is the significance, for Dewey, of whether our activities have or do not have aesthetic quality? Though the answers to these questions are interrelated, I will answer each question consecutively. Afterwards, a conclusion will follow.

JOHN DEWEY'S STARTING POINT

What is John Dewey's starting point for doing aesthetics? In essence, Dewey's starting point is experience, but he does not mean "experience" as understood by modern philosophy, i.e. something subjective or the content of consciousness. Instead he means lived experience as we find it in our everyday interactions and situations.[9] Dewey wanted a philosophy of art to begin with aesthetic experience, namely, those events in our lives that stand out because of their aesthetic quality, scenes that grab our attention and arouse our interest along the way. For example, the mockingbird sings perched on the blooming Rose of Sharon, the couple walks their collie down the sidewalk, and the kids play hide-and-seek in the front yard.[10] It is from those ordinary

---

[9] For Dewey's view of experience see his 1917 essay, "The Need for Recovery in Philosophy" in *The Middle Works of John Dewey*, 1899-1924, vol. 10, ed. Jo Ann Boydston (Carbondale, IL: Southern Illinois University Press, 1980) or *The Philosophy of John Dewey*, ed. John J. McDermott (Chicago: The University of Chicago Press, 1973, 1981), 58-97.

[10] Dewey states:
In order to understand the esthetic in its ultimate and approved forms, one must begin with it in the raw; in the events and scenes that hold the attentive eye and ear of man, arousing

moments that aesthetic qualities emerge. In fact, any given ordinary activity could possess aesthetic qualities.[11] Dewey writes:

> The sources of art in human experience will be learned by him who sees how the tense grace of the ball-player infects the on-looking crowd; who notes the delight of the housewife in tending her plants, and the intent interest of her Goodman in tending the patch of green in front of the house; the zest of the spectator in poking the wood burning on the hearth and in watching the darting flames and crumbling coals.... The man who poked the sticks of burning wood would say he did it to make the fire burn better; but he is none the less fascinated by the colorful drama of change enacted before his eyes and imaginatively partakes in it. He does not remain a cold spectator.[12]

But notice how the statement, "The sources of art in human experience will be learned," relate to the participants. Sources of art in human experience are found in commonplace activities involving certain qualities such as "tense grace" that is "infecting the on-looking crowd," the "delight" of the housewife, the "intent interest" of the groundskeeper in tending the green grass, and the "zest of the spectator." Any activity in principle can have aesthetic quality and not merely isolated experiences in an art gallery, museum, opera house, or theatre.

Dewey's approach to aesthetics has several consequences. First, since his starting point is "everyday events, doings, and sufferings," then what counts as aesthetic is wide-ranging.[13] It is in the usual occurrences of our days that sources of art are learned.[14] We observe and listen to an event, activity, or object in "raw experience" and, with attentive use of the five physical senses, arousal of interest takes place, enjoyment begins to be cultivated, and

---

his interest and affording him enjoyment as he looks and listens: the sights that hold the crowd–the fire-engine rushing by; the machines excavating enormous holes in the earth; the human-fly climbing the steeple-side; the men perched high in air on girders, throwing and catching red-hot bolts [Dewey, *Art as Experience*, 3].

[11] Ibid., 3.
[12] Ibid., 2
[13] Idem.
[14] Ibid., 3.

observations of learning are made.[15] We experience pleasure.[16] Descriptive and active words such as "engagement," "interest," "finding satisfaction," "genuine affection of resources" in any given activity in common life are often employed.[17]

This broad view of aesthetic engagement stands in stark contrast to the more narrow approach that would claim that aesthetic experiences only occur in relation to particular art forms such as painting, dance, and music, special exhibitions, concert halls, and museums.[18]

Since fewer limits are applied, his view is also emancipating, for we are free from exclusive classifications that generate a narrow our vision or outlook in philosophy of art. The usual rigid classifications in philosophy used to describe the aesthetic experience are questioned once we pay attention to our daily affairs and the values we ascribe to certain activities such as finishing a game, harvesting vegetables from a garden, and drinking coffee with a dear friend. Rigid classifications such as a mere examination of the formal properties of the art-piece (use of colors lines, etc) or the opinion that an art-piece must be handled as if it is not representative of anything, go against our personal experiences and create arbitrary methods regarding the value of art. Consequently, other important aspects of art are excluded. For example, we are no longer free to value the feelings of connection that emerge from an encounter with an art-piece.

---

[15] Idem.

[16] Ibid., 4.

[17] Idem.

[18] For example, George Dickie contends that authorities or members of the "artworld," which include art critics, curators, and specific patrons, have to bestow their approval on certain objects or artists in order for something or some one to be considered artistic or/and aesthetically valuable. See George Dickie, *The Art Circle: A Theory of Art* (New York: Haven, 1984). In his view of aesthetic judgments, Immanuel Kant defined the aesthetic attitude one is to possess "disinterested and sympathetic attention to and contemplation of any object of awareness whatever" [Jerome Stolnitz, *Aesthetics and the Philosophy of Art Criticism* (Boston: Riverside, 1960). Thus, from Kant, Clive Bell argued that a pure aesthetic experience is one whereby a painting must be dealt with as if it "were not representative of anything" [Clive Bell, *Art* (London: Chatto & Windus, 1947)]. In other words, there is to be no concern for such things as content because it would violate indifference to such things as conceptualization. This formalist notion that art is not to be expressive of emotion in order to focus on its form stands exclusive and reductionistic [*A Companion to Aesthetics*, ed. David Cooper (Malden: Blackwell, 1992, 1995), 23-7; 243-9]. In contrast, Dewey asserts: "In order to understand the esthetic in its ultimate and approved forms, one must bring with it in the raw; in the events and scenes that hold the attentive eye and ear of man, arousing his interest and affording him enjoyment as he looks and listens" [Ibid., 3]

There also exists a bilateral relationship between our personal experience and our situational setting. Like the health of the mother and the health of her unborn baby, we also discover that our impulses, choices, and reactions affect the conditions of our experience while the particular contexts affects us.[19]

In fact, Dewey contends that we are who we are because of our interactions with our environment, and we are subject to the nutritious qualities found within. But this awareness goes beyond recognizing this inter-penetrating relationship. We must actively engage our situation as an adventurer; we must take a risk and see what consequences come our way.[20] But this awareness goes beyond recognizing this inter-penetrating relationship. We must actively engage our situation as an adventurer; we must take a risk and see what consequences come our way.[21]

The context-bounded aspect of everyday life means that we must also pay attention to the interaction and relations that are found in the context of a concrete situation. For example, if we seek to understand the nature of a flower, we will not only study the root, stems, leaves, and petals, but we will also consider how the soil, water, sunlight, and air interact with the flower.[22] This is an interesting approach because

---

[19] R. W. Sleeper, *The Necessity of Pragmatism: John Dewey's Conception of Philosophy* (Urbana, IL: University of Illinois Press, 1986, 2001), 188; Philip W. Jackson, *John Dewey and the Lessons of Art* (New Haven, CT: Yale University Press, 1998), 45.

[20] John J. McDermott illustrates this interpenetrating relationship quite well by using uterine metaphors. We are not merely "in the world" like a movie is in a cover where no bilateral transactions and developments are taking place. No, we should "consider ourselves as being in a uterine situation, which binds us to nutrition in a distinctly organic way." We are "floating, gestating, organisms, transacting with our environment, eating all the while" [McDermott quoted in Richard E. Hart's, "Landscape and Personscape in Urban Aesthetics," 151]. While I certainly agree we affect our setting and our setting affects us, I contend our identity should be rooted in Christ (e.g., Ephesians 1:5; Romans 6:4-6; 15:7; Colossians 2:9-10; 3:1-3; Galatians 6:19-20; 1 Corinthians 6:17; 1 Peter 2:9). We are made in God's image (Genesis 1:26-27) and we best understand ourselves, each other, and even our environment, by intimately knowing Him, reflecting Him and His ways by the choices we make, the values we embrace, and even the pleasures we pursue. As a result of our intimacy with and obedience to Him, we will enrich our situational setting in the most dynamic ways.

[21] Dewey, *Art as Experience*, 61.

[22] Dewey states:
It is quite possible to enjoy flowers in their colored form and delicate fragrances without knowing anything about plants theoretically. But if one sets to understand the flowering of plants, he is committed to finding out something about the interactions of soil, water, and sunlight that condition the growth of plants [Ibid., 2].

we have inherited the habit to analyze a situation or object by dissecting it into its various parts.[23] As a result of such analysis we tend to give more careful attention to the individual parts than to the whole. But if we fail to understand how these parts relate together or interact, we not only neglect other relevant truths, but we also fail to understand the nature of that situation or object.[24] Furthermore, when we consider an object apart from its context or analyze its various parts without taking into account its interacting factors, we commit the philosophical fallacy, that is, neglecting context.[25]

Moreover, we disregard our own context in which our inquiries are made.[26]

The importance of context helps us understand why the worth and meaning of an art-product mean something to one person but something else to another, or have different meanings to the same person.[27] In other words, when we ascribe meaning to an art-product

---

[23] Edward C. Moore's comment is helpful:

It is a natural tendency in thought to analyze a complex situation, to break it up into its parts. Parts being simpler to understand than wholes, we tend to study the parts more carefully and, by this emphasis, to give them an honorific position and eventually to hypostatize them. We ignore their relations to the whole and treat as a feature of reality what is only a feature of our limited understanding. Throughout more than two thousand years of the history of thought, we have crystallized these partial aspects of experience until they have come to form such a dominant background of our thinking that we cannot conceive the universe in any other way-except as a result of a rigorous training in one of the arts or science, and even then we tend to lapse into the older view when we get out of the field in which we may be a specialist [*American Pragmatism: Pierce, James, and Dewey* (New York: Columbia University Press, 1961), 186].

[24] Dewey states:

Flowers can be enjoyed without knowing about the interactions of soil, air, moisture, and seeds of which they are the result. But they cannot be understood without taking just these interactions into account-and theory is a matter of understanding [Dewey, *Art as Experience*, 11].

[25] LW 6:5.

[26] Dewey writes:

When artistic objects are separated from both conditions of origin and operation in experience, a wall is built around them that renders almost opaque their general significance, with, which esthetic theory deals. Art is remitted to a separate realm, where it is cut off from that association with the materials and aims of every other form of human effort, undergoing, and achievement [Dewey, *Art as Experience*, 2].

[27] Dewey states:

A work of art no matter how old or classic is actually, not just a potentially, a work of art only when it lives some individualized experience. As a piece of parchment, of marble, or canvas, it remains (subject to the ravage of time) self-identical throughout the ages. As a work of art, it is recreated every time it is esthetically experienced…. But what is true of it is

or an object, we do so within a particular context or situation. For example, I may use a knife to eat, tighten a flathead screw, or defend an individual from harm.[28] These varied meanings we ascribe is not merely with objects, but can be with any given activity, relationship, or event. Therefore, we have an enriching way to look at objects, activities, and relationships within a situational setting. In other words, Dewey exhorts us to understand the particular context and community out of which a certain activity, event, or object is constructed and its relationships to other things in everyday living.

AN AESTHETIC EXPERIENCE

Now having considered Dewey's starting point, that is, experience itself, we now direct our attention to the second question of our exposition of John Dewey's aesthetics: "what distinguishes aesthetic experiences or activities from others?" In order to better understand the nature of an aesthetic experience, we will begin by distinguishing modes of experience from that which is aesthetic. We will then consider the relationship between art and experience.[29]

Let us now turn to Dewey's description.

There is a common pattern to all experiences, regardless of the degree of uniqueness of each one.[30] For example, every experience

---

equally true of the Parthenon as a building. It is absurd to ask what an artist 'really' meant by his product: he himself would find different meanings in it at different days and hours and in different stages of his own development. If he could be articulate, he would say, 'I meant just that, and that means whatever you or any one can honestly, that is in virtue of your own vital experience, get of out it.' Any other idea makes the boasted 'universality' of the work of art a synonym for monotonous identity. The Parthenon, or whatever, is universal because it can continuously inspire new personal realizations in experience [Ibid., 113].

[28] Monroe C. Beardsley, *Aesthetics: From Classical Greece to the Present* (Tuscaloosa: The University of Alabama Press, 1966), 338.

[29] The contrast I am about to make is in an effort to understand Dewey's view of aesthetic experience. It is for pedagogical purposes only. Dewey warns against the idea of assuming that they are separate experiences or should be categorized into distinct categories. Dewey asserts that the distinction between what aesthetic and artistic cannot be "pressed so far as to become a separation" [Dewey, *Art as Experience*, 49]. Interestingly, Dewey notes:

Perfection in execution cannot be measured or defined in terms of execution; it implies those who perceive and enjoy the product that is executed. The cook prepares food for the consumer and the measure of the value of what is prepared is found in consumption. Mere perfection in execution, judged in its own terms in isolation, can probably be attained better by a machine than by human art. By itself, it is at most technique, and there are great artists who are in the first ranks as technicians (witness Cézanne), just as there are great performers on the piano who are not great esthetically, and as Sargent is not a great painter [Idem].

[30] Dewey claims:

is the result of the organism and environment interacting with one another in an open-ended, temporal process.[31] In moment-by-moment living we are either at odds with our environment and face tension or we are able to make terms with our environment and enjoy equilibrium. When we are able to make terms with our environment, then in that moment we not only achieve balance, but form, namely, an ordering that occurs out of relations that both interlocks and sustains one another. There is unity between all the integral factors. Thus, when the experience runs its full course we have completion, satisfaction, or consummation.

But not all experiences lead to completion. Many of our hopes and dreams fall short of completion. Like a car that is stuck in a deep rut or out of gasoline, we are often unable to achieve equilibrium or make terms with our environment. For example, interruptions, unforeseen events, broken promises, lack of strength, trivial diversions, or a focus on the past or the future to the neglect of the present, can impede us.[32]

One critical reason why many of our experiences are unaesthetic or considered to be aberrant is that our own choices prevent them. All too often we surrender ourselves to whimsical impulses or do

---

The outline of the common pattern is set by the fact that every experience is the result of interaction between a live creature and some aspect of the world in which he lives. A man does something; he lifts, let us say, a stone. In consequence he undergoes, suffers, something: the weight, strain, texture of the surface of the thing lifted. The properties thus undergone determine further doing. The stone is too heavy or too angular, not solid enough; or else the properties undergone show it is fit for the use for which it is intended. The process continues until mutual adaptation of the self and the object emerges and that particular experience comes to a close. What is true of this simple instance is true, as to form, of every experience. The creature operating may be a thinker in his study and the environment with which he interacts may consist of ideas instead of stone. But the interaction of the two constitutes the total experience that is had, and the close which completes it is the institution of a felt harmony [Ibid., 45].

[31] Philip Jackson's understanding of Dewey's conception of experience is helpful:
Dewey invites us to think of experience differently. He asks us to abandon the convention of looking upon experience as something that happens exclusively with us, that is, as an essentially psychological concept. In its place he would substitute a conception far more inclusive, one that embraces what is being experienced as well as the experiencer. Here is the way he puts it: 'Instead of signifying being shut up within one's private feelings and sensations,... [experience] signifies active and alert commerce with the world; at its height complete interpenetration of self and the world of objects and events' (LW 10, 25). Experience, in other words, is transactional. It is not just what registers on our consciousness as are as much a part of experience as we are ourselves. When we are fully immersed in experience, its components so interpenetrate one another that we lose all sense of separation between self, object, and event [*John Dewey and the Lessons of Art*, 3].

[32] Dewey, *Art as Experience*, 45.

something in a mechanical way, and it is in those moments that our experiences become unaesthetic.[33] We will observe these choices and outcomes more closely when we look at the aesthetic problems within local churches.

In essence, there are two extremes in moment-by-moment experiences.[34] We may liken these unaesthetic choices to polarized poles.[35] On the first pole there is no appropriate "aliveness," that is, no active engagement, no qualitative interest in excellence, and no genuine affection for the task at hand. We do things in a mindless and mechanical mundane way. For example, we announce our songs mechanically with no sense of active engagement, wondrous spirit, or creativity. On the second pole there is no order to our choices, only chaos, excess, or randomness.[36] For example, consider ineffectiveness that flows from a person who gives a rambling message with no logical outline.[37] These non-aesthetic poles are enemies to an aesthetic experience because balance cannot be established.[38] Like riding a motorcycle down a freeway, a tilt too far to one side will inevitably lead to a crash.

---

[33] Ibid., 42.

[34] Dewey states:
Thus the non-esthetic lies within two limits. At one pole is the loose succession that does not begin at any particular place that ends-in the sense of ceasing-at no particular place. At the other pole is arrest, constriction, proceeding from parts having only a mechanical connection with one another. There exists so much of one and the other of these two kinds of experience that unconsciously they come to be taken as norms of all experience. Then, when the esthetic appears, it so sharply contrasts with the picture that has been formed of experience, that it is impossible to combine its special qualities with the features of the picture and the esthetic is given an outside place and status [Ibid., 41-2].

[35] Idem.

[36] Dewey gives other examples of these two unaesthetic extremes. When we organize our room in a manner that is routine [Ibid, 81] or when we are overwhelmed by passion [Ibid, 51], we have committed ourselves to an unaesthetic experience.

[37] Ibid., 81.

[38] Dewey's description of these poles are helpful:
They are the humdrum; slackness of loose ends; submission to convention in practice and intellectual procedure. Rigid abstinence, coerced submission, tightness on one side and dissipation, incoherence, and aimless indulgence on the other, are deviations in opposite directions from the unity of an experience. Some such considerations perhaps induced Aristotle to invoke the 'mean proportional as the proper designation of what is distinctive of both virtue and the esthetic he was formally correct. 'Mean' and 'proportion' are, however, not self-explanatory, nor to be taken over in a prior mathematical sense, but are properties belonging to an experience that has a developing movement towards its own consummation [Ibid., 42].

Unfortunately many of our experiences are "cut short of completion" because of a failure to achieve an appropriate balance.[39] Too much or too little effort, or too much or too little receiving causes this failure.[40] In contrast, in order for an experience to run its full course unto completion or satisfaction whereby unity is achieved, there must also be an active-consequence bilateral interplay between the situation and us. But if these two are not related to each other to form a unity, then it will not be a complete experience.[41] For example, when a pastor proclaims a message, he is giving effort and his congregation is receiving. But if the congregation is not appropriately giving, then the pastor will not be appropriately receiving.

This interplay, which is involved in a typical pattern of experience, may be described as the "doing and undergoing."[42] To help us understand this interactive relationship, consider Dewey's illustration. When a person decides to lift a stone, the lifting can be described as the "doing." In the "undergoing," "consequence," or "receiving," he feels or "suffers something: the weight, strain, texture of the surface of the thing lifted."[43] Thus an interaction takes place between one's efforts and the consequences one receives from those efforts. This process between the "doing and undergoing" continues until there is an adjustment or mutual adaptation that emerges and comes to

---

[39] Dewey contends:
There may be interference because of excess on the side of doing or of excess on the side of receptivity, of undergoing. Unbalance on their side blurs the perception of relations and leaves the experience partial and distorted, with scant or false meaning. Zeal for doing, lust for action, leaves many a person, especially in this hurried and impatient human environment in which we live, with experience of an almost incredible paucity [scantiness], all on the surface. No one experience has a chance to complete itself because something else is entered upon so speedily. What is called experience becomes so dispersed and miscellaneous as hardly to deserve the name. Resistance is treated as an obstruction to be beaten down, not an in invitation to reflection. An individual comes to seek, unconsciously even more than by deliberate choice, situations in which he can do the most things in the shortest time [Ibid., 46].

[40] Regarding "undergoing" Dewey states:
Experiences are also cut short from maturing by excess of receptivity. What is prized is then the mere undergoing of this and that, irrespective of perception of any meaning. The crowding together of as many impressions as possible is thought to be 'life,' even though no one of them is more than a flitting and a sipping. The sentimentalist and the day-dreamer may have more fancies and impression pass through their consciousness, than has the man who is animated by lust for action. But his experience is equally distorted, because nothing takes root in mind when there is no balance between doing and receiving [Idem].

[41]. Idem.
[42] Ibid., 45.
[43] Idem.

a close.[44] We are not to imagine that the "doing and undergoing" is merely one of an alternative pattern, like pistons operating in a car engine. Rather, we must think of them in relationship together, for the action in doing and the consequences in undergoing are joined together.[45] "The interaction of the two constitutes the total experience that is had, and the close which completes it is the institution of a felt harmony."[46]

To be sure, this moment of completion, or the "close" may either be positive or negative. For instance, when a loved one passes away, when a fierce storm occurs, or when a friendship ruptures, we might have completion, and memorialize it in our mind, but it will not be remembered as a joyous moment.[47] But sharing a fantastic meal together, seeing a sunset, or visiting with an old friend, can be both a positive and unforgettable experience.

Let us now elaborate on Dewey's view of aesthetic experience. Like an ordinary experience, an aesthetic moment is a temporal process of causes and effects that occur in the active engagement with one's environment. If we can adjust to the environment and the environment adjusts to us, then energies, emotions, relationships, and other factors begin dynamically accumulating, rhythmically building, and integrally organizing to the point that tensions in experience generate reinforcing balances that culminate into completion. But unlike an ordinary experience, an aesthetic is characterized with aliveness, growing clarity, endurance, fascination, intensity, balance between two opposing forces, and a memorable appreciation for the experience.[48] In sum, the genetic traits of aesthetic experience involve

---

[44] Idem.
[45] Ibid., 46.
[46] Ibid., 45.
[47] Ibid., 37-9. On this point of suffering Dewey makes an important statement:

There is,...an element of undergoing, of suffering in its larger sense, in every experience. Otherwise there would be no taking in of what preceded. For 'taking in' in any vital experience is something more than placing something on the top of consciousness over what was previously known. It involves reconstruction which may be painful. Whether the necessary undergoing phrase is by itself pleasurable or painful is a matter of particular conditions. It is indifferent to the total esthetic quality, save that there are few intense esthetic experiences that are wholly gleeful. They are certainly not to be characteristic as amusing, and as they bear down upon us they involve a suffering that is none the less consistent with, indeed a part of, the complete perception that is enjoyed [Ibid., 42-3].

[48] But how does an aesthetic experience emerge from ordinary experience? Dewey states:

the components of an ordinary experience except these components are charged, cemented, and rounded out by heightened emotions.

For example, when I paint with oils I must consciously undergo the effect of every brush stroke.[49] I have to be able to "see each particular connection of doing and undergoing in relation to the whole" that I desire to create.[50] In order to achieve this balance I need intelligence, direct sensitivity, and skill.[51] But even with my capacities, there are times when the circumstances abruptly change, and I make a costly mistake. As a result, I feel tension and no matter how hard I try, it is impossible to recover from that mistake. Not only is the painting beyond repair, but also my experience runs short of what it could have been.[52] In contrast, in order for the experience to be complete, balance is required with each stroke I take and each effect I encounter. With each sensitive effort I have an appropriate consequence. The tensions between my doing and undergoing are balanced. My experience with the art-product continues to build until all the factors are integrally translating into an ordered, organized movement, or interlocking unity. At that point, the experience I am having with the art-product reaches fulfillment.[53] To be sure, this experience will always lie between the poles of "aimlessness and mechanical efficiency."[54] Moreover, it is in that "mean" where unity of all these constituent parts is achieved.

A generalized illustration may be had if we imagine a stone, which is rolling down, to have an experience. The activity is surely sufficiently 'practical.' The stone starts from somewhere, and moves, as consistently as conditions permit, toward a place and state where it will be at rest-toward an end. Let us add, by imagination, to these external factors, the ideas that it looks forward with desire to the final outcome; that it is interested in the things it meets on the way, conditions that accelerate and retard its movement with respect to their bearing on the end; that it acts and feels toward them according to the hindering or helping function it attributes to them; and that the final coming to rest is related to that went before as the culmination of a continuous movement. Then, the stone would have an experience, and one with esthetic quality [Ibid., 41].

[49] Ibid., 47.
[50] Idem.
[51] Idem. Dewey claims:

To apprehend such relations is to think, and is one of the most exacting modes of thought. The difference between the pictures of different painters is due quite as much to differences of capacity to carry on this thought as it is to differences of sensitivity to bare color and to differences in dexterity of execution. As respects the basic quality of pictures, differences depends, indeed, more upon the quality of intelligence brought to bear upon perception of relations than upon anything else-thought of course intelligence cannot be separated from direct sensitivity and is connected, though in a more external manner, with skill [Ibid., 47].

[52] Ibid., 18.
[53] Ibid., 40
[54] Idem.

Furthermore, "An experience has a unity that gives it its name, that meal, that storm, that rupture of friendship."[55] Thus there will be a "single quality that pervades the entire experience in spite of the variation of its constituent parts."[56] Therefore, in looking back at the memory of painting, I identify the whole experience with a single pervading quality: "Stunning!"[57] That exclamation was not a result of any ordinary activity that ran its course. It was an aesthetic experience, a heightened moment that was enlightening, intense, and memorable. It stands out among my ordinary activities. First, with the use of imagination I had a desire for fulfillment to some end. Second, as the process unfolds, I find myself interested in the problems I meet on the way and there is an active engagement with all that I encounter. And third, my adjustment to the forces of obstacles and successes leads to final satisfaction. While it is impossible to go back in time and experience art-pieces the way the original spectators did, enduring art-products like the ceiling of the Sistine Chapel, Gogh's "Starry Night," or certain places like the temple area in Jerusalem, can elicit new aesthetic experiences.[58] Why? Enduring art-products give us a sense that we belong to something larger than ourselves.[59] This experience can be so intense that "we are carried out beyond ourselves to find ourselves."[60] Dewey states that in a particular moment, a work of art can operate "to deepen" and bring forth this unusual "clarity," this sense of an "undefined whole that "accompanies every normal experience."[61] In that moment we are "citizens of this vast world beyond ourselves, and any intense realization of its presence with and in us brings a peculiarly satisfying sense of unity in itself and with ourselves."[62] The aesthetic

---

[55] Ibid., 38.

[56] Idem.

[57] Idem.

[58] Ibid., 113. Dewey's evaluation of art works that endure in contrast to those that become dated will become critical later as we discuss problem churches and their inability to bridge the cultural gap.

[59] Ibid., 202.

[60] Idem.

[61] Ibid., 203.

[62] Ibid. Since consummation occurs when temporal balance is achieved by two opposing tensions, the rhythmic aspects of equilibration and disequilibration all play an integral role in shaping who we are and what we do. First, Dewey states that because of our experience with discontinuity (out of step with environment) and continuity (made terms with our environment), we gain an awareness of this constant rhythm in life. Second, those conditions, discontinuity and continuity, then become material out of which form our purposes. Third,

experience can be so "eye-opening" and "intense" that we are awakened to new connections, new experiences, and new possibilities.[63]

One critical factor that distinguishes Dewey's conception of aesthetic experience apart from other modes of experience is that aesthetic experiences can involve any given activity; it is not only experienced in the art gallery, the museum, or the opera house. In the common places of life, roots of the aesthetic find expression such as recreational places, in the home, or in the mechanic's shop.[64] In fact, the value of an object of art does not lie in the actual artistic object itself but in the experiential activity through which it was produced and perceived. But how do art-products relate to aesthetic experience?[65] "Art is a quality that permeates an experience"; it is not the experience itself.[66]

In summary, an aesthetic experience is a participatory unity between the art-product and the individual whereby there is a "felt harmony" that enriches a person's life.[67] While we explore how aesthetic experiences may occur in corporate worship, Dewey is clear that aesthetic experiences are not consigned to art museums, concert halls, and theatres; aesthetic experiences can emerge, come about, and be discovered in the *ordinary* activities, events, and scenes of our lives.

---

emotions serve as a sign of where we are in that temporal process of continuity of discontinuity. Fourth, discontinuity fosters reflection and a desire to experience continuity once again. Fifth, our desires are translated from mere emotions into purposes or goals. Sixth, in view of the goals to experience continuity again, we develop endurance to face resistance and tension. And seventh, we will cultivate tension in order to achieve balance [Ibid., 203].

[63] Dewey states:
The rhythm of loss of integration with environment and recovery of union not only persists in man but becomes conscious with him; its conditions are material out of which he forms purposes. Emotion is the conscious sign of a break, actual or impending. The discord is the occasion that induces reflection. Desire for restoration of the union converts mere emotion into interest in objects as conditions of realization of harmony. With the realization, material of reflection is incorporated into objects as their meaning. Since the artist cares in a peculiar way for the phase of experience in which union is achieved, he does not shun moments of resistance and tension. He cultivates them, not for their own sake but because of their potentialities, bringing to living consciousness an experience that is unified and total [Ibid., 14].

[64] Ibid., 3-4

[65] Richard Shusterman, "Pragmatism" in *The Routledge Companion to Aesthetics*, 103.

[66] Dewey, *Art as Experience*, 1.

[67] For example, in an illustration of a thinker in his study where he is interacting with ideas, Dewey states:
But interaction of the two constitutes the total experience that is had, and the close which completes it is the institution of a felt harmony [Ibid., 45].

Interestingly, Dewey's observations about harmony resonates with a claim made by Blaise Pascal (1623-1662):

"Beauty is a harmonious relation between something in our nature and the quality of the object which delights us."

DEWEY'S CRITICISM OF THE MUSEUM CONCEPTION OF ART

Dewey begins *Art as Experience* with a problem he intends to address in an effort to recover the continuity of aesthetics with the normal processes of living, that is, the isolation of fine art from common life.[68] In essence, when we separate an art-product from the life of a community, namely, its indigenous origins and use, by relegating it to a museum, putting it on a pedestal, or allowing it to achieve classical status, we build a wall that divides it from origins and use in experience.[69] As a result of isolation, the art-product becomes the "property rights" of the privileged few (division), aesthetic anemia (emptiness) spreads, and opportunities for art-products to enrich, improve, and transform lives (enrichment and poverty) are removed.[70] Since these art-products are not integrally related into daily living, people will likely seek to fulfill their aesthetic hunger by beholding what is "cheap and vulgar."[71]

To be sure, Dewey's problem is not with museums per se.[72] He recognizes the need to preserve art for future generations.[73] No, the problem is the isolation of fine arts from regular life. Dewey contends that art should be placed in the commonplaces of life, where it may be dynamically experienced and shared by all. We will discover that Dewey's call for recovery is practical.

Let us now explore his critique against the isolation of art from everyday life by examining the problems of origin and use, enrichment

---

[68] Dewey writes:
When an art product once attains classic status, it somehow becomes isolated from the human condition under which it was brought into being and from the human consequences it engenders in actual life-experience [Ibid., 1].

[69] Dewey claims:
When artistic objects are separated from both conditions of origin and operation in experience, a wall is built around them that renders almost opaque their general significance, with which esthetic theory deals [Ibid., 2].

[70] Ibid., 7.
[71] Ibid., 4.
[72] Idem.
[73] Ibid., 7.

and poverty, and division and need. Afterward, we will examine the benefits of integrating art-products with the organized community. As we explore this first problem, we will also uncover why an "art-product" is distinguished from "a work of art" and how "beauty" is described.

THE PROBLEM OF ORIGIN AND USE

The isolation of art from ordinary living is tragic because "art is a quality of activity."[74] Origin and use revolves around the causal conditions for the emergence of art within normal activity.[75] When we do not recognize that art materializes out of its environment and has a dynamic and on-going relationship to ordinary life, then philosophical fallacies are revealed. For example, the analytic fallacy occurs when conclusions are made about art-products apart from the context from which they are brought into being and used. These conclusions are not merely authoritative, but are quite possibly elevated and given a classification that is final.[76] Dewey also states that reductionism in aesthetic criticism is one of the great fallacies because it is oversimplification.[77] Additionally, the fallacy of selective emphasis takes place when we pass over our own cultural context from which our judgments are made.[78]

In contrast, let us consider the conditions for the emergence of the Parthenon in Athens. The Parthenon is a great example since it was originally a place to worship the Greek goddess Athena. Dewey writes:

---

[74] Ibid., 232.

[75] Ibid., 11.

[76] When isolated art-products are judged on the basis of its formal properties, emotions it provokes, or the message it generates to or within the receptor. In essence, they commit themselves to analytic reductionism for they are not taking into account the causal, contextual conditions of which the art-products emerge [Pappas, *John Dewey's Ethics*, 26].

[77] Dewey, *Art as Experience*, 328.

[78] For example, some like Clive bell abstract an art-piece from a specific context and apply to all contexts (e.g., Clive Bell's thesis of Significant Form). Ibid., 26-7. For example, Clive Bell forgets his own cultural context in which line and form were emphasized to the neglect of other relevant factors that are deemed valuable (e.g., origin and use). The relations and combinations of lines and colors are what Bell describes as "Significant Form." Bell promotes reductionism by arguing that what is aesthetically valuable is *only* a particular combination of lines and colors that stir our aesthetic emotions [*Art*, 3rd ed. (Oxford, UK: Oxford University Press, 1987), 4].

By common consent, the Parthenon is a great work of art. Yet it has esthetic standing only as the work becomes an experience for a human being. And, if one is to go beyond personal enjoyment into the formation of a theory about that large republic of art of which the building is one member, one has to be willing at some point in his reflections to turn from it to the bustling, arguing, acutely sensitive Athenian citizens, with civic sense identified with a civic religion, of whose experience the temple was an expression, and who built it not as a work of art but as a civic commemoration. The turning to them is as human beings who had needs that were a demand for the building and that were carried to fulfillment in it; it is not an examination such as might be carried on by a sociologist in search for material relevant to his purpose. The one who sets out theorize about the esthetic experience embodied in the Parthenon must realize in thought what the people into whose lives it entered had in common, as creators and as those who were satisfied with it, with people in our homes and on our own streets.[79]

We are able to make at least four observations about the Parthenon's origin and use. First, the Parthenon was created out of common need for a place to worship. It was not created as "art for art sake." Nor was it meant to postulate a culturally charged, anti-establishment, counter-cultural message.[80] The civic need was identified with religion and the Temple was an expression of that relationship to the community. So important was this religious need that the Parthenon was built overlooking the whole of Athens.

Second, this building was born out of personal and collective identity. Not only did the Parthenon emerge out of a common desire to worship Athena, the goddess to whom the Greeks collectively endeared themselves, but it was also born out of their collective desire or contextual demand to be associated with the worship of the Greek gods as a people-group. But this sociological activity was even more than just a mark of identification with the Greek goddess. The Temple affected the quality of citizens' lives. Every person would be able to

---

[79] Dewey, *Art as Experience*, 3.
[80] Ibid., 25.

physically, relationally, and emotionally connect with the Parthenon as he or she went about day-to-day living. Thus, the Athenian Temple became a storehouse of memories, a place of motivation, and a way of life.

Third, the Parthenon is a continual embodiment of meaning. Because of the transactional activity people enjoy with the Parthenon, new meaningful experiences and relationships are made. In fact, the Temple was constructed in such a way that it "continually inspire[s] new personal realizations in experience."[81] Architecture like the Parthenon can express "enduring values of collective human life."[82] This is substantiated by the fact that after almost twenty-five hundred years since its creation, millions of people continue to visit the site annually.

Treasures like the Parthenon not only shaped the people's collective identity, but also their development as persons. Why? The Parthenon was an art-product that was able to continuously inspire new realizations and relationships, dynamically enlightening activities, inquiries, purposes, and values for the citizens as they interacted with their environment in all of its stable and precarious ways.[83] The materials were constructed in such a way that it marks an experiential "way of envisaging," of "feeling" so that it "most readily" and effectively becomes material for the on-going construction of transactional interplays[84] This explains why Dewey also uses the word "universal" to describe enduring art products.[85]

---

[81] Ibid., 113.

[82] Dewey asserts:
It [architecture] 'represents' the memories, hopes, fears, purpose, and sacred values of those who build in order to shelter a family, provide an altar for the gods, establish a place in which to make laws, or set up a stronghold against attack. Just why buildings called palaces, castles, homes, city-halls, forums, is a mystery if architecture is not supremely expressive of human interests and values. Apart from cerebral reveries, it is self-evident that every important structure is a treasury of storied memories and a monumental registering of cherished expectancies for the future [Idem].

[83] Ibid., 113-4

[84] Another example may be helpful. Even though the statue of David by Michelangelo may not mean to us what it meant to the artist and its original audience, it is an art-product that is able to "speak" both generationally and cross-culturally. This is evident by the millions of people from different cultures who visit Florence every year and memorialize their particular encounter with Michelangelo's David. Thus, an enduring art-product reaches a status of celebration because it is formed out of material in such a way that it can easily and intensely "enter into the experiences of others" [Idem].

[85] Ibid., 113. Dewey states, "But as a work of art, it is recreated every time it is aesthetically experienced.... The Parthenon, or whatever, is universal because it can continuously inspire new personal realizations in experience...." [Ibid., 113]. Interestingly, in his article, "Aesthetic Universals," Denis Dutton attempts to identify universal features of aesthetics in reaction to recent trends in favor of aesthetic relativism. In essence, Dutton regards art as a natural

Fourth, the Parthenon was created and designed out of stone with "artistic engagement." The people not only identified with the Temple in worship, but the creators valued its construction. This is reflected in the superb workmanship of this temple.[86] The work does not appear to be done in a mundane or chaotic way. Instead, I suspect the stone carvers were artistically engaged given their attentiveness to form and expression. Not surprisingly, the Parthenon is considered by many to be the most perfect Doric temple ever built.[87] For Dewey, "art is a quality of doing and of what is done."[88]

Since the Parthenon became an enduring product of art, valued in every generation since its construction, it has become a source of civic

category of human activity and experience. He comments that Leo Tolstoy believed that the universal essence of art is its communicative capacity to tie people to one another, Friedrich Schiller argued that art derives from a human impulse to play, and Clive Bell discovered the essential nature of art in "Significant Form." But all such attempts to identify universal features of art share an element in common, namely, they presuppose the existence of a fundamental human nature. This human nature involves interests and desires which are uniformly and cross-culturally present in the constitution of human persons [*The Routledge Companion to Aesthetics*, 203-4].

[86] Dewey, *Art as Experience*, 339. William Temple offers an interesting insight about art and its endurance. However, instead of using the word "endure" or "universal" when speaking of such celebrated art-products, he uses "finality." Nevertheless, he makes an interesting statement that resonates with John Dewey's statement that "esthetic experience is a manifestation, a record and celebration of the live of a civilization, a means of promoting its development, and is also the ultimate judgment upon the quality of a civilization [Ibid]. For Temple, art receives a status that even science cannot achieve:

It takes a considerable time for a secure aesthetic judgment to be formed, and with regard to contemporary art there is much debate. But when common judgment is reached after long periods of discussion, it is secure as scientific theories never are. Many may be uncertain in this second quarter of the twentieth century about the aesthetic rank of Epstein as a sculptor or T.S. Eliot as a poet. But there is no serious dispute about Pheidias or Aeschylus, about Giotto, or Piero, or Botticelli, about Velasquez or Rembrandt about Dante or Shakespeare. No doubt I 'date' myself by the precise list which I select; Beethoven to Bach; but every name thus mentioned is securely established in the list of Masters; and the actual works of the earliest touch us now as they touched the hearts of those he knew them first…. It takes longer for the aesthetic judgment to become stable than for the scientific, but when it reaches stability it also achieves finality as other does not [*Nature, Man, and God* (New York: Macmillan, 1956), 158-9].

One might suggest that in a decadent culture enduring art-products would be readily disregarded. While a culture may degenerate into "rottenness," I suspect the art-products are venerated because they become a "work of art" in our experience. In other words, they speak to us in experience. But the key is to have them incorporated into in everyday living, not isolated, because if they are isolated, then they will be *ignored* by the masses and only experienced by a privileged few.

[87] John Julius Norwich, *Great Architecture of the World* (New York: Random House, 1975, 2001), 63.

[88] Dewey, *Art as Experience*, 222.

pride and future inspiration for other meaningful activities. To this day the connection between Athens and the Parthenon is so tightly woven that it is difficult to think about Athens without reflecting upon the Parthenon. Athens is identified with the Parthenon both artistically and historically.[89] We will discover that the local church should seriously consider how it is and can be identified with the community in which it is embedded.

But why distinguish an "art-product" from a "work of art?" According to Dewey, an "art-product," such as the Parthenon is not a "work of art." Rather, a "work of art" occurs when a person, such as the Athenian stone carver or the citizen cooperates with the product, so that the "outcome is an experience that is enjoyed because of its liberating and ordered properties."[90] Thus, a "work of art" is in the conduct of activities like carving stone or looking out at the Parthenon from one's porch.[91] In fact, we can extend "a work of art" to include any given activity such as gardening, playing sports, or preparing a dinner party. Or stated differently, works of art refer to aesthetic experiences within any given activity. An art-product is a physical object with the potential of becoming a "work of art" in experience. A work of art takes place when the person relates to the art-product (transactional activity) in experience. That relationship is "pregnant" with new and open possibilities, developments, processes, and relationships. Potentialities unfold and we change as we encounter, engage, and absorb these new relationships within a spatial-temporal context.

The idea of an art-product having the potential of becoming a "work of art" begs the question, "*What is beauty?*" Beauty is described by Dewey as experiencing a "marked presence of relations of fitness and reciprocal adaptation among the members of the whole whether

---

[89] Ibid., 5.
[90] Dewey claims:
A work of art no matter how old and classic is actually, not just potentially, a work of art only when it lives in some individualized experience. As a piece of parchment, of marble, of canvas, it remains (subject to the ravages of the time), self-identical throughout the ages. But as a work of art, it is recreated every time it is aesthetically experienced....The Parthenon, or whatever, is universal because it can continuously inspire new personal realizations in experience [Ibid., 113].

[91] Ibid., 222.

it be an object, situation, or deed."[92] It is a heightened emotionally charged experience of ordered relations.[93] Moments like these can come about suddenly as when we turn a bend and are immediately introduced to a valley down below that is arrayed in fall colors or when one is floating down a stream and all of a sudden a large cloud gives way to the sun and rays of light strike the water teeming with life, revealing a kaleidoscope of colors and reflections that are overwhelming.[94]

THE PROBLEM OF ENRICHMENT AND POVERTY

Marshall McLuhan once observed, "We become what we behold."[95] What McLuhan echoes in media is what Dewey proclaims about the transactional relationship with our environment.[96] Isolating art from the life of an organized community is a serious problem because our environment impacts our personhood, purposes, and pursuits. Art-products such as the Parthenon stand as an enduring or universal piece of architecture and a continual a source of embodied meanings to the life of the community. But if enduring art-products are isolated from everyday living, then enriching opportunities for fulfillment, personal

---

[92] Ibid., 135.

[93] Dewey states:
Beauty, conventionally assumed to be the especial theme of esthetics.... Is properly an emotional term, though one denoting a characteristic emotion. In the presence of a landscape, a poem or picture that lays hold of us with immediate poignancy, we are moved to murmur or to exclaim, 'How beautiful.' The ejaculation is a just tribute to the capacity of the object to arouse admiration that approaches worship.... beauty is the response to that which to reflection is the consummated movement of matter integrated through its inner relations into a single qualitative whole [Ibid., 134-5].

[94] Ibid., 17-8. This does not mean that consummatory experiences occur apart from tension. Some experiences involving activities, events, or art-products may be so surprising, dramatic, and unforeseen that the immediacy of the moment is consummatory. It may also mean that in that particular moment all of one's senses were equally "alive," meaning, that one is fully present, that is, all there, with the past being absorbed into the present and where sudden and complete interpenetration is occurring affecting every aspect of one's being.

[95] Marshall McLuhan, *Understanding Media: The Extensions of Man*, critical edition, ed. W. Terrence Gordon (Corte Madera, CA: Gingko Press, 1964, 1994, 2003), 32.

[96] Dewey states:
As the developing growth of an individual from embryo to maturity is the result of interaction of organism with surroundings, so culture is the product not of efforts of men put forth in a void or just upon themselves, but of prolonged and cumulative interaction with environment. The depth of the responses stirred by works of art show their continuity with the operations of this enduring experience. The works and responses they evoke are continuous with the very process of living as these are carried to unexpected happy fulfillment [*Art as Experience*, 28].

realizations, and delightful perceptions are diminished both personally and as a society.[97] Therefore, we will discover that the problem of isolation affects the moral, creative, and human qualities and conditions of civilization itself.[98] This will involve examining aesthetic experience and the functionality of art.

Isolation deprives people of potential aesthetic experiences in two compounding ways.[99] The isolation of art diminishes opportunities to have aesthetic experiences with art-products that influence character formation. And second, the isolation of art impoverishes community. The functionality of art is the practical ability of the art-product to serve and meet our needs as well as brings out the best in us (e.g., creativity, intelligence, skills). By isolating art-products from its origin, use, and function, we are impoverishing ourselves personally and sociologically, since art is a means to transform our lives collectively.

---

[97] Ibid., 16-17; 19.

[98] Dewey states, "The final measure of the quality of that culture is the arts which flourish. Compared with their influence things directly taught by word and precept are pale and ineffectual [Ibid., 359]." Contrary to the concerns of thinkers like Plato and Tolstoy, the moral aim of art is perhaps the most underappreciated and belittled value in today's society. But when we commit our will to the true good of others (agape love) in art, films, music, and other art products, artistic activities, and other artistic constructions, we encourage or promote intellectual and moral virtue. Consequently, when art products with the highest moral aims/values are found in the common places of daily living, even in pluralistic communities, we will all collectively benefit from them. Art can inspire greatness, stir our affections for intellectual, moral, and spiritual truths over and against our selfish bodily appetites and pleasures, bring exposure to what we want to willfully ignore and suppress as individuals and communities, engender peace, and foster hope. Given the transcendent character of natural, moral law over time, space, and culture [see J. Budziszewski's *What We Can't Not Know (A Guide*: San Francisco: Ignatius Press, 2003, 2011)], we have a good starting point to integrate moral aims into the wide array of art forms we create, value, and share. Coupled with natural, moral law's integration of Aristotle's virtue ethics into a correspondence thesis, what art products could foster or envision for the common good of the community are not only exponential but also worthwhile-not only for our present conditions, but also for our posterity. Given the empirical fact of our depravity, the pursuit of nonsensical amusement, the celebration of that which is crude, kitsch, profane, and sacrilegious, these pursuits are necessary if we are to even attempt to recover from this decadent, sensate age. Art products in ordinary places of living that promote moral qualities such as altruism, benevolence, courage, forgiveness, justice, liberty, love (agape), peace, unity, and wisdom could assist in tempering the worst in us while bringing out our very best for our collective good when they become "works of art" as Dewey observes. Thus, this mandate should be our aesthetic "categorical imperative," especially given the vaporous condition of our lives, the nature and consequences that flow from cultural rottenness, and the opportunity to propel intellectual and moral virtue into the very foundations of our society [Dewey, *Art as Experience*, 6; 26; 341- 341-3].

[99] Ibid., 13; 24-5; 39-40; 44; 48.

For example, Dewey observes:

> The material of aesthetic experience in being human-human in connection with the nature of which it is a part-is so social. Esthetic experience is a manifestation, a record and celebration of the live of a civilization, a means of promoting its development and is also the ultimate judgment upon the quality of a civilization. For which it is produced and is enjoyed by individuals, those individuals are what they are in the content of their experience because of the cultures in which they participate.[100]

Notice the theme of interpenetration between in the last sentence, "For which it is produced and is enjoyed by individuals, those individuals are what they are in the content of their experience because of the cultures in which they participate."[101] The words "produced" and "enjoyed" by individuals are intimately connected to the culture in which they live, move, and develop. Whether our immediate conditions are polluted with that which is "cheap and vulgar" or enriched by that which is "noble and enduring," we are affected by our surroundings.[102] Consider these two contrasting examples: The decay of art in the Alexandrian period and the reconnection of art and life with the Church.

According to Dewey, the decay and degeneracy of art in the Alexandrian period (330-200 BC) are reflected in the civilizations' poor imitations of "archaic models."[103] But these poor reproductions revealed a greater problem. They were a "sign of the general loss of civic consciousness that accompanied the eclipse of city-states and the rise of conglomerate imperialism."[104] As a result, theories of art and the focus on grammar and rhetoric displaced creativity. In fact, Dewey claims that, "theories about art gave evidence of the great social change that had taken place."[105] He goes on to say:

---

[100] Ibid., 339.
[101] Idem.
[102] John J. McDermott, quoted in Richard Hart's, "Landscape and Personscape in Urban Aesthetics," 151.
[103] Dewey, *Art as Experience*, 342.
[104] Idem.
[105] Idem.

Instead of connecting arts with an expression of the life of the community, the beauty of nature and of art was regarded as an echo and reminder of some supernal reality that had its being outside social life, and indeed outside the cosmos itself-the ultimate source of all subsequent theories that treat art as something imported into experience from without.[106]

In contrast, Dewey observes that the Church, even more than the Roman Empire, "served as the focus of unity amid the disintegration that followed the fall of Rome."[107] He remarks that the arts were reconnected with common life and became a bond of union. Through its services and sacraments, the Church "revived and adapted in impressive form what was most moving in all prior rites and ceremonies."[108] He states that a "sense of unity was constituted" in the daily lives of the people and that the sacraments, song, pictures, rite, and ceremony all possessed an "esthetic strand, more than by any other one thing."[109] Therefore, we should promote art-products that enrich our community in everyday life.[110] We will closely examine the role of current churches within their respective communities and how that relationship contributes to the health of the church today. But advancing such pieces that penetrate and effect the best in us, individually and collectively, becomes more pressing and difficult because of the next interrelated problem associated with the isolation of art from common life: the problems of division and emptiness.

---

[106] Idem.

[107] Idem.

[108] Idem.

[109] Idem. Dewey states:
Sculpture, painting, music, letters were found in the place where worship was performed. These object and acts were much more than works of art to the worshipers who gathered in the temple. They were in all probability much less works of art to them than they are today to believers and unbelievers. But because of the esthetic strand, religious teachings were the more readily conveyed and their effect was the more lasting. By the art in them, they were changed from doctrines into living experiences [Idem].

[110] Art that is enriching will promote such qualities as a social conscience, interpersonal relationships, artistic excellence, and collective expressions of values.

THE PROBLEMS OF DIVISION AND EMPTINESS

These two problems are grouped together because separating art-products from everyday life engenders both "class division" and "aesthetic hunger" among the life of the community. By "division" I am referring to class distinctions that are promoted when art is detached from common life.[111] Artistic objects lose their significance among us in everyday living because we come to think of art as only being found in places like galleries, museums, and homes of wealthy people.[112] Thus the idea, whether intended or not, is that fine art is a luxury of the wealthy. This seclusion of art from common life leaves a vacuum whereby we are likely to seek satisfaction from art-products that are qualitatively anemic and detrimental to community and ourselves.[113] Stated differently, the isolation of art promotes aesthetic anemia, "emptiness," or what Dewey calls "aesthetic hunger."[114] When enduring art-products are isolated from community, we develop a hunger that translates into pursuing art-products and works of art that are of both crude and of poor quality. We find the emptiness to be multi-faceted. Let us take a closer look at six consequences that flow from isolation of art from the greater community.

First, "a superior cultural status" can be cultivated when places like museums are built and art-products are collected, invested, owned, and publicly supported by the wealthy.[115] The idea is promoted that art is "not part of a native and spontaneous culture"[116] but belongs only to those who possess "a superior cultural status" or who reflect a "holier-than-thou attitude."[117] While this posture may not be specifically directed to people, it can be directed toward their "interests and occupations."[118] Hence, isolating art from commonplaces can promote aesthetic segregation among the lower socio-economic classes of society.[119]

---

[111] Ibid., 7.
[112] Dewey, *Art as Experience*, 2.
[113] This concern is not original. Plato, for example, was a fierce critic of aesthetics because of the impact it can have upon both people and the city-state. See *The Republic* by Plato: 401 B; 424 B; 605 A.
[114] Dewey, *Art as Experience*, 4.
[115] Idem.
[116] Idem.
[117] Idem.
[118] Idem.
[119] Ibid., 4.

Second, since capitalism delivered "newfound riches," people adorn their homes with costly and rare art-products.[120] As a result, in order to "certify" "good standing in the realm of higher culture," one must collect art-products.[121] Further, art-products became "insignia of tastes and certificates of special culture."[122]

Third, museums become showcases of "trophies of war" when nations pillage or conquer another and take away their art-products.[123] Consequently, art is reduced to "specimens of fine art and nothing else" as contextual origins and indigenous expressions are neglected.[124] Even though the isolation of art has served countries well (e.g., when Japan nationalized her temples), the exhibiting of one's loot from conquest reveals a relationship between the modern segregation of art, nationalism, and militarism.[125]

Fourth, when art-products are isolated from common life, artists too are affected. Since they are not integrally valued and related to the collective needs of the community, they become marginalized or venerated. As a result, individuality apart from community life emerges. They reflect this consequence by creating art-products that champion "self-expression," "independence," and "obscurity."[126]

Fifth, the isolation of art from its origin and use creates a gap between ordinary and aesthetic experience, a confusion of aesthetic values and perception.[127] By relocating art to a museum, philosophies about art find expression and development apart from common life

---

[120] Idem.
[121] Idem.
[122] Ibid., 8.
[123] Ibid., 7.
[124] Idem.
[125] Idem.
[126] Ibid., 8.
[127] Dewey writes:
Put the action of all such forces together, and the conditions that create the gulf which exists generally between producer and consumer in modern society operate to create also a chasm between ordinary and esthetic experience. Finally, we have, as the record of this chasm, accepted as if it were normal, the philosophies of art that locate it in a region inhabited by no other creature, and that emphasize beyond all reason the merely contemplative character of the esthetic. Confusion of values enters in to accentuate the separation. Adventitious matters [added from outside sources rather than intrinsic], like the pleasure of collecting, of exhibiting, of ownership and display, simulate esthetic values. Criticism is affected. There is so much applause for the wonders of appreciation and the glories of the transcendent beauty of art indulged in without much regard to capacity for esthetic perception in the concrete [Ibid., 8-9].

(e.g., "the contemplative character of the esthetic").[128] Confusion of values erupt when outside sources such as the collecting and exhibiting of art simulate aesthetic values in contrast to those values that intrinsically emerge out of ordinary experiences. Additionally, so much commendation is given to certain theories about art (e.g., formalism) that there is no capacity to see aesthetic qualities in the "events and scenes" that surround people.[129]

And sixth, division is directly linked to aesthetic hunger. When enduring pieces are unavailable to the community at large, this hunger grows and is likely to seek fulfillment in that which is poor and profane.[130] Because we are part of and impacted by our environment, our aesthetic condition worsens. This leads us to the idea of "emptiness."

The greater the isolation of enduring art-products is from human experience, the larger the need to fill this aesthetic void.[131] Consequently, we are likely to pursue what is "cheap and vulgar."[132] Perhaps the question is begged, what is the measurable difference between the true aesthetic experience and the opposite pursuit of harmful, vulgar forms? Though Dewey does not cite clear examples of the vulgar, he simply reinforces the idea of the true aesthetic moments being enriching and beneficial to the community. This necessarily rules out many "art-forms" that are offensive to the sensibilities or emerge from a historic civilization in its decline.[133]

But in order to see the other side of Dewey's criticism of the museum approach to art, we need to discuss the benefits of making art-products accessible to the community. Art-products have the power to break strongholds and bring people together, as well as the

---

[128] Ibid., 8.
[129] Ibid., 3.
[130] Ibid., 4.
[131] Dewey observes that our "impulsions" are the "beginnings of complete experience because they proceed from need; from a hunger and demand that belongs to the organism as a whole and that can be supplied only be instituting define relations (active relations, interactions) with the environment" [Ibid., 61].

[132] It is as if we are starving and what is remaining to eat is either poor in nutrition or decomposing. But the isolation of the art-product not only generates an aesthetic appetite and will likely drive us to pursue what is poor and putrid, but will also become our staple, that is, our "daily bread," since enduring art-products are not an integral part of our daily experience. Then once we are habituated to that way of eating, we may find it difficult to change. In fact, we may not even want to change.

[133] Ibid., 342.

command to affect and infect the collective life of the community.[134] Let us consider the benefits in order.

Art is able to "break through barriers that divide human beings, which are impermeable in ordinary situation" and bring them together.[135] It is out of common-life that art naturally emerges, no matter the context. Art is both a universal and unbounded form of language.[136] This seems obvious given cross-cultural appreciation of art (e.g., Japan's appreciation of Western classical music).[137] Friendship and affections find completion in artistic engagement. This also seems plain since the sources of art flourish in corporate settings and activities (social gatherings and celebrations). Art can generate communion which may take on a "definite religious" quality. Relationship between art-products and community can promote sacred spaces, meaningful rituals, endeared convictions, and shared activities. Art-products emerge from that union of fellowship and become an extension that reverberates all sorts of incidents and scenes of life (e.g., Gothic cathedral, Vietnam Memorial). The union between people becomes a reward and a hallmark, testifying to the power of art. Lastly, art-products are a reminder, a prompt, an memory aid, of the establishment of that union (e.g., the wedding ring) and its future. Art serves as a reminder of the importance of always being together. Art forged out of past unions prods us to promote and pursue future unions. Art-products tie the past and future together.[138]

---

[134] Dewey claims, "The materials of his thought and belief come to him from others with whom he lives. He would be poorer than a beast of the fields were it not for traditions that become a part of his mind, and for institutions that penetrate below his outward action into his purposes and satisfactions" [Ibid., 281].

[135] Ibid., 254. Dewey claims:
Since art is the most universal form of language, since it is constituted, even apart from literature, by the common qualities of the public world, it is the most universal and freest form of communication. Every intense experience of friendship and affections completes itself artistically. The sense of communion generated by a work of art may take on a definite religious quality. The union of men with one another is the source of the rites that from the time of archaic man to the present have commemorated the crises of birth, death, and marriage. Art is the extension of the power of rites and ceremonies to unite men, through a shared celebration, to all incidents and scenes of life. This office is the reward and seal of art. The art weds man and nature is a familiar fact. Art also renders men aware of their union with one another in origin and destiny [Ibid., 282].

[136] Dewey also states, "Continuity of meaning and value is the essence of language. For it sustains a continuing culture [Ibid., 249]."

[137] Denis Dutton, "*Aesthetic Universals*," 203-13.

[138] Dewey states, "Rite and ceremony as well as legend bound the living and the dead in a common partnership" [Dewey, *Art as Experience*, 341].

Therefore, sources of art are "part of the significant life of an organized community."[139] "The collective life that was manifested in war, worship, the forum, knew no division between what was characteristic of these places and operations, and the arts that brought color, grace, and dignity, into them."[140] Each of these communal modes of activity "united the practical, the social and the educative in an integrated whole having esthetic form."[141] In fact, social values are introduced into experience in impressive ways (e.g., dance, rituals). Important aspects of the life of the community are connected.[142] Dewey states:

> Art was in them, for these activities conformed to the needs and conditions of the most intense, most readily grasped and longest remembered experience. But they were more than just art, although the esthetic strand was ubiquitous [ever-present].[143]

And third, the power of art also has the power to affect and infect the collective life of the community. This occurs because of the interpenetrating relationship between people and their environment.[144] But this sensitivity is two-fold in that Dewey, like Plato before him, recognized the power that art-products can have in a person's experience.[145] In fact, the isolation of art or the idea of "art for art

---

[139] Ibid., 5-6. Dewey provides a number of examples of this union. In the following excerpt look closely at the descriptive words and phrases that identify this union promotes: "organically one," "one with the social purpose," intimate parts of the rites and ceremony in which the group life was consummated," "torn loose" and its relationship to "significant character," "celebrated and enforced traditions," "instructing their people," "commemorating glories," and "strengthening their civic pride" [Ibid., 6]:
Painting and sculpture were organically one with architecture, as that was one with the social purpose that the buildings served. Music and song were intimate parts of the rites and ceremonies in which the meaning of group life was consummated. Drama was a vital reenactment of the legends and history of group life. Not even in Athens can such arts be torn loose from this setting in direct experience and yet retain their significant character. Athletic sports, as well as drama, celebrated, and enforced traditions of race and group, instructing their people, commemorating glories, and strengthening their civic pride [Idem].

[140] Ibid., 5-6.
[141] Ibid., 341.
[142] Idem.
[143] Idem.
[144] Ibid., 341-3.
[145] Dewey echoes Plato's concerns of the power of aesthetics in community when he states, "Plato's demand of censorship of poetry and music is a tribute to the social and even political influence exercised by those arts" [Ibid., 341].

sake alone" divorced from interests of life would have been non-existent to ancient Greeks because art-products reflect the emotions and ideas of community. Instead, such art-products as music, poetry, and theatre, which plays an integral part of the organized life of the community, can powerfully affect our emotions, conjure ideas in our minds, and prod our wills to action.[146] Moreover, art-products can propel an idea into culture and turn something into a sweeping sensation that influences the very foundations of society.[147]

EVALUATING CHURCH ACTIVITIES

Now having considered Dewey's starting point, what distinguishes aesthetic experiences or activities from others, and his threefold criticism against the isolation of art-products from common life, we will now consider the fourth and last major question to our exposition of John Dewey aesthetics: "what is the significance for Dewey of our activities and practices having or not having aesthetic quality?"

An aesthetic experience, once more, is a heightened process of continuity that is enlightening, intense, memorable, involving active participation, perception, and appreciation. Unfortunately, too many of our daily activities are non-aesthetic, namely mechanical, mindless, mundane, or chaotic, disordered, or random. Dewey writes:

> Thus the non-esthetic lies within two limits. At one pole is the loose succession that does not begin at any particular place that

---

[146] Dewey asserts:
Under such conditions [where there were no such divisions], it is surprising that the Athenian Greeks, when they came to reflect upon art, formed the idea that it is an act of reproduction, or imitation. There are many objections to this conception. But the vogue of the theory is testimony to the close connection of the fine arts with daily life; the idea would not have occurred to any one had art been remote from the interests of life. For the doctrine did not signify that art was a literally copying of objects, but that it reflected the emotions and ideas that are associated with the chief institutions of social life. Plato felt this connection so strongly that it led him to his idea of the necessity of censorship of poets, dramatists, and musicians. Perhaps he [Plato] exaggerated when he said that a change from the Doric to the Lydian mode in music would be the sure precursor of civic degeneration. But no contemporary would have doubted that music was an integral part of the ethos and the institutions of the community. The idea of 'art for art sake' would not have been even understood [Ibid, 6].
I suspect one of Dewey's criticisms would be reductionism, namely, reducing the aesthetic value of art to objective properties such as harmony, symmetry, and proportion.
[147] Ibid., 26.

ends-in the sense of ceasing-at no particular place. At the other pole is arrest, constriction, proceeding from parts having only a mechanical connection with one another. There exists so much of one and the other of these two kinds of experience that unconsciously they come to be taken as norms of all experience. Then, when the esthetic appears, it so sharply contrasts with the picture that has been formed of experience, that it is impossible to combine its special qualities with the features of the picture and the esthetic is given an outside place and status.[148]

Because non-aesthetic activities are so common, when we encounter an aesthetic activity, we categorize the aesthetic experience outside of our normative activities. It is not a part of the flow of our daily experience, and, as a result, we do not seek it out in daily living. We plan vacations and excursions out of our ordinary routine to find aesthetic moments. Non-aesthetic experiences are not merely activities that are mechanical or random. They are enemies to what is aesthetic because they keep us from actively engaging, maintaining interest in our tasks, and finding satisfaction in those activities, practices, and rituals. Dewey contends:

> The enemies of the esthetic are neither the practical nor the intellectual. They are the humdrum; slackness of loose ends; submission to convention in practice and intellectual procedure. Rigid abstinence, coerced submission, tightness on one side and dissipation, incoherence, and aimless indulgence on the other, are deviations in opposite directions from the unity of an experience. Some such considerations perhaps induced Aristotle to invoke the 'mean proportional as the proper designation of what is distinctive of both virtue and the esthetic he was formally correct. 'Mean' and 'proportion' are, however, not self-explanatory, nor to be taken over in a prior mathematical sense, but are properties belonging to an experience that has a developing movement towards its own consummation.[149]

---
[148] Ibid., 41-2.
[149] Ibid., 42.

So without the intention of creating aesthetic experience, we become accustomed to the humdrum and look to the sensational, the exaggerated, for relief. We, of course, take our habituations, expectations, and needs into all the places we travel. Clearly, and most unfortunately, one of the most poignant areas where non-aesthetic activities, practices, and rituals are expressed is often found in our local church. Mechanical prayers, disinterested greetings, meaningless traditions, disconnected Scripture readings, and similar, overused patterns of speech in sermons and even among the people as they worship and fellowship, are only a few examples. But Dewey calls us to a different path.

Like any other aspect of culture, Dewey entreats us to take seriously the aesthetic dimensions of the church. Why? The answer, in part, is that Christian worship is a social activity that serves a purposeful function. For instance, when Jesus Christ and the disciples gathered in the upper room to celebrate the Passover (Luke 22:19) or when the apostle Paul discussed "the Lord's Supper" in First Corinthians 11, we discover that religious activity is associated with purpose, namely, the corporate worship of God.[150] But these two social activities were not merely regular practices, they were worshipful rituals combined with artistic commitment: "Do these things in remembrance of me." Thus, should we pursue these religious activities in a manner that is mechanical or disorganized? Dewey's analysis of what is and what is not aesthetic will not merely expose the mundane and chaotic, but also engender a heightened interest in doing every activity with artistic engagement, whether great or small. In fact, if we apply Dewey's analysis to the local church, then we have a practical resource, a beneficial tool, to help us examine the way we look at church worship activities and the manner in which we do them.

A WAY OF SEEING AESTHETIC PROBLEMS

Dewey's tool benefits the way we look at church activities. If experience itself is a church's starting point in the area of aesthetics, a reorientation occurs that affects the way we observe, engage, and critique church life. Aesthetic qualities are not isolated in abstract reasoning,

---

[150] James F. White, *Introduction to Christian Worship*, 3rd edition, rev. and expanded (Nashville, TN: Abingdon Press, 1980, 2000), 21.

disconnected, isolated, or cut off from "human effort, undergoing, and achievement."[151] In other words, for Dewey, we are not looking for aesthetic qualities in mere objects themselves such as the church's architecture or in an otherworldly realm. Rather, we are looking for aesthetic qualities in the way we do church worship. The manner in which we care for the property, announce upcoming gatherings, and sing a hymn or praise song can have aesthetic qualities.[152] The ordinary activities and events that surround us become extraordinary.

This vivacious disposition not only enriches and gives importance to those activities, but also provokes awareness of and the need to address the non-aesthetic. So, regardless of the ritual or event, do we find the individual activities meaningful or do they fall short of what they could be in our corporate experience? And, if not, how can we intentionally pursue change?

Dewey does not merely ask us to discern what is aesthetic and non-aesthetic. He entreats us to examine our relationship to and with our worship service, rather than separating from it. We will become sensitive to the active interplay of the choices we make and the effects we undergo from those choices. Hence, do we pursue our church services in a manner that is routine or mechanical or are we sensational and chaotic in our approach? In either case, qualitative enrichment does not take place. In the former case, the church service will be forgettable as a dream; there will be no memorable experience that generates change. In the latter case, the aesthetics may be memorable, but is devoid of meaningful nutrition. In both cases, there is no character development, whether personally or collectively. But in contrast, when there are aesthetic qualities, there will be sincere appreciation, genuine pleasure, perception, and satisfaction. A doing and undergoing will take place in that moment which will result in a transformative experience.

Dewey also calls us to develop an appreciation for "resistance" or "tension." Why? Because it is from tension that continuity and nutritious growth occur.[153] Dewey states, "Equilibrium comes about

---

[151] Dewey, *Art as Experience*, 2.
[152] Ibid., 3.
[153] Ibid., 13.

not mechanically and inertly, but out of, and because of, tension."[154] In contrast, constant contentment results in a cessation of growth. When we are "out of step" with our environment, we develop a longing to be "back in step" with it. Thus, our desires are combined with our will to improve our situation. We will face the tension and attempt to overcome it in order to achieve continuity once again in this rhythmic composition of life and experience. With each recovery from discontinuity with our environment, we will grow and develop as persons.[155] Therefore, we will not approach tension the same way. So, when a church faces a tough problem, such as changing the form or style of music in order to be germane to the changes of culture, we will attempt to overcome it, realizing that qualitative growth lies on the other side. New horizons are only a risk away. In addition to these aspects of the change in outlook, the reorientation will also infect our values. We find new worth in the exposition of Scripture and in the singing of songs as well as the way a church luncheon is arranged, the church property is cleaned, and the order of a worship service is ordered. Dewey was able to see beauty in the ordinary activities, events, and scenes of our everyday lives. He invites us to pause and see if aesthetic values are only located in ceremonial communion, baptism, and proclamation of Scripture. He reminds us to see that the sources of art are found and learned in church life: the tense grace of the musician, the delight of the audio-visual technician, and the zest of the sweet church lady who never meets a stranger.[156] In sum, everyday activities in church life become "pregnant" with values. There is no little person and no little activity. This outlook leads us to consider the second significance of aesthetic qualities: method.

A WAY OF GOING ABOUT OUR CHURCH ACTIVITIES

Aesthetic qualities are not only found in our everyday events and activities, they also emerge in the manner in which we engage our church activities. They are expressed when a given activity in the worship service becomes a "work of art." Aesthetic experience combines an activity such as singing and converts it into a medium of

---
[154] Idem.
[155] Ibid., 143.
[156] Ibid., 3.

expression.[157] "Art denotes a process of doing or making."[158].

For example, I seek to write a sermon, pray with others, or lead a communion service. I could pursue this activity mechanically with no keen interest or passion, or I could pursue this chaotically, without any order at all. Either choice is available to me. But either choice will be an unaesthetic experience. It could be a forgettable or a disastrous experience. On the other hand, if I intentionally pursue this task with utmost concentration, devote my efforts to doing it well, find satisfaction at each juncture, and care for my materials and reference tools with sincere respect, then I will be artistically engaged.[159] Guided by purpose, I take what is an indeterminate situation and creatively work through each problem I encounter. There is a two-fold relational transaction that is taking place. A doing and undergoing, a punctuated rhythm of intakings and outgoings occur. Adjustment is taking place as I am affected by the conditions of the changing environment and the environment is being affected by my efforts. My emotions are building with each problem and each success (development). Eventually the experience culminates in a sermon that is defined by a single pervading quality with me exclaiming, "Wow, that is powerful!"

Significance or worth takes place when I engage any church activity such as singing, reading Scripture aloud, or praying corporately for people in the church in a way whereby the tensions I face are reinforced into a balance that culminates into a complete experience identified by unity. Thus, in a given activity Dewey invites us to pour ourselves into our activities. Though we may fail, the impulse for success in view of past successes and the feelings of discontinuity motivate us to try. Our lives will be enriched and our community will benefit as well.

ENLARGING OUR WAY OF SEEING CHURCH ACTIVITIES

Dewey's tool enlarges our aesthetic aim in church activities. Rather than merely looking at the church's art products to see aesthetic qualities, Dewey invites us to become the canvas. In other words, art is in us, how we inquire, and go about our lives. Becoming the canvas involves three related ideas. First, the essence of art is found in the transactional

---
[157] Ibid., 290-1.
[158] Ibid., 48.
[159] Ibid., 4.

experience between our settings, not merely the art-product itself and ourselves. Second, aesthetic value is found in the integration of the aesthetic experience. Aesthetic experience should be a practical objective. And third, aesthetic experience should be our legacy.

First, given the reality that we will inevitably die, we should seize each and every moment to live a meaningful life (Ecclesiastes). Even though death haunts our very footsteps and we can be swallowed up by the unexpected, the opportunity lies before us to take advantage of the day. Like Soren Kierkegaard (1813-1815) and Howard Hendricks (1924-2013), Dewey exhorts us to not die before we actually die. This dying before death is an unaesthetic life primarily characterized by boredom or disorder, performing activities that are mechanical or random, and embracing what is mundane or what is excessive. Instead of living an unaesthetic life, and recognizing that not every single moment can be aesthetic, he urges us to take the risk and attempt to translate an indeterminate situation into an experience of consummation. If balance and completion can be achieved, then we will look upon that moment as being enriching, memorable, and satisfying.[160]

Second, aesthetic integration should be our practical target. For Dewey, aesthetic status is measured by the completeness of that integration.[161] Instead of merely focusing on the art-product and valuing its aesthetic properties, Dewey asks us to look at the integration of experience between the environment and ourselves.[162] Our goal for aesthetic experience is in ordinary aspects of church life whereby our activities, practices, and rituals are integrated into aesthetic form.[163] Here activity becomes meaningful, enriched, and purposeful rather than unaesthetic.[164]

---

[160] Dewey writes, "It is this degrees of completeness of living in the experience of making and of perceiving that makes the difference between what is fine or esthetic in art and what is not" [Ibid., 27].

[161] Ibid., 289.

[162] Ibid., 288.

[163] Ibid., 341.

[164] I personally contend that we are to also be concerned with the vertical level. Once again, we are to offer our utmost to the God of the Bible, reflecting His beauty in all that we do. For Christians, we should never pursue one without the other. Once again, the horizontal activities can hinder our beholding of God.

And third, aesthetic experience should be our legacy. Dewey states, "Art is the extension of the power of rites and ceremonies to unite men, through a shared celebration, to all incidents and scenes of life."[165] Therefore, the opportunity is also available for us to enrich our present and future generations by emphasizing educative, social, and practical activities that will promote enduring art-products. Dewey states:

> The works in which meanings have received objective expression endure. They become part of the environment, and the interaction with this phase of the environment is the axis of continuity in the life of civilization.[166]

If it were not for those art-products that emerged out of desire, need, celebration, and worship, significant past events, lives, and stories would be lost in oblivion.[167] The art-products connect the past to the present and imbue our minds with possibilities. For example, the aesthetic manner in which Scripture was copied down by scribes, the creativity expressed as seen in historical churches with stained glass windows, the use of religious symbols that adorn the church pillars, floors, and walls, the stories that Christians created, such as John Bunyan's *Pilgrims Progress*, John Milton's *Paradise Lost*, or J. R. R. Tolkien's *Lord of the Rings*, and the hymns by Fannie Crosby and Charles Wesley, all connect the past with the present.

Therefore, Dewey's tool of sorting out what is and what is not an aesthetic activity, practice, or ritual, offers a beneficial, advantageous way to analyze church activities, the manner in which we do them, and why we do them. But this aesthetic approach of studying corporate worship can also be extended to our personhood, who we are, and the moment-by-moment decisions we make. We can choose whether or not to enrich our everyday experience by developing a disposition that

---

[165] Ibid., 282.
[166] Ibid., 340.
[167] Ibid., 340-1. Dewey notes:
Apart from rite and ceremony, from pantomime and dance and the drama that developed from them, from dance, song, and accompanying instrumental music, from the utensils and articles of daily living that were formed on patterns and stamped with the insignia of community that were akin to those manifested in the other arts, the incidents of the far past would now be sunk in oblivion [Idem].

is "fully alive," advancing a purposeful integrated aim that is spiritually and aesthetically virtue driven, encouraging spiritual and aesthetic values of character formation, and leaving a spiritual and aesthetic legacy that nourishes those within our spheres of influence- all unto the glory of God.

CONCLUSION

What we discover in our study of John Dewey's aesthetics is that from ordinary events of everyday living, sources of art emerge, aesthetic qualities are expressed, and lives are improved. Museums are not the only places where aesthetic appreciation and values are declared. Art-products can also be found in the ordinary activities of life where our senses are attentive, our affections moved, and our minds inspired. And since we are related to our environment and our environment is related to us, we can enjoy the ongoing opportunities to develop our lives by focusing on those everyday activities in a manner that is qualitatively nutritious rather than in a manner that is non-aesthetic, that is, routine or disorganized. But unfortunately, one such place where aesthetic experiences are neglected or taken for granted is found in one the most central and influential aspects of the organized community, namely, the church. We will now direct our attention to the aesthetics of the local church.

> *Let each of us examine his thoughts; he will find them wholly concerned with the present or the future. We almost never think of the present, and if we do think of it, it is only to see what light it throws on our plans for the future. The present is never our end. The past and present are our means, the future alone our ends. Thus we never actually live, but hope to live, and since we are always planning how to be happy, it is inevitable that we should never do so.*
> ~ Blaise Pascal

AESTHETIC PROBLEMS IN TRADITIONAL CHURCHES

"To bring back truth, on a practical level, the church must encourage Christians to be not merely consumers of culture but makers of culture."
~ J. Gresham Machen

Using Dewey's aesthetics we will investigate four types of problem churches. While there are thousands of evangelical churches that are organically healthy, centered on Jesus Christ, clearly identified with the careful exposition, proclamation, and appropriate application of Scripture, promote aesthetic possibilities in their activities, and actively engage the community in ways that are sacrificial, genuine, and practical, these four churches serve to illustrate common aesthetic problems many churches face. First, Dewey's insights reveal an imbalance in the manner in which churches conduct their religious activities. Churches promote reductionism by focusing on one religious activity to the neglect of other related areas. This imbalance also finds expression when churches conduct their worship service in a non-aesthetic manner that is either mechanical or chaotic. And secondly, some of these churches separate themselves from community. What we will discover is that imbalance and separation promote deficiencies in meeting the practical, educative, social, and spiritual needs of the whole person and the community. While no church offers the perfect worship experience, those that are dominated by the non-aesthetic are cultivating aesthetic hunger in the attendees.

The four problem churches are as follows: the first type, the elite church, promotes an aesthetic that is exclusively reserved for its members. As a result, this church widens the culture gap that exists between itself and community. The second type, the broken church, has separated or divorced itself from community in order to maintain its own values. The third type, the humdrum church, ignores the aesthetic, for its members are preoccupied with the routine, afraid of and unwilling to embrace change, and glorify the past to the neglect of the present or the future. The fourth type, the sensational church, promotes a non-nutritious aesthetic, namely one that is characterized by indulgence and entertainment. Dewey's insights on what is and is not aesthetic, offers a beneficial tool of analysis for both the diagnosis and recovery from non-aesthetic activities. To be sure, each of these four churches examined is a real church.

With each examination, I will offer a description, highlighting particular issues for the respective church that contribute to its non-aesthetic imbalance and relationship to community. Depending on the church, different details will be included; however the role of church leadership and the members will be taken into account in each scenario. I will then offer an aesthetic analysis that will highlight strengths and address some significant problems that are common to many evangelical churches no matter their location.

THE ELITE CHURCH

This elite church is situated in a major cosmopolitan city. It was established prior to World War II and gained a reputation in the community for being politically conservative, affluent, educated, and intellectually driven. The simple architecture and the use of space emphasize a worship service that revolves around Scripture.[168] The actual worship service is centered on exegetical teaching, instruction in Bible doctrine, and a simple explanation of salvation, all drawn from a plain, normal, literal grammatical-historical method of interpretation. Little attention is given to the cultivation of interpersonal relationships, corporate fellowship, and personal testimonies.

Though there is a board of deacons that manages the business of the church, the senior pastor is its centralized and vocal authority. He is formally trained in Hebrew and Greek, biblical exposition, and systematic theology. The accurate proclamation of the Scripture is carefully protected by the pastor. There is little or no use of lay leaders to instruct adults in the exposition of Scripture. They

---

[168] White, *Introduction to Christian Worship*, 166.

demand the highest doctrinal integrity and exegetical competence in the instruction of the Bible.

Music, which is comprised of specifically chosen traditional hymns (all considered doctrinally sound) on a short rotating basis, is played by an organist or pianist and sung corporately. Typically, two hymns are sung and are led by a volunteer music leader. The music is then followed by an exegetical, historical, theological exposition of a particular book of the Bible. Some even refer to the entire worship service as a "Bible class."

In fact, the instruction itself is advanced. The predominant use of classifications, categories, formulations, and emphases upon the Greek and Hebrew etymology, grammar, syntax, and biblical history is the content of each message. An overhead may be used to show the parsing of Hebrew and Greek words and the words' syntactical relationships. Booklets, which are available at no charge, not only reflect summaries of certain doctrines presented by the pastor, but are also illustrated with charts, diagrams, and pictures. There is little use of other authorities, specialists, and insights from other evangelical traditions.

The pastor of the elite church tends to be the focal point of authority since he is the pastor-teacher of the Bible. He demands total attention. In fact, he gained a reputation for calling members of his congregation out for chewing gum, yawning, and falling asleep.

In contrast, trivial attention is given to the art of preaching sermons. In terms of the exposition of Scripture, form gives way to content in importance. Graphic designs, entertainment, multimedia, and movie and music clips are not utilized. The introduction is centered upon a thesis statement rather than a real human need or an illustration designed to "hook" the listener. The conclusion is often a restatement of the introduction. Minor emphasis is given to personal application; the Holy Spirit will make it personal for each person. The pastor stands from the pulpit and proclaims the content of his message to his congregation. The congregants are listening, writing down the pastor's textual observations and rich biblical and theological insights as they follow along in their Bibles.

The role of the audience in the church is one of a learner receiving instruction through didactic teaching. They locate their seats and listen attentively. Outside of funding missionaries and disseminating biblical and doctrinal instruction to other ministries throughout the world, no significant attention is directed toward corporately meeting the practical needs of others in the community. No activities are situated around community celebrations, social causes or protests, or other public events.

In sum, the church worship services may be described as the "Service of the Word."[169] The worship service not only reflects one central aspect of the Protestant Reformation, namely, Scripture alone, but everything else about their "bible classes" points to the acquisition of biblical and theological knowledge. Why? Scripture alone is infallible, fully authoritative, and sufficient for the life of the believer.

What are we to make of a church whose expression of worship is the careful diffusion of doctrine?[170] If we apply Dewey's analysis of what is aesthetic and what is not against the backdrop that our environment affects us and our environment is affected by us, an aesthetic experience can find expression. But two non-aesthetic problems stand out. In essence, an aesthetic experience can occur in the way the teaching lesson is constructed and how the congregation receives it. But on the other hand, one factor that could keep the experience from being aesthetic revolves around the type of didactic teaching that is taking place. The second problem involves the cultural gap between the church and community. In fact, we will discover that this latter problem takes us back to Dewey's criticism of the isolation of art-products from common life. When art-products are removed from common life, both deprivations of potential aesthetic activities occur (problem of enrichment and poverty) and fulfillment of aesthetic hunger is likely to be sought in what is crude or profane.

a. Strength. Enriching aesthetic activity can take place in the dissemination of and response to Scripture in the life of the member. When the Bible lesson is constructed in certain a way that

---

[169] Ibid., 166-7.
[170] Richard Vialdesau, *Theology and the Arts: Encountering God through Music, Art, and Rhetoric* (New York: Paulist Press, 2000), 167.

it readily marks an experiential "way of envisaging," it effectively becomes material for the construction of transactional interplays.[171] As a result, people can walk away from that lesson and claim that the church service was "powerful!" If connections were made, then the experience is memorialized. In sum, this singular aesthetic is very attractive and persuasive, emphasizing this church's distinctiveness among those who are shallow in biblical exposition, target felt-needs only, or exchange the proclamation of Bible and theology as it is for kitsch like proclamations, sentimentalities, and underdeveloped sermons. The life of the Christian mind is valued, prizing the dynamic relationship between the mind, the act of the will, and the affections of the heart (Proverbs 23:7; Psalm 19:7-11; John 17:17; Romans 12:1-2; 2 Timothy 4:1-15).[172]

The depth of this teaching can offer aesthetic opportunities for those who are unsatisfied with shallow and informal studies of Scripture they find elsewhere. As a result this church not only offers a popular teaching ministry, but also has produced some very learned Christians. Moreover, families even move to this city from other places in order to receive this in-depth instruction face-to-face. In sum, this singular aesthetic is very attractive and persuasive, causing the church to stand out among many others.

b. The problem of reductionism. Because the church's singular focus is on expositional teaching and systematic formulations of doctrine, it neglects other relevant truths and other meaningful areas of the life of the church such as the importance of interpersonal relationships, corporate fellowship, testimonies, and wide use of personal and spiritual giftedness. The displacement of individual existential, felt, practical, and other personal needs and contextual situations in which people are imbedded can take place in favor of biblical and theological doctrine. Though well meaning, the inherent value of people, personhood, and situatedness can be pushed into the background in preference for rightly knowing bible doctrine. The reasons for this shift are multifarious. To be sure, people are messy, their problems weighty, and can even be reflective of what

---

[171] Dewey, *Art as Experience*, 113-4.
[172] Ibid., 45. Peter Kreeft, *Christianity for Modern Pagans: Pascal's Pensees* (San Francisco: Ignatius Press, 1993), 176.

we try to ignore and suppress within ourselves. In fact, doctrine can be used as a mask of self-deception, and a path of diversion. Like Blaise Pascal once observed, "Without diversion there is no joy; with diversion there is no sadness. That is what constitutes the happiness of persons of rank, for they have a number of people to divert them and the ability to keep themselves in this state." [173]

While never minimalizing the importance of correctly understanding and appropriately applying the teachings of Scripture, allowing Bible doctrine to become one's worldview that reflects the disposition of Jesus Christ in moment-by-moment living (hence the need to intimately and thoroughly know biblical, systematic theology), the ever-present temptation is to prize doctrine over and against people (1 John 3:16-17). In his classic work, *True Spirituality*, Francis A. Schaeffer (1912-1984), who lamented over and reconsidered Christian life and thought given the theological and political controversies he experienced within his own denomination, wrote these words of reflection:

> The Christian is to be a demonstration of the existence of God. But if we as individual Christians, and as the church, act on less than a personal relationship to other men, where is the demonstration that God the Creator is personal? If there is no demonstration in our attitude toward other men that we really take seriously the person-to-person relationship, we might as well keep quiet. There must be a demonstration; that is our calling: to show that there is a reality in personal relationship, and not just words about it. If the individual Christian, and if the church of Christ, is not allowing the Lord Jesus Christ to bring forth his fruit into the world, as a demonstration in the area of personal relationships, we cannot expect the world to believe. Lovelessness is a sea that knows no shore, for it is what God is not. And eventually not only will the other man drown, but I will drown, and worst of all, the demonstration of God drowns as well when there is nothing to be seen but a sea of lovelessness and impersonality. As Christians, we are not to be in fellowship with false doctrine. But in the very

---

[173] Idem.

midst of the battle against false teaching, we must not forget the proper personal relationships. [174]

In fact, doctrine can even become an idol in one's life just as principles from modernism and modernity were extracted from meeting people where they are. We value systems over and against people for which they were initially intended. In her work, *Finding Truth*, Nancy Pearcey's insights into idolatry is helpful. She writes, "An idol is anything in the created order that is put in the place of God."[175] Earlier she states: "An idol is anything we want more than God, anything we rely on more than God, anything we look to for greater fulfillment than God. Idolatry is thus the hidden sin driving all other sins."

Therefore, we must love God from out of one's whole heart, mind, soul, and strength and love [*agape*] our neighbors as ourselves (Mark 12:28-34). Like two sides of one coin, understanding and real life applications are needed in both corporate worship and daily living. Reductionism and imbalance must be exchanged for the inherent values of biblical exposition and people as people made in God's image.

c. Didactic pedagogy problem. Even though aesthetic experiences do sometimes occur in the teaching, an imbalance can emerge as a result of the nature of teaching style that is practiced at this church. Two types of disproportions are obvious, and both involve the doing and undergoing.

First, when the pastor proclaims (effort) and the congregation passively receives, the pastor does not receive a proportional response. As a result, he is impoverished by the interaction with his audience even though he may receive aesthetic experiences in his preparation. Secondly, the audience does not have the opportunity to actively engage the pastor. Other than note taking, the congregation is in a passive posture (spectator). As a result, people can be aesthetically deprived. Not only is their excessive doing from the pastor and

---

[174] Francis A. Schaeffer, *True Spirituality* (Carol Stream, IL: Tyndale House Publishers, 1971, 2011), 135.
[175] Nancy Pearcey, *Finding Truth: 5 Principles for Unmasking Atheism, Secularism, and Other God Substitutes* (Colorado Springs, CO: David C. Cook Publishing, 2015), 42.

excessive receiving experienced by the congregation, but there is also deficient receiving from the pastor and deficient doing by the congregation. In contrast, if both the pastor and members are able contemplate the Scripture together, actively engaging each other as they study a given portion of Scripture, then there is an opportunity for proper adjustment and mutual relations reinforcing one another into the sort of communication that has aesthetic quality, a proper balance between doing and undergoing. Additionally, more interaction would accommodate different learning styles, thus arousing interest, and both parties would be actively affecting each other.

Associated closely with this imbalance is the fact that the exposition is the church's singular aesthetic strength. In other words, since this church reduces its aesthetic to one activity, affectionate care must be given to both the handling and delivering of the exposition of Scripture each and every time because everything (aesthetically speaking) is dependent on the quality of the message taught. If artistic engagement is not employed every time a sermon is prepared and proclaimed, then the experience will likely fall short of becoming a complete experience for all involved. There is no room for error; no other aesthetic aspect of the church can help maintain the balance. It is too easy for a pastor to rely on his past experiences, memory, training, and the loyalty of his congregation, and as a result, can construct and conduct his sermon in a manner that is mechanical. This likelihood becomes more pronounced by the fact that the pastor is in a personal state of imbalance due to excessive doing and deficient undergoing.

d. Culture gap between church and community. The manner in which this service is conducted reveals three critical cultural gap problems. First, the church restricts accessibility to the community. For instance, the presentation, as well as the material itself, is not easily understandable to the theologically ignorant or untrained. The church attempts to remedy the situation by suggesting that visitors entreat themselves to past-recorded lessons and the study of its free literature. But the adjustment to this "aesthetic of the Word" is the responsibility of the attendee. In order for the visitor to come to a position where tension gives way to continuity, indoctrination must take place. Interestingly, there is no helpful guide to explain some of the more important and repetitive technical words used by the pastor.

Secondly, since the structure of the worship service is inflexible, lacking creative intelligence and lively spontaneity (but not disorganization), focused on the dissemination of Scripture in view of the life of the mind, there is no varied or wide array of possibilities to aesthetically reach people where they are. When a local church only practices transient, dated expressions of worship, whether it is by church leadership or congregants, it fails to recognize that the gap between itself and community will continue to grow. The church becomes static in its art forms whereas culture continues to change. Interestingly, creativity, which many theologians consider to be an aspect of being made in the image of God, is squelched in the church.[176]

Focusing the congregation's attention to the content of the mind to the neglect of other religious activities such as corporate opportunity of fellowship has had most profound results. The people tend to have difficulty in establishing interpersonal relationships outside of their immediate context. They are skeptical and feel threatened by any other teaching, foster an unusual loyalty to the pastor, are not able to meaningfully engage in theological diversity (e.g., reasonable and competitive interpretations), and are overly critical of other expressions of biblical worship.

If the church refuses to expand its activities where aesthetic experiences can occur outside of the receiving of Scripture, then it not only misses opportunities to be enriched in other meaningful ways, but it will also fail to contribute to the well-being of the community. For example, if there is no meaningful outreach to meet practical needs why would the community even look to the church? This gap becomes even more explicit when certain ways of doing are employed for the sake of tradition, personal preference, or habituation. When activities are done poorly, people are less likely to be inspired, aroused, or moved. As a result, the church is unattractive to the community, if not ignored. Like an art-product relegated to

---

[176] Nicholas Wolterstorff, *Art in Action* (Grand Rapids, MI: Eerdmans, 1980), 50-9.

the museum, church itself becomes isolated from common life and is only enjoyed by the few.

Thirdly, a lack of opportunity to formulate interpersonal relationships in church-related activities (e.g., pot-luck meals; small groups; service opportunities) will further divide the elite church from community. The human need for relationships is virtually ignored and opportunities for the assimilation of outsiders are diminished. Further, with the sole focus on Bible lessons, the members themselves are not enriched corporately as a church in meeting the practical needs of the community.

Overall, the elite church is one that promotes an aesthetic that is perhaps formally elaborate, but divorced or isolated from community. In view of its activities, this church is somewhat inaccessible to the community. While the elite church offers a singular activity where aesthetic experiences could occur, it fails to recognize the non-aesthetic imbalance that results from its form of didactic teaching. As a result, all miss opportunities to dynamically learn, reflect, and grow together. The result is holistic malnourishment. There is the ever-present concern that a message may be prepared and delivered in a manner that is mechanical. The church promotes individualism while disregarding the significance of collective relationships and interactive goals. Because the church's aesthetic is for a learned or trained churchgoer, the corporate opportunity to actively connect, engage, and improve the organized life of the community is negligible.

A response to this church's aesthetic problems would be to recognize the value of other activities or avenues of aesthetic experience. Do not commit reductionism by focusing on one activity to the neglect of others. Fellowship gatherings, small group discussions, testimonies, creative use of music, pastoral interactions, and the enablement of lay leaders are only a few examples of activities where artistic engagement may occur. While the church should seek to rightly know, richly proclaim, and appropriately apply Scripture and biblical, systematic theology, the church must also must seek to promote interpersonal relationships where community, personal differences, and continuities are valued among its people. The church must open up more opportunities to serve the community in an open manner, promoting organic transactional activities that will increase awareness of the relationship of the church and its environment, which will hopefully lead to practical benefits for all involved.

THE BROKEN CHURCH

Proximal to one of the largest cities in America, this evangelical church is surrounded by master-planned communities, schools of stellar reputation, a very active civic organization, and other resources that make this community inviting for growing families. This small church is the remnant of a large traditional church. The leadership decided to relocate the church due to a substantive influx of immigrants. Because of relocation issues, changes in church leadership, and internal turmoil, membership eventually reduced from a few hundred to less than twenty families.

Unlike the elite church, the church's constitution is such that the practical authority of the church does not reside in the senior pastor, or "teaching pastor," but in the "ruling elders." These elders are volunteers elected and annually reaffirmed by the congregation. Unanimous elder consent is required to move forward in the ministry or change direction even slightly. In major decisions such as hiring or terminating a pastor, the congregation has final authority. Although the pastor must attend all meetings and offer suggestions and guidance, he does not have a vote. He is not subject to annual reaffirmation. This system of "checks and balances" is the backbone of the church and the leadership is, without apology, bound to it. Interestingly, this type of church government is in direct response to a nearby elite church whereby all the authority resides in the senior pastor.

The worship service revolves around contemporary songs and the delivery of a structured sermon. Three vocalists, all volunteer, lead the music using a keyboard, guitars, and drums. The children are taught through an object lesson at the stage. The pastor, who is well educated, offers an expository message that typically lasts 40 minutes and contains a number of illustrations and personal applications. An outline of the sermon is provided and a visual screen is utilized to aid in clarity.

The church offers a number of ministries centered on the teaching of Scripture and fellowship opportunities. In addition to weekly small groups that meet in the homes of the members, Sunday school classes for all ages are offered, as well as a special mid-week class geared toward preparing young people for intellectual and moral issues they might face after high school graduation. Organized fellowship activities such as games, banquets, and other events are ongoing. Conferences are held featuring guest speakers. Additionally, the church routinely has once a month dinner gatherings in multiple homes and visitors are usually invited.

As far as the role of the audience in this church, high commitment is expected but not demanded. In part, this is due to strong family values embraced by the church membership. Because families are so interwoven into each other's lives, people are very knowledgeable about each other's situations. Transparency is valued. Moreover, the willingness to minister and be ministered to is naturally expected. Communication with each other is highly valued. One member said, "In many ways we adults are literally like brothers and sisters."

In spite of the advantages it offers to its members in comparison to the elite church, this church does not thrive due to the weaknesses and imbalance generated from its failings. This church possesses one of the most valuable strengths any community could possess, which is intimate relationships. The teaching in each setting, as well, is usually delivered in an engaging and nutritious manner. Unfortunately, this church is overwhelmed by a problem that cannot be overcome by the loving relationships or substantive teaching, namely, separation from the community at large. During the research phrase for this study, the leadership has chosen to sell the church property and gather in homes. Many families have moved to other churches even though they are still involved in the lives of one another and are called upon or show up when a particular crisis occurs.

a. Strengths. Aesthetic experiences repeatedly occur within the church in view of important relationships made among the church families. From the young to the old, families are involved in each other's lives. From those relationships, families are helped and strengthened, resources are shared, and individual as well as corporate growth occurs. Moreover, these relationships generate a shared value of communication, which can possess aesthetic qualities. For example, they are able to be genuine with each other, accepting of each other's oddities, interests, and issues. They value the harmony of differences that makes up their congregation.[177] In other words, they prize a balance between their differences and continuities. In that balance rhythm and shared growth find expression.[178]

While the exposition of Scripture each Sunday is didactic in nature, opportunities naturally came about to discuss the message and communicate with the pastor. Moreover, cooperative opportunities of learning for all who were involved in the Sunday school programs, youth activities, and small group ministries are maximized. There is never the appearance of mechanical or random teaching; all are given ample learning and growing experiences.

b. Separation from community. This church is broken and possibly unable to recover from its disconnection from the community. To some extent the church leadership is ignorant of the relationship between the members and community. They feel like a real close-knit family rhetorically asking questions like, "Why should we bring people into the church when we are happy with the church as it is?" Moreover, the larger community is, for the most part, ignorant of the church and its opportunities. While relational friendship is one the deepest human needs, there is no strategic method of communicating to the society that this church could offer an answer to that need. Thus, separation from community has been central to its lack of health. But the nature of this separation is multifaceted.

First, the church leadership has not seen its unwillingness to embrace the community as an obstacle to growth. This was evident by the decision to move from the original location because of the diverse people-groups that were migrating to the area. The leaders chose, most diplomatically, to set themselves apart (protecting their governing structure and their membership), and did not embrace the growing diversity that surrounded them, thus setting a precedent. So they moved to another suburban community that they thought

---

[177] Pappas, *John Dewey's Ethics*, 236-9.
[178] Idem.

would better reflect their way of life. In doing so they believed the church would be in a better position to grow.

Second, the church did not reach out to its new neighborhood in an organized, meaningful way. Random attempts were typically fruitless. Just like the former community, the growing neighborhood became diverse as Asian Americans and Indian-Americans began to buy new homes. Perhaps in the best interests of this church it would have been better served had a pastor or staff member been acquired who reflected the cultural background of the neighborhood residents in order to bridge this growing disparity. Moreover, the church could have made itself or its facilities more available to meet the diverse needs of the public. These opportunities were always extended to selective organizations that did not offer potential for church growth.

And third, the governmental leadership structure is an obstacle to change. If one of the elders or the pastor formulates an idea to address the growing problem, then he is placed in a difficult position of having to convince every ruling elder since unanimous consent is required. Since the elders are closely involved in the lives of the members, they have always been very sensitive to their opinions and reactions to change. Some significant church participants believed that this church should serve as a "place of seclusion" from the outside world, to be a place where their children could grow without being influenced by outsiders whose family values may be different. These factors have contributed to the immobilization of the church as a whole.

3. Aesthetic Insights. The broken church typifies many churches that are separated from their community. Dewey's analysis serves as a warning. If separated too long, the church will either break or merely subsist. Has the church become disconnected, forgotten by community?[179] Has the church neglected the value of the greater community, namely, the culture in which the church is located? If so, then the church is broken. But Dewey's analysis can serve as a corrective tool for potential vitality.

If a church is facing this type of problem, then realizing that it is out of step with the march of its environment is an important

---

[179] McDermott, *The Drama of Possibilities*, 207.

step. Recovery, if obtained, will lead to organic growth. Had this church found creative and meaningful ways to embrace and relate to its diverse neighborhood, the church's situation would have likely improved.

But churches in this situation must realize that change is a constant, both within and beyond its walls (e.g., membership changes, personal turmoil, and new experiences). Therefore, the church needs to understand its own state and its relationship to the community. Like a Bedouin nomad who guides his animals in the desert wilderness, the leadership must be willing to adjust properly to tension, whether whether suddenly or slowly

If we examine the elite church and broken church together, we are able to glean the following insights. While both churches can have in particular instances activities with aesthetic quality, they both tend to suffer from isolation or separation from community, which is not conducive to having the most enriching aesthetic experiences. Both churches place restrictions on outsiders, but in a different way. The elite church demands that people adapt themselves to the pastor's didactic style and authority. The broken church separates itself in an effort to be culturally homogeneous and protective of its families. These "unwritten" mores can be unaesthetic because they can restrict natural church development. In fact, whenever a church has too many or too little customs, rules, or orders, it can be difficult for organic aesthetic experience to emerge. While the broken church succeeds in personal relationships, it has chosen not to corporately and actively participate in community. Sadly, it appears that this separation between church and community might cost the church its corporate existence.

To be sure, the shared weaknesses among the previous case studies are the lack of experiences; they understand the position they hold within community. If I return to the example of the Parthenon, potentialities for aesthetic experiences on different levels abounded. The workers themselves who were engaged in their artistry were experiencing ongoing aesthetic moments, but, just as importantly, the finished product enables others in the community the potentiality of an aesthetic experience as well. In contrast to that scenario, the leadership and members of these churches may be affording themselves esthetic occurrences, but they are not ones that lend themselves to further potential aesthetic connections to the community. We will now consider the humdrum church, which relishes in the routine

THE HUMDRUM CHURCH

This evangelical church is strategically located in a town of approximately 35,000 people. The church origins date to the early 1980s with several families meeting together in a business office. Just within a few years the church grew to over a hundred people. Similarly to the elite church, the church's ministry revolves around the exposition of Scripture.

The church's authority resides in an elder board. The board functions in cooperation with the solo pastor as spiritual leaders, ministering and caring for the congregation. All elders have voting power and decisions are made by majority vote. The church also has a board of deacons who assists in the business affairs of the church. Like the previous churches studied, the pastor is well educated. A part-time youth director is also employed. Each elder has oversight over a number of families and is often in contact with them. The church leaders value efficiency such as, time-management, comprehensiveness, and attention to details. Often they discuss finer points of theological doctrine.

The congregational members are largely successful, and most over the age of 40. The men often wear jackets and ties and the women tend to wear fashionable outfits. In fact, the church seldom struggles with financial concerns.

The church's building is an older property. The simple brick architecture reflects the central theme of the worship service, primarily the teaching of Scripture. The traditional church auditorium is simple with stained glass, windows, red carpet, and symbolic tapestries on each side of the wall. An organ and piano are positioned on either side of simple rectangular pulpit. The oak communion table sits just below the pulpit. The landscape is attractive with an assortment of flowers. A large playground is next to the church. The church is visible from one of the main roads in town.

The order of service is strictly adhered to: hymn, announcements, two more hymns, Scripture reading, prayer, children sermon, hymn, message, closing hymn, and benediction. The music is traditional with hymns and spiritual praise songs from the seventies and eighties and is led by volunteer amateurs. The pastor presents an expository message lasting anywhere from thirty to forty minutes. This church offers a program called children's church. After the pastor gives the children's message, and without even an announcement, the children file out to their respective classes. They receive a Bible lesson and an opportunity to sing and play.

In terms of other activities, this church features an active youth program organized by a part-time staff worker, a college student, who functions under the direct authority of the pastor. He offers an interactive program of biblical studies and fellowship. The church also offers an adult Sunday school class in the fellowship hall. The teaching process is typically collaborative in nature and the audience is mature. Many come early to Sunday school in order to fellowship with church friends that they have known for perhaps decades. Lastly, the church is involved in supporting social causes ranging from sending and supporting medical teams to third world countries to contributing financially to special community needs. They are also involved in supporting many missionaries.

The pastor is quiet and unassuming. His message is expositional in nature. Like the elite church, rarely is there an introduction that touches upon a real need. The conclusion is a restatement of the introduction. While the message is often rich in expositional details there are few illustrations and personal applications. The illustrations used are often the same ones he has used before. This pastor is always available and present when in need. He strives to live a simple life. He dislikes surprises of any sort and exercises enough authority to ensure no potential problems or threats arise in the programs.

The responsibility of the audience is to regularly attend, participate in a specific manner when called upon, and maintain unity, never disturbing the peace. Like the elite church, being a voice of objection or dissension generates alienation or marginalization from the church. People who enjoy structure and the church model of yesteryear are naturally drawn to this atmosphere.

2. Aesthetic analysis. This church is to be commended for its fellowship among its members. This church is also to be extolled for its willingness to think beyond its own needs. Notwithstanding, the church's worship service champions the routine.

a. Strengths. With its mature audience, the church has many relationships that have withstood the test of time and have grown deep. Hugs are shared liberally and visitors, though infrequent, are made to feel welcome. Careful attention to the needs of members and deep conversations and encouragement from friends often leads to aesthetic experiences.

b. The problem of the routine. In every possible way, the church's worship follows the same mechanical format or order every week. For example, the lighting is never adjusted, the hymns and songs are on a short rotation list and are sung and played the same way, and the manner in which the sermon is designed and delivered does not change. No anticipation of what will come next in the church's worship service is needed. When in doubt, a detailed bulletin lists every step in the order of worship. Hence, if anything occurs out of the ordinary, such as a vacation for the pastor, several advance notices are provided, or, in some cases, an apology is offered. There is also no tension. All is calm, composed, and placid.

The non-aesthetic mechanical nature of the church's worship service involves several factors. First, the leadership of the church is fearful of change. Slight changes that have occurred, only by accident (e.g., organist becomes unexpectedly ill), overwhelm the pastor with personal tension and anxiety. He admits that any form of change is very emotionally and physically difficult.

Similarly, many members of the congregation seem to have embraced the personality of the pastor, preferring the routine. This is reflected in the transactional activity of the church setting. In fact, anything that happens unexpectedly, for example, a first-time visitor raises her hands in worship, is thus memorable, even though the experience will fall short of completion. Thus, in both parties, the church leadership and the congregation, stability means peace, and tension is always perceived negatively. Like Dewey states, "Resistance is treated as an obstruction to be beaten down, not as an invitation to reflection."[180] Even though the pastor occasionally confesses that changes need to be made to make the service more enriching and inviting to younger people, the unrest it would cause within himself and those in his congregation would be too turbulent and overwhelming to seriously consider.

Second, security is found in regularity. Fearful of the unexpected, the order of the service is rigidly followed. For instance, there are rarely any exceptions to the church's order of service. The clock governs every move. Further, habitual prayers are offered. A new hymn is preceded by an explanation (an apology?) for its appearance. Risks are avoided.

Third, the church clings to and glories in the past. The church relishes its own tradition and contends that the best way to worship God is to follow what it has always known. If another church seeks to be cultural relevant to its community, it will be judged by the humdrum church to be necessarily equated with biblical compromise unto secular trends in culture with the use of contemporary genre and such instruments as electronic guitars and drums. I wonder if the fear to adjust to a more spontaneous and dynamic order of service involves the notion that the people would have to give up the nostalgic sentiments they collectively share. They are not only honoring their heritage, but their weekly experience evokes past memories with loved ones.

Fourth, familiarity is valued over creativity. There are many members in the church who have amazing testimonies, who are wonderfully gifted in such as areas as art and music, and have contagious personalities. They are left as untapped resources, that is, unused, unexposed, or unable to be given a platform. Involvement with the unknown is too risk, so creativity is stifled. As a result, we only see the same people doing the same jobs, singing the same songs, and playing the same instruments in the same way. According to Dewey, the danger is that familiarity induces indifference, apathy, and inactivity.[181] Additionally, the fear of change also generates

---

[180] Dewey, *Art as Experience*, 66.
[181] Ibid., 108. Dewey puts it this way:

alienation because if someone visits the church, then, like the elite church, he must conform to one way of doing things. If he does not conform, he is not welcome to stay.

Fifth, there is very little room for a life-changing experience. Because the worship service is done in a very mechanical way, there is very little room for someone's life to be touched deeply, that is, enraptured in an aesthetic moment. Should they be touched by the music or the sermon, it is interpreted as highly emotional, unwarrantedly mystical, and intellectually pointless. Thus, any aesthetic moment that may be found is better kept to oneself. Furthermore, there is no "altar call" or "invitation" extended at the end of the service. No part of this sacred hour can be corrupted by the unpredictable nature of people and there is no need to affirm the teaching or the order of service other than the fact that all went smoothly and finished on time.

Lastly, the church's aesthetics is constructed in such a way that it is non-nutritive to those in its sphere of influence. While the worship service brings the past to the present, there is no anticipation, that is, no vision for something new in the worship service. No element of experimentation to the church's aesthetics or openness to new ideas is encouraged.[182] Instead, new ideas are met with the refusal to change. While its repudiation to adapt to a more spontaneous and dynamic setting may be vacuous to some members, the leadership is willing to accept that over the possibility of losing other members who are enraged by a slight modification. The church is, for the most part, immobilized by the unknown and prejudiced by the familiar.[183]

Why is the routine non-aesthetic? There is no curiosity, no suspense, and no movement towards consummation through a connected series of qualities. The music, the prayers, the exposition, the children's lessons, and the interior decorations do not qualitatively change and contribute to one another. There is no tension. There

---

How, then, can objects of experience avoid becoming expressive? Yet apathy and torpor [inactivity] conceal this expressiveness by building a shell about objects. Familiarity induces indifference, prejudice blinds us; conceit looks through the wrong end of a telescope and minimizes the significance possessed by objects in favor of the alleged importance of the self [Ibid].

[182] Ibid., 51.
[183] Ibid., 108.

is only a mechanical connection.[184] As a result, there is no active interplay of rhythm, imagination, and unity. There are no forces that are carrying these qualities to a decisive moment in one's life to produce an organic moment of consummation. Consequently, the church worship service falls short of a complete experience. The habituated non-aesthetic routine becomes normative in the life of the church. Qualitative impoverishment is the result and every service is forgettable. Though its members may become aware of the cultural gap, all that can be offered to the community is rather mundane.

3. Aesthetic insights. This church needs to rethink its position on change. Look at risk and tension from a different perspective. Though change for change sake is not profitable, change to meet a growing need is natural and necessary for growth. If heels are stubbornly dug into the ground too long, the church will find that it no longer has a place within the ever-changing community. The humdrum church could suffer the same fate as broken church. Lastly, incorporating objects of art can be used to assist in changing the worship service from inactivity to active engagement. Dewey writes:

> Art throws off the covers that hid the expressiveness of experienced things; it quickens us from the slack of routine and enables us to forget ourselves by finding ourselves in the delight of experiencing the world about us in its varied qualities and forms. It intercepts every shade of expressiveness found in objects and orders them in a new experience of life. Because the objects of art are expressive, they communicate. I do not say that communication to others is the intent of an artist. But it is the consequence of his work-which indeed lives only in communication when it operates in the experience of others.[185]

THE SENSATIONAL CHURCH

The other extreme and enemy to aesthetic experience is the sensational. Often in reaction to the non-aesthetic routines that typify many worship services, many pursue churches that emphasize

---
[184] Ibid., 41.
[185] Ibid., 108.

the sensational, and by this I mean promoting a worship experience that not only attracts a great deal of interest, but also overwhelms the senses. But like the humdrum church, this church champions a non-aesthetic experience that is not truly beneficial.

This is a non-denominational church averaging several hundred people per week. The location is located in a strategic place in a major cosmopolitan city in order that it may impact the community. The leadership boasts inclusivity and diversity.

The children are organized neatly into colorful classrooms and taught with the best of materials. Children's education is taken very seriously and no expense is spared to offer the very best. The leaders want the program to be a thrilling and entertaining experience to keep them wanting to come back. One person stated that if the church loses the interest of the parents, they would likely continue to attend for the sake of their children. The youth set-up is similar to a movie theatre. The best of technology is used to offer them an environment where the students can feel cool and hip. Large screens, sound equipment, the use of lighting, and live music dominate the scene.

The enclosed auditorium is designed like an amphitheatre. The circular stage is positioned in the center of the auditorium at the lowest level. Chairs are situated around the auditorium except for one section where the baptismal tank and the music band is located.

A "praise team" who is racially diverse performs the music. Both genders are evenly represented. Interestingly, their clothing is coordinated with each other and they are positioned around the perimeter of the circular stage facing the audience. Digital screens are hanging down from the ceiling. These monitors are facing the audience around the circular stage. The words of each and every song are displayed on screens above and around the circular stage. Hymnbooks are unnecessary. Members of the praise team are positioned under each monitor.

As one approaches the entrance, a racially diverse group provides a warm greeting. They direct all who enter toward a corridor that unfolds into a circular auditorium. Even before entering, upbeat music and singing can be heard. The children are guided to their classrooms.

Before the church service officially begins, announcements are made on the monitors.

When the service begins, the praise team invites all to sing. The music lasts at least thirty minutes. Each praise team member sings under the screen. The music is so loud that the singers on stage, and no one from the audience, can be heard. The lighting is dimmed and all attention is driven to the stage. The music is professionally done and timed perfectly. There is a keyboard, several electric guitars, two drummers, and a piano. The music is spontaneous, ready and willing to adjust to the direction of the praise leader and pastor.

At the beginning of the pastor's message, he asks the congregation to lift up their Bibles and repeat a statement of belief in the authority of Scripture. After the passionate crowd enthusiastically cooperates, they set the Bibles in their laps or on the floor and read the passage on the overhead screen. The pastor speaks on issues to which many congregants are sympathetic, as revealed by frequent head-nods, lifted hands, and words of affirmation. But soon after the beginning, the pastor often abandons his study notes in order to "speak from the heart." He claims that the Lord guided him to do so. Reminiscent of the elite church, no one questions his authority. Scripture passages are proclaimed in the pastor's message but there is no coherent pattern to the proclamations. Historical and literary context is not considered. While his rhetoric is passionate, his major points are often disconnected from one another. But the congregation and pastor begin to mutually respond to each other with shouts of proclamations and supporting applause. However, the statements proclaimed by the pastor and heartily received by the congregation are "attitude" claims of such things as abundance, success, and peace. In essence, if we would take ownership of these positive statements, no matter how fierce and determined the opposition is, these "truths" would translate into empowering success in every aspect of our lives. They are guaranteed to work if we have enough faith. During my visit, I noted that along the edge of the circular stage the pastor would make direct eye contact with the attendees. Eye contact was very important to him.

The service always closes with an invitation to come down and experience God's blessings. The stage is soon filled with people, both the young and old. Many of those who remain in their chairs lift up their arms, pray, and sing along with the praise team who slow the pace to a meditative style. The praise team interacts with the direction, rhetoric, and movements of the pastor. Afterwards, the service concludes with prayer and upbeat music inviting the attendees to come back next week.

1. Aesthetic analysis. The worship service of the sensational church may primarily be described as non-aesthetic because of a two-fold imbalance. First, the sensational church is preoccupied with indulgence in activities. Second, the church activities are overly focused on excessive undergoing (receptivity), crowding as many fanciful impressions as possible into one event.[186] This excessive undergoing overwhelms the senses and captivates the emotions, causing people to hunger for the sensational rather than balance in experience. When people are called to publicly respond to the worship experience, then all of a sudden, the excessive undergoing dramatically shifts to excessive doing. In other words, the roles are now reversed. Here the audience's doing is governed, that is, now informed by their own undergoing. As a result, the pastor and worship team receives excessive undergoing and deficient doing. Just as the humdrum's worship service is engrossed with the non-aesthetic routine, the sensational church is preoccupied with the indulgent and is imbalanced.

a. Strengths. The activities of the church are commendable in many respects. We will focus on two strengths. First, the people in this church are the first to respond to crises in community. They open their doors when the community floods, go out of their way to help the misfortunate, and attempt to enrich the lives of those in their sphere of influence. They are sensitive to racial tensions and gender issues by emphasizing unity in all their activities. They are also involved in public protests, fighting against vices in our community, and supporting public officials such as police and fire. For them, these are expressions of worship.

---

[186] Ibid., 46.

Moreover, this church embraces technological changes, striving to incorporate the latest technology in their worship service and educational programs. Unlike the elite and humdrum church, it welcomes technological revolutions and assimilates new advances into the worship experience. In fact, the use of technology is striking.

Music is performed brilliantly. The interaction between the praise team and the audience is rhythmic with both feeding off of each other. Nothing would be described as mediocre. To be sure, aesthetic qualities are expressed. The greeters, musicians, praise team, and pastor are all engaged in their jobs, all interested in doing well, and seem to express genuine affection. Their body language is focused, using their whole bodies in worship, and they are able to adjust as the circumstances change under the pastor's direction. Though it seems the integral factors such as the music, setting, use of technology, and style possess aesthetic qualities, they fall short of a complete aesthetic experience because of imbalance.

b. The problem of imbalance. In essence, the worship experience tilts to the excessive and the focus centers on the audience experiencing and indulging in the sensational, namely, saturating the audience with sensations in order to generate an emotional response. Then suddenly, the focus dramatically changes from the excessive in receiving to excessive in responding to the service before others. The emotional response is then equated with a religious experience with God.

The aesthetics of a sensational church is cut short from maturation because what is valued is an emotional response from the congregation. The loud music, the use of colorful lights, the emotional rhetoric, the sentimental words, and the use of technology are choreographed to provoke people to respond. Like a pep rally, the music begins very upbeat and is excitable and slowly builds up to a crescendo through the use of rhetoric and music, targeting felt needs, desires, and dreams. The crescendo is followed by an emotional release. Thus, the emotional release is considered be an encounter with God. This release becomes the overriding goal of the sensational church and entertainment, that is, using various means to hold our attention, is the means to provoke this response.[187]

---

[187] I am not trivializing the importance of entertainment as a significant aspect of our

But an emotional release of this sort should not be equated with qualitative enrichment. Dewey writes:

> With respect to human emotion, an immediate discharge that is fatal to expression is detrimental to rhythm. There is no enough resistance to create tension, and thereby a periodic accumulation and release. Energy is not conserved so as to contribute too an ordered development.[188]

Rather, this goal is reductionistic because all aspects are singularly focusing on the build up of emotions to the neglect of other areas of personhood, such as the mind, under the guise of religious experience. Qualitative enrichment improves the whole person simultaneously, like the growth of an unborn baby; it is not merely a release of emotions.

While there are elements of passion in aesthetic perceptions, when we are overwhelmed by our passions, there is no order or balance. Instead of an appropriate dignity, a balanced sensitivity involving the whole person and the environment, there can be an unruly ex-

---

lives. But my question is how does one know when the target response is directed to the emotions rather than the whole person? Am I being enriched by the experience or am I being emotionally manipulated. For example, at the beginning of sensational service, the music is clearly a performance. The lights are on the stage. Audience participation at that point is virtually unnecessary. The opening music is meant to excite us with pounding drums and praise team members jumping up and down. The only acceptable emotion is utter joy and happiness. Then near the end of the service, after the message, the intense and slower music is used, and tears begin to flow from the praise team members and the speaker. Are they manipulating us to a sort of introspection that will lead us to a public response or are they interested in authentic development? Are these emotions authentic or are they manipulated? Interestingly, the entertainment industry is not obligated to explain themselves in our Western culture. Their purpose is to evoke an emotional response for financial gain and do not stand accountable for what else they might provoke. In other words, they do not necessarily care if your life is enriched or degenerated as a result of their entertainment. While aesthetic desensitization is outside of the purpose of this work, it has relevance to the extent that churches modeling themselves after the entertainment industry. See Richard Shusterman, "Entertainment: A Question for Aesthetics" in *British Journal of Aesthetics* 44:3 (2003): 289-307, for an excellent philosophical discussion regarding the classification, importance, and role of entertainment in common life. Consider this statement by Marshall McLuhan:

> For any medium has the power of imposing its own assumption on the unwary. Prediction and control consists in avoiding this subliminal state of Narcissus trance. But the greatest aid to this end is simply in knowing that the spell can occur immediately upon contact, as in the first bars of a melody [*Understanding Media: The Extensions of Man* (New York: McGraw-Hill, 1964), 30].

[188] Dewey, *Art as Experience*, 162.

citement with some people collapsing on the floor, others literally howling at the top of their lungs, running around the auditorium in circles, or are marked with uncontrollable laughing.[189] The lights, sounds, and scenes of the service penetrate those emotions, tipping people toward this emotional indulgence. In contrast, consider Dewey's insight:

> When complete release is postponed and is arrived at finally through a succession of ordered periods of accumulation and conservation, marked off into intervals by the recurrent pauses of balance, the manifestation of emotion becomes true expression, acquiring esthetic quality—and only then.[190]

The ability to induce people into such a response reaffirms how sensitive we are to our context. Though Plato and Dewey have recognized the power of aesthetics to induce emotions and displace order, the sensational church capitalizes on this relationship between people and environment in a very organized way to generate specific conditions and promote certain results. Other churches, especially the humdrum, fail to really understand the impact that the setting makes in promoting aesthetic enrichment to the whole person.

Regarding the response to the experience, the elite church overemphasizes the private whereas the sensational church overemphasizes the public. In other words, there is an expectation of a long line of people who have "walked the aisle" to receive prayer, power, forgiveness, or miraculous intervention. Some desire to publicly express a new decision or direction or simply to sing with lifted arms at the front rather than in their own seats. So the indulgence finds expression in public professions and requests. The response at the altar call affirms and justifies the pastor's message and identity even though the reaction of the congregation is not organic. Therefore, the excess in receiving throughout most of the worship service immediately shifts to becoming excess in the doing. In other words, the saturation of stimuli is meant to lead to an indulgent response, and the attention to the dramatic continues each and every week.

---

[189] Ibid., 51.
[190] Ibid., 162.

But we have to be careful in our analysis of indulgence less we neglect the history of revivalism (e.g., First and Second Great Awakenings in America), Quaker worship services, and the enriching aspects of Pentecostal and charismatic movements. There is a dynamic relationship between having an emotional release and having a spiritual experience.[191] Thus, in our evaluations of the actual exercise of indulgent excess, we must investigate the end-results. For example, let us briefly consider the insights of the American philosopher Jonathan Edwards (1703-1758). He carefully and comprehensively examined sensational aspects of worship during and following the First Great Awakening. But what we will discover is that Edwards' judgment of these events is agreeable with Dewey's

---

[191] For example, consider the following response by Jonathan Edwards in his analysis and defense of intense moments of spiritual ecstasy. Edwards writes:

It is no argument that a work is not of the Spirit of God that some who are the subjects of it have been in a kind of ecstasy, wherein they have been carried beyond themselves, and have had their minds transported into a train of strong and pleasing imaginations, and a kind of visions, as thought they were rapt up even to heaven and there saw glorious sights. I have been acquainted with some such instances, and I see no need of bringing in the help of the devil into the account that we give of these things, nor yet of supposing them to be of the same rapture into paradise. Human nature, under these exercises and affections, is all that need be brought into the account. If it may be well accounted for, that persons under a true sense of a glorious and wonderful greatness and excellency of divine things, and soul-ravishing views of the beauty and love of Christ, should have the strength of nature overpowered, as I have already known that it may; then I think it is not at all strange that amongst great numbers that are thus affected and overborne, there should be some persons of particular constitutions that should have their imaginations thus affected. The effect is no other than what bears a proportion and analogy to the other effects of the strong exercise of the minds. It is no wonder, when the thoughts are so fixed, and the affections so strong-and the whole soul is so engaged, ravished, and swallowed up-that all the other parts of the body are so affected, as to be deprived of their strength, and the whole frame ready to dissolve. Is it any wonder, that, in such a case, the brain in particular (especially in some constitutions), which we know is most especially affected by intense contemplations and exercises of mind, should be so affected, that its strength and spirits should for a season be diverted and taken off from impressions made on the organs of external sense, and be wholly employed in a training of pleasing delightful imaginations, corresponding with the present frame of the mind? Some are ready to interpret such things wrong, and to lay too much weight on them, as prophetical visions, divine revelations, and sometimes significations from heaven of what shall come to pass; which the issue, in some instances I have known, has shown to be otherwise. But yet, it appears to me that such things are evidently sometimes from the Spirit of God, though indirectly; that is, their extraordinary frame of mind, and that strong and lively sense of divine things which is the occasion of them, is from his Spirit; and also as the mind continues in its holy frame, and retains a divine sense of the excellency of spiritual things even in its rapture, which holy frame and sense is from the Spirit of God, thought the imaginations, through the imaginations that attend are but accidental, and therefore there is a commonly something or other in them that is confused, improper, and false [Jonathan Edwards, *Jonathan Edwards on Revival* (Carlisle, PA: The Banner of Truth Trust, 1994), 97-8].

call for qualitative enrichment of the whole person if we keep the end-results in mind.

Jonathan Edwards warns against being lead by impulses and impressions and by evangelists who despise the proper role of the mind and learning.[192] However, he defends revivalism and the unusual emotional outbursts and responses that occur and the ways in which preachers appeal to the emotions. For instance, in *The Distinguishing Marks of the Works of the Spirit of God*, he contends that unusual signs such as trembling and passing out do not validate or invalidate the work of the Holy Spirit.[193] He states, "Therefore it is not reasonable to determine that a work is not from God's Holy Spirit because of the extraordinary degree in which the minds of persons are influenced."[194] He later states, "A work is not to be judged of by any effects on the bodies of men; such as tears, trembling, groans, loud outcries, agonies of body, or the failing of bodily strength."[195] But, on the other hand, in the same work, Edwards argues that love for Jesus, mortification of worldly lusts, renunciation of sin, pursuit of and high esteem for Scripture, a sensitive accountability before God in view of their lives, and authentic Christ-like love to God and others, are distinguishing markings of the true work of the Holy Spirit.

In sum, Edwards argues that lives, which are holistically transformed by the Holy Spirit are those that receive authentic religious experiences.[196] In fact, he writes, "Can it not be determined whether it [work of God] tends to awaken their consciences, or to stupefy them; whether it inclines them more to seek their salvation, or neglect it; or lead them to deism; whether it makes them have more regard for the great truths of religion, or less?"[197] Thus, Edwards looks at the end-results of such experiences to determine if they are beneficial to the whole person.

---

[192] George M. Marsden, *Jonathan Edwards: A Life* (New Haven, CT: Yale University Press, 2003), 233.
[193] Jonathan Edwards, *Jonathan Edwards on Revival*, 75-147.
[194] Ibid., 89.
[195] Ibid., 91.
[196] Ibid., 109-120.
[197] Ibid., 121.

In a similar way, Dewey's aesthetics generates questions such as "Are people qualitatively enriched by such experiences whereby their lives are practically improved? Is there a proportional balance that nutritiously impacts the whole person, not merely one's emotions?"[198] Therefore, our examination into excessive indulgence must not merely involve the actual instance of overwhelming emotions but the beneficial, qualitative results that follow.

In certain traditions, such as those in African and African-American churches, the relationship between homilies, rhetorical cadence, rhythm, songs, and dance play integral roles to experiencing meaningful expressions of worship. The use of technology such as the drums, keyboards, organ, choir, and congregational attire are all integrally relating and contributing to authentic worship for the whole person. While the release of emotions is critical to having an aesthetic experience, what sets these activities apart from the sensational church is that there is not only an appropriate doing and undergoing, but the authentic aesthetic experience is naturally and organically comes from within the contextual activity. In other words, the experience is not contrived or artificial, imposed upon the activity.

---

[198] In his work, *Love God with All your Mind: The Role of Reason in the Life of the Soul*, J. P. Moreland offers a helpful and logical case for the role of the mind in spiritual transformation [(Colorado Springs, CO: NavPress, 1997)]. Interestingly, Moreland states:

God is worthy of the very best efforts we can give Him in offering our respect and service through the cultivation of our total personality, including our minds. Seen in this light, dedication to intellectual growth is not merely done for the edification of the worshiper, but as an act of service rendered to God. Halfhearted study in high school or college represents a failure to grasp the fact that loving God with the mind is part of worship. Such halfhearted study is an unworthy offering to the Lord [Ibid., 159]. Later he defines worship:

Worship is the not under the control of human beings, nor is the form it takes up to their whims. Rather, worship is a response to a God who initiates toward His people, gives them life, and shows Himself active on their behalf [Ibid., 161]. One of the applications Moreland makes from his discussion about the use of the mind has bearing on our study of religious worship services. Moreland asserts:

Frequently, our worship services place worship prior to the teaching of the Word. Now there is nothing wrong with this in itself. However, if worship is response, then if a service starts with worship, the people of God have not been given something to which to respond. In my view, we ought to vary the order of our services with a time of teaching followed by congregational testimonies about how God has used the sermon topic in people's lives. Once God's people have their minds filled with truths about God, His Word, and His ways, and once they have had a chance to meditate for a moment on these truths and the way they have been applicable to someone else's life, then the congregation is prepared to respond in worship.... The emotions and will can be more sincerely and intentionally directed toward God if the mind has been given the chance to recall, understand, or reflect on truth [Idem].

Moreover, unlike healthy churches, technology in sensational churches is used to induce an artificial experience of indulgence, to entertain people, saturating their senses. Therefore, because of the transactional relationship between our environment and personhood, the strategic placement and use of technology must be considered. Questions must be asked such as, "What are the purposes for the calculated use of technology?" "Is technology being used to entertain people or is it contributing to the development of the experience within the environment?" Interestingly, Marshall McLuhan claims:

> With the arrival of electronic technology, man extended, or set outside himself, a live model of the central nervous system itself. To the degree that this is so, it is a development that suggests a desperate and suicidal autoamputation, as if the central nervous system could no longer depend on the physical organs to be protective buffers against the slings and arrows of outrageous mechanism. It could be well that the successive mechanizations of the various physical organs since the invention of printing have made too violent and superstimulated a social experience for the central nervous system to endure.[199]

Just like the instruments of a movie theatre are adjusted appropriately to bring a target response, we must examine the purposes of technology and see how it might be better used to promote an organic aesthetic experience and not induce a simulation, a fabricated activity upon the congregation that merely overwhelms senses and affects the emotions. All too often we can think we are having an aesthetic experience when it is one that is only simulated. This is a terrible problem because the values of aesthetic experience are being confused, if not displaced in some churches, by excessive entertainment. Like a narcotic drug, we can so easily become addicted to entertainment that we long for more of that indulgence, which is not healthy, than we do for organic aesthetic experiences. It is not a difficult step to become desensitized and even bored over time as a result of too much exposure to indulgent entertainment.

---

[199] McLuhan, *Understanding Media*, 53.

Therefore, we should not only inquire into proportionality, but also critically examine the role of technology in relationship to the end-results. Is technology balanced with substantive learning? Is there proper doing and undergoing in view of technology and the senses? Stated differently, if there was a power outage, is an aesthetic experience even possible?

In sensational churches there is also an imbalance in the actual messages proclaimed. For example, when the pastor set aside his Bible and turned to statements that reflect what may be described as the actualization of positive thinking, he relegated the reality of pain, sadness, suffering, and trauma to something that is detrimental to our well being. While suffering cannot always be alleviated, it can, nevertheless, generate benefits that bring greater meaning to how we live our lives and serve our community (e.g., cancer survivor ministering to others). In contrast, healthy churches treasure authenticity, the reality of pain, and the beauty of relying upon other members to get through difficulties, whether great or small. Recovery from discontinuity generates growth. The same book of the Bible that states prayers offered in faith will make the sick person well (James 5) also declares in chapter 1 to count it all joy when one encounters various trials. Therefore, positive thinking does not take reality as it is by ignoring or reducing in importance the roles of tension and discontinuity. As a result, the benefits of suffering may be undervalued and the benefits of "American" success may be overplayed, creating an artificial setting that does not harmonize with the rest of experience in common life.

c. The problem of reductionism. Since the church's singular focus is creating a dramatic experience, it neglects other relevant areas of expository teaching, church history, and systematic theology. In particular, the leadership tends to downplay the importance of the mind in favor of what they call "heart knowledge." In other words, they focus on the subjective aspects of the Christian experience divorced from critical thinking, deliberating, and judging.

In sum, the sensational church has many aesthetic qualities, but there is no proper balance. As a result, lives are not organically enriched. Rather, like the humdrum church, the members are impoverished. The building may be huge, the music loud, the lights flashy, the images colorful, the suits sleek, and the preacher's proclamations energetic, but in the end, the aesthetics are devoid of nutritional content because the pastor and his team primarily sought to tap into the emotions, not the whole person. As a result, their aesthetic indulgences generate suspicion in the community because they manipulate the emotions in attempt to motivate genuine life-change. Other pastors merely seek to entertain and reinforce "positive" and "non-disturbing ideas." Still others use entertainment as an element of control. Expectations by the church leadership, such as financial giving in order to be blessed by God, even lead some to mock the church, fostering greater alienation between the church and community, even in spite of the fact that the church strives to serve the community. Though it strives to be "relevant," this type of church is qualitatively anemic.[200]

3. Aesthetic insights. Our advice to the sensational church would be to aim for balance in both doing and receiving and appropriately engage the heart, mind, and will within a setting that does not contribute to excessiveness in worship. Further, church leadership should not foster dependency upon the church service to offer an aesthetic experience. It is not necessary to have all these electronic devices, loud music, and visual stimuli, in order to have an aesthetic experience. Instead, pause and look around and experience wonder, delight, and zeal as one does in the ordinary activities, events, and scenes of life. Religious expression of worship should be an organic process and not one that is artificially induced. Lastly, like the humdrum church, the sensational church should not avoid or ignore how tension and pain can contribute to aesthetic experience. Dewey puts it this way:

> Struggle and conflict may themselves be enjoyed, although they are painful, when they are experienced as means of developing an experience; members in that they carry it forward, not just because they are there. There is ...an element of undergoing, of

---

[200] See Os Guinness, *Prophetic Untimeliness: the Challenge to the Idol of Relevance* (Grand Rapids, MI: Baker, 2003) for a thought-provoking discussion about the topic of relevance.

suffering in its large sense, in every experience. Otherwise there would be no taking in of what preceded. For 'taking in' in any vital experience is something more than placing something on the top of consciousness over what was previously unknown. It involves reconstruction which may be painful. Whether the necessary phase is by itself pleasurable or painful is a matter of particular conditions.[201]

CONCLUSION

While there are many vibrant evangelical churches today that eagerly strive to worship God and interact with community in enriching, meaningful ways, many other churches struggle to attract newcomers and grow corporately. Though they recognize the widening gap, they are unwilling to change, afraid of the risk of hurting current members or attracting new members that do not "fit the mold" of what they desire.

Using Dewey's analysis of what is and what is not aesthetic, we are able to uncover aesthetic problems that many churches face. In each of these cases studied, actions and consequences are not joined together in appropriate balance. This imbalance finds expression when the routine or sensational are valued above harmony between what we do and what we receive. As a result, aesthetic experiences are cut short from what they could be. Moreover, these imbalances promote a cultural gap between the church and community because, in part, the church is not able to offer substantive aesthetic enrichment to everyone in the larger society in which it is embedded. Therefore, coupled with excesses and deficiencies, the elite, broken, humdrum, and sensational churches aggravate the cultural gap between church and community. But in turn, the gap also impacts the members themselves. It has caused frustrated people to break away from church and ways of doing church. Many are disillusioned and unfulfilled. As a result, two evangelical movements recently arose, namely, the "seeker-sensitive" critique and the "emergent/emerging" critique. We will now direct our attention and address the advantages and failures of these two critiques using Dewey's tools of aesthetic analysis.

---

[201] Dewey, *Art as Experience*, 42.

> ...*works of art are objects and instruments in action. They are objects and instruments of action whereby we carry out our intentions with respect to the world, our fellows, ourselves, and our gods. Understanding art requires understanding art in man's life.*
>
> ~ Nicholas Wolterstorff [202]

---

[202] Wolterstorff, *Art in Action*, 3.

REINGINEERING THE LOCAL CHURCH: THE SEEKER-SENSITIVE AND EMERGING/EMERGENT MOVEMENTS

> "Organized Christianity that fails to make a disturbance is dead."
> ~ G. Campbell Morgan

The aesthetic problems in the elite, broken, humdrum, and sensational churches, such as religious activities divorced from enriching community, activity for activity sake, and sensational manipulation, have led many to conclude that the traditional ways of doing church are vacuous in addressing people's needs. The disparity between the aesthetic practices of the traditional church and community are too great and the lack of a meaningful worship experience is too profound. As a result, two new approaches have advanced in recent years: the "seeker-sensitive" movement and the subsequent "emerging church" movement(s). Both advocate reengineering the traditional church in the United States in order to bridge the culture gap and offer worship activities to new generations that are more effective in reaching people where they are. These ideas are controversial, critical, and engaging. They have profound influences that cannot be ignored in any philosophical study of contemporary church aesthetics.

Our purpose is to explore these two reactions with particular attention to the ways they seek to bridge the culture gap and engage in religious activities. After I describe these two approaches, I will then discuss some of the values each movement embraces. Then in the next chapter I will use Dewey's analysis to examine the aesthetics and explain why I believe their attempts to bridge the culture gap are inadequate.

A DESCRIPTION OF THE SEEKER-SENSITIVE CHURCH

The "seeker-sensitive" approach attempts to correct the problems of traditional churches by using marketing theories to restructure the local church. For the sake of evangelism, that is, spreading the gospel message, the seeker-sensitive church attempts to be "culturally inviting."

"A seeker church is one that tailors its programs and services to attract people who are not church attenders."[203] Thus, seeker churches strip traditional churches of their usual or normal aesthetics of historical and liturgical elements and ecclesiastical designs, icons, and interior structures. In place of these "barriers," they utilize contemporary forms of worship and cutting-edge technology, target "felt-needs" (what people consciously lack and desire) through mass marketing, and restructure the design of the church to conform to the other aspects of suburban or urban life. In essence, they remove any object or design that may prove to be an obstacle to potential guests.

Bill Hybels, a 23-year-old college student and youth minister, who was disgruntled by the "staleness in traditional churches," envisioned a church that "could speak to the contemporary concerns of suburban professionals like himself."[204] He rented a movie theater on Sunday mornings and within a year his congregation grew from over 100 high school students to a congregation of 1,000 young people. The church's name is Willow Creek Community Church. Three years later it was 3,000 people strong, and by 1994 it boasted 15,000 attendees and found itself on a 120-acre campus in an affluent Chicago suburb, South Barrington, Illinois. [205] It became the second-largest Protestant church in the Unites States with approximately a 7,000-seat auditorium and sophisticated audio-visual technology.[206] This church became the leader behind the seeker-sensitive movement. In 2000 Willow Creek was drawing 17,000 people a weekend.[207] The church now averages

---

[203] Kimon Howland Sargeant, *Seeker Churches: Promoting Traditional Religion in a Nontraditional Way* (New Brunswick, NJ: Rutgers University Press, 2000), 2. When asked, "What is the seeker-sensitive movement?" Bill Hybels responds by saying, "It is nothing more than a growing awareness among thousands of church leaders that local churches lost their evangelistic effectiveness many decades ago and that something should be done about it" [Michael G. Mauldin and Edward Gilbreath, "Selling Out the House of God?," *Christianity Today* (18 July 1994): 21].

[204] Edward Gilbreath, "The Birth of a Megachurch," *Christianity Today* (July 18, 1994): 23. Lynne & Bill Hybels, *Rediscovering Church: The Story and Vision of Willow Creek Community Church* (Grand Rapids, MI: Zondervan, 1995), offers a personal account of the formation of this church and how churches can apply their unique philosophy and methodology to other congregations.

[205] Idem.

[206] Eric Reed, "Church: Willow Creek Readies for Megagrowth" *Christianity Today* (April 24, 2000): 54.

[207] Gillmor, Community is Their Middle Name," 48.

23,000 attendees every weekend. In 2009 the annual budget was reported to be $54 million dollars.[208] In 2000, the church also branched out, offering four satellite campuses for those who live more than 30 minutes from the main campus.[209]

As a result of its incredible success in church growth, other churches began to follow and in 1991 an alliance was established among like-minded churches known as "Willow Creek Association" (WCA). By the year 2000 it was comprised of 5,600 seeker-sensitive churches in 90 denominations.[210] The membership by 2009 was reported to be at 12,000. This association hosts conferences, offers curriculum and materials, and provides networking resources for churches to benefit from each other's experiences.[211] In fact, approximately 65,000 church leaders attend WCA conferences every year.[212]

In 2000 Willow Creek announced a $70 million dollar new building project on the church's now 155-acre suburban Chicago campus. Plans were drawn for 49,000 square foot office building, a classroom building for workshops, and a new auditorium with over 7,000 seats.[213] In a 2009 on-line article, the Briefing Room notes:

> Its [Willow Creek] truly awe-inspiring auditorium boasts over 7,200 seats, which technically make it the largest theater in the world. Thanks to state-of-the-art sound, LED display, and projection systems, not one of the seats could be fairly described as 'bad,' a fact that makes Willow Creek's services so engaging.[214]

Hybels broke away from traditional sets of physical and visual practices of worship. By exercising creativity, innovation, and strategy, he sought to identify, connect, and impact people who are described as the "unchurched." These are people who are unfamiliar, estranged, or

---

[208] William C. Symonds, "Marketing," *Stanford Business* (February 2009): 16.

[209] Ibid., 18.

[210] Gillmor, "Community Is Their Middle Name," *Christianity Today* (November 13, 2000): 54.

[211] Michael S. Hamilton, "Willow Creek's Place in History" *Christianity Today* (November 13, 2000): 67-8.

[212] Idem.

[213] Verla Gillmor, "The Next 25 Years," *Christianity Today* (November 13, 2000): 54.

[214] Heather Davis, "Daniel Subwoofers Handle the Low-End for Willow Creek Church," *The Briefing Room*, April 14, 2009 <www.blogsvconline.com/2009/04/14/danley-subwoofers-handle-the-low-end-for-willow-creek-church/>. Retrieval date: 1 June 2010.

have ill feelings toward the Christian faith. Therefore, the seeker-sensitive movement strives to change the "unchurched" perception. As a result, Sunday morning worship activity shifted from one of edifying believers to evangelism by creating an atmosphere that is culturally inviting and using various means to communicate the gospel in a manner that is entertaining. In fact, Hybels contends that Willow Creek is "following the pattern of the first-century church."[215]

How Hybels restructured an evangelical worship service is interesting. Consider the following observations. Edward Gilbreath remarks:

> Willow Creek does not look like 'church.' There are no crosses, steeples, or stained-glass windows. And the church's weekend 'seeker services,' geared to attract the unchurched, dispense with reciting creeds or using hymnals and employ professional-quality drama and contemporary Christian music.[216]

In his 1996 article in the *Atlantic Monthly*, "Welcome to the Next Church," Charles Trueheart observes:

> No spires. No crosses. No robes. No clerical collars. No hard pews. No kneelers. No biblical gobbledygook. No prayer rote. No fire, no brimstone. No pipe organ. No dreary eighteenth-century hymns. No forced solemnity. No Sunday finery. No collection plates.[217]

The church resembles a convention center with a large auditorium surrounded by an even larger parking lot. The buildings

---

[215] Gilbreath, "The Birth of a Megachurch," 23. When asked what are the biblical marks of a healthy church, Hybels responds:
One way we describe it is that the church exists for the four-fold purpose of exaltation, evangelism, edification, and social action. Then there's the Acts 2 model, where the first-century church devoted itself to teaching, fellowship, prayer, and Communion. Sometimes we just go down these grids looking for those marks of a biblical church, then we keep lining Willow Creek up against them to see how we're doing [Ibid., 22].

[216] Ibid.

[217] Charles Trueheart, "Welcome to the Next Church," *Atlantic Monthly* (August, 1996): 37-58.

are similar to downtown structures; they are purposefully architecturally divorced from the historical legacy of church architecture. There are no features that may promote barriers between church and community.

In a 2000 *Christianity Today* article, "Community is their Middle Name," Veria Gillmor notes, "The services' 'wow' factor is aided by 50 vocalists, a 75 piece choir, seven rhythm bands, a 65-piece orchestra, 41 actors, a video production department, and an arts center with 200 students that serves as a farm club for future talent."[218] In an Op-Ed article in the *The New York Times*, columnist David Brooks describes the seeker-sensitive churches this way:

> To fill the pews, they [churches] often emphasize the upbeat and the encouraging and play down the business about God's wrath. In today's megachurches, the technology is cutting-edge, the music is modern, the language is therapeutic, and the dress is casual. These churches are seeker-sensitive, not authoritarian.[219]

In order to be culturally inviting, the church produced programs around the "felt-needs" of "consumers" and used contemporary cultural ideas, lingo, and pop icons to provoke curiosity. The tremendous growth it has experienced in sheer numbers has been overwhelming. As a result, Willow Creek generated a church marketing movement phenomenon, employing professional expertise, skills, and statistics to bridge the culture gap and make a positive impact in community. In fact, many people describe the seeker-sensitive movement as "pragmatic evangelicalism."[220]

The "unchurched" are sure to feel comfortable and entertained and even awe-struck as they absorb the huge building, professional

---

[218] Gillmor, "Community Is Their Middle Name," 49.

[219] David Brooks, "The National Creed," *The New York Times* (December 30, 2003), 21.

[220] *Listening to the Beliefs of the Emerging Churches: Five Perspectives*, ed. Robert Webber (Grand Rapids, MI: Zondervan, 2007), 15. For example, Webber writes:

This wide spread presence of pragmatic evangelicalism has made traditional evangelicalism look like a 'throwback to a 'past era,' and as the traditional church, its building, its worship, and its evangelism went into decline, so did its theology. It isn't that the megachurch and the new evangelicalism reputed the old theology; it was more a case of the transference of interest. The theological issues of traditional evangelicalism became nonissues. The mega church, seeker tradition, contemporary worship, and the need-driven church became post-evangelical, or at least post-traditional evangelical. So pragmatic evangelicalism, responding to

music, sophisticated multimedia, and skits. Non-confrontational uplifting messages are delivered, referencing popular culture and addressing practical needs. In fact, the pastor, who is dressed in casual attire, often uses humor, skits, imagery, and music to draw upon and augment a particular point or topic(s) to be addressed. The church's leadership believes this consumer approach attracts people who are searching for answers and brings them into a relationship with Christ. The hope is that the church can capitalize on the contagious fervor to reach out and serve the greater community.[221]

If we were to enter into a church like Willow Creek for the first time, we would immediately be struck by the size of the sanctuary and the large projection screens. Typically in a church like Willow Creek, soothing recorded music is playing in the background while announcements, images, and photographs are displayed on the giant screens. Reminiscent of the sensational church, the volume of music continues to build as the time of the service draws near. Then the singing begins. The volume and energy exponentially rise and the singers and musicians, who are outstanding, offer a well-produced show. The lyrics to the music are projected across the screens with images to reinforce the message. Monologues, skits, and other dramatic tools are used. Every transition is smooth. The pastor comes forward to offer an entertaining message, typically examining a conscious need or desire.[222] Oftentimes, he sits on a bar stool and in a friendly, endearing tone, offers an encouraging and inspiring message.

Unlike the church, the actual message from the pastor is not abstract, conceptual, or theoretically driven. The message is typically top-

---

the unraveling of society, created new practical solutions-corporate churches, entertainment worship, need-driven programs, therapeutic faith. Theology became relevant. Pragmatics become prominent. The divorce between theology and practice was complete. Traditionalists maintained their intellectual theology, their evidential apologetics, their propositionalism, and their foundationalism. Pragmatics, on the other hand, were concerned with practice, meeting the needs of the people through a pragmatic agenda. They have drawn hundreds of thousands of converts around the world. They have instituted numerous small groups for Bible study and accountability. Their churches are thriving, welcoming, hospitable places, open to all groups, serving the needs of broken families, single mothers, abused spouses, alcoholics, drug addicts, and the aged. And these churches are to be commended for these and other successes in meeting needs [Ibid].

[221] Matt Branaugh, "Willow Creek's 'Huge Shift'," *Christianity Today* (June 2008): 13.
[222] Scott Thumma & Dave Travis, *Beyond Megachurch Myths: What We Can Learn from America's Largest Churches* (San Francisco: Jossey-Bass, 2007), 149.

ical and at times expositional. It is practical in content. Self-depreciating humor and real-life stories are used. Illustrations from film, music, sports, games, and television shows are incorporated throughout the message. Cultural and political issues such as the importance of recycling may even be discussed. The pastor possesses excellent speech, an engaging personality, and a sincere disposition.

Unlike the elite, broken, humdrum, and sensational churches, seeker-sensitive churches seek to intentionally design the worship experience in a way that preserves a person's anonymity. In other words, they do not want to place the "seeker" in an awkward position. For example, the attendees are rarely asked to participate in corporate singing. In his book, *Introduction to Christian Worship*, James F. White, observes that there is very little singing by the congregation. Rather, "professional musicians provide 'entertainment evangelism' with music that resonates in nostalgic style to whatever age group is targeted."[223] These musicians are highly competent. In fact, the service itself is performance driven. Scott Thumma and Dave Travis note:

> Within this stream [attendees are merely observers], the performance value of the worship presentation is very important. The entire worship experience includes a 'down-to-the-second' production sheet with each element carefully scripted, rehearsed, polished, and delivered on the mark during the service. Afterward, the worship leaders gather to review the experience, tweak any elements for future worship services that weekend, and learn from any glitches before the next weekend. Some of these churches have even created the staff position of 'weekend producer' to plan and execute all elements of the service.[224]

---

[223] White, *Introduction to Christian Worship*, 129. According to *Christianity Today*, Os Guinness fears that when the church embraces these tools of modernity they invite potential chaos. Guinness states:
Totally planned, professionally orchestrated, single-purposed environments' may be as 'effective' for evangelism in megachurches as they are for selling in megamalls. But when everything is controlled… who controls the church and who controls the controllers [Mauldin and Gilbreath, "Selling Out the House of God?," 21].

[224] Thumma & Travis, *Beyond Megachurch Myths*, 149.

They also state:

> The overall level of the worship experience must be perceived as excellent for the local context. The church is not only being judged in relation to other churches, but is also being compared to larger cultural criteria. In the minds of its attendees, the church's worship service is measured against nightclubs, movies, television, and entertainment venues.[225]

Interestingly, addressing the criticisms by representatives of traditional churches that Willow Creek is "watering down" the gospel by both making no real demands on listeners and by cultivating an entertainment atmosphere, Hybels responds:

> The word entertainment, of course, is emotive by its nature. And yes, we do use drama, contemporary Christian music, and multi-media presentations. But they are never used for the sake of titillation. I think it's good to ask: 'Who was the master composer? Who created the arts? Whose idea was it to communicate the truth through a wide variety of artistic genres? I think it was God. Then why has the church narrowed its options and selected a talking head as its only form of communicating the most important message on the planet? Even though preaching is the primary way the truth of God has been and should be communicated, we add texture and feeling and perspective to it through the use of music and media and drama. And anyone who has witnessed our presentations would never use the words 'mere entertainment.[226]

James White, a professor of liturgical studies at Drew University, contends that the seeker service "may not be considered worship at all but a form of evangelism."[227]

---

[225] Ibid., 154.
[226] Gilbreath, "The Birth of a Megachurch," 23.
[227] White, *Introduction to Christian Worship*, 165.

Worship as Experience

How does a church like Willow Creek go beyond attracting thousands of people with its elaborate performance-driven service to directly ministering to the needs of the people? In an investigation of seeker-sensitive megachurches like Willow Creek, John Mickelthwait and Adrian Wooldridge state, "So they have begun to adopt techniques that allow churches to be both big and small, spectacular and intimate, at the same time."[228] Willow Creek emphasizes active participation in small groups whereby interpersonal relationships and support may be offered to one another. This is perhaps the most important aspect of its ministry because it is in small groups, that is, gatherings composed of several people or families, where relational friendships are made, nurturing support is offered, and instruction is given.

The church also offers community-care ministries in which congregational members may serve. These include programs such as coping with divorce, career transition, marital restoration, postpartum depression, and meeting the needs of those who are physically or mentally challenged. The church also offers diverse outreach opportunities to engage and enrich the lives of those in the community who are homeless, poor, and in prison.[229]

For example, in the Divorce Recovery program, 450 people sign up for each 10-week session and approximately 35-40% of those attending describe themselves as seekers. Willow Creek offers more than 100 ministries with 29 of them being community-care programs.[230] These programs foster a sense of belonging and purpose to the attendees who are involved.

Though Willow Creek church is reported to have a staff of 200 full-time paid employees, the church largely functions by volunteers. For example, most of the church's in-depth instruction occurs in "small groups" are done by lay-leaders. This structure stands in stark contrast to the elite church. Why allow the church's activities be led by volunteers? For one, the church discovered that "service is its own reward." Trueheart notes:

---

[228] John Micklethwait and Adrian Wooldridge, *God is Back: How the Global Revival of the Faith is Changing the World* (New York: Penguin Press, 2009), 187.

[229] Gilbreath, "The Birth of a Megachurch," 23.

[230] Gillmor, "Community Is Their Middle Name," 50.

What brings people to their gift of service is a desire to do something that—perhaps unlike their day job, perhaps unlike their evenings—matters. Among the things that they didn't realize they wanted when they came back to church, in the view of many people I met, was not just a changed life but also the chance to change the lives of others.[231]

In his sociological account of the seeker-sensitive movement, Charles Trueheart declares, "Centuries of European tradition and Christian habit are deliberately being abandoned, clearing the way for new, contemporary forms of worship and belonging."[232] This entirely new way of doing church is unprecedented in the history of Christian worship.

Why is this change needed? In his book, *A Church for the 21st Century*, Leith Anderson, for example, calls the traditional church to change from being fixed on that which is theoretical and standardized, and become practical by learning how to customize to meet the needs of a particular community. Knowing the demographical and geographical context in which the community is embedded is required in order to develop a healthy strategy for change. In contrast, Anderson argues that traditional churches (e.g., the elite, broken, and humdrum) are having no effect on the world outside of their own walls. In fact, he contends that if these traditional churches cling to old ways, they will suffer decline. Death is inevitable. Therefore, he defends the reinvention of the church.[233]

---

[231] Charles Trueheart, "Welcome to the New Church," *Atlantic Monthly* (August 1996): 54.
[232] Ibid., 37. Trueheart goes on to say:
The Next Church, as the independent and entrepreneurial congregations that are adopting these new forms might collectively be called, is drawing lots of people, including many Americans with patching or blank histories of churchgoing. It constitutes, its champions believe, a distinctly American reformulation of church life, one that transcends denominations and the bounds of traditional churchly behavior. As such, it represents something more: a reconfiguration of secular communities, not just sacred ones. Social institutions that once held civic life together-schools, families, governments, companies, neighborhoods, and even old-style churches-are not what they used to be (if ever they were what we imagined). The new congregations are reorganizing religious life to fill that void. The Next Church in its fully realized state can be the clearest approximation of community, and perhaps the most important civic structure, that a whole generation is likely to have known or likely to find anywhere in an impersonal, transient nation [Ibid., 37-8].
[233] Leith Anderson, *A Church for the 21st Century: Bringing Change to Your Church to*

While Bill Hybels was disenchanted and broke away from the manner in which traditional churches conducted services; he contends that he has not forsaken the church's ancient heritage. In fact, Hybels states, "We've set up all our leadership structures and goals to grow a full-functioning Acts 2 community, as opposed to just an evangelizing machine that doesn't drive the roots down deep and do all the other things it's supposed to do."[234] In another interview, Hybels states:

> I find most traditional churches are not organized according to spiritual gifts. They don't have discipleship and small-group emphasis. I find that traditional churches do not understand or practice biblical worship. I see most traditional churches as teaching centers that seek to influence people primarily for an hour a week, as opposed to a biblically functioning community that has a full-orbed approach to bringing people to Christ, assimilating them into the body of Christ, discipling them, helping them find their spiritual gifts, and sensitizing them to the needs of the world.[235]

He later states:

> I don't mean it to sound hostile. I think the reality is more like a continuum than polar opposites. Some traditional churches are seeker-hostile and very narrow in the scope of their ministry. There are also many traditional churches that are effective in evangelism and have well-rounded ministries, without necessarily being contemporary and seeker driven.[236]

Meet the Challenges of a Changing Society (Minneapolis, MN: Bethany House, 1992), 26. For example, Anderson writes:

While the New Testament speaks often about churches, it is surprisingly silent about matters that we associate with church structure and life. There is no mention of architecture, pulpits, length of typical sermons, or rules for having a Sunday school. Little is said about style of music, order of worship, or times of church gatherings. There were no Bibles, denominations, camps, pastors' conference or board meeting minutes. Those who strive to be New Testament churches must seek to live its principles and absolutes, not reproduce the details. We don't know many of the details, and if we reproduced the ones we do know, we would end up with synagogues, speaking Greek, and the divisive sins of the Corinthians [Ibid].

[234] Idem, 37.
[235] Idem, 22.
[236] Idem.

How this church impacts the lives of others is interesting. Consider the testimony of Teresa Russo-Cox. Russo-Cox serves as a volunteer for the church's hairdresser ministry. When interviewed, she had been a professional hairdresser for 25 years and an educator for Paul Mitchell hair products. One day she was invited by one of her clients to join her at Willow Creek.

"I was raised Catholic but had left church," Russo-Cox says, "When I first walked into Willow, I thought, 'What is this all about? No icons? No robes?' I remember John Ortberg spoke on 'Shhh, God is Speaking.' My heart was beating fast, and I knew God was speaking to me. Right there I rededicated my life to Christ."[237]

Afterwards, Russo-Cox became like a hungry baby and could not get enough "spiritual food" to make up for the previous years. Therefore, she took a class on "How to be a Contagious Christian" and one on spiritual gifts.[238] Interestingly, she later said that she and her husband were about to lose their home because of a bad business decision. As a result, a volunteer counselor in Willow's "Good Sense Ministry" set them up on a budget and enabled them to get their finances under control.[239]

Her husband became active in the Christian Auto Repairman Serving ministry that provided 300 free car repairs. Moreover, this ministry was able to restore 120 cars out of the 1,200 that were donated to provide vehicles for needy families. On the other hand, Russo-Cox created a hairdressers ministry whereby she and thirty other professional hairdressers volunteer to wash, cut, and style hair for abused and battered women and for women who are alone and pregnant, as well as for homeless people.[240]

Therefore, this story and thousands like them reveal the purpose behind the seeker-sensitive movement and its incredible success in view of the thousands of people who attend every week:

> The idea behind all this was to create a kind of nondenominational church that would use an interesting program and comfortable

---
[237] Idem.
[238] Idem.
[239] Idem.
[240] Idem.

surroundings to draw in the unchurched. Once drawn in, they would be enveloped in a comprehensive network of activities designed to give them a supportive community and deeper instruction in the Christian faith.[241]

Its success is often attributed to its innovation and ability to target felt-needs. One editorial put it this way:

> The modern megachurch is now famous for 'innovation' and 'growth through strategies, programs, tools, and resources' so that the churches can 'multiply their impact.' That's the reason for its success in America, where business principles and organizational techniques sit atop the altar of Success. These principles have indeed led to many Americans being brought into the kingdom of God.[242]

But it does not merely seek to target needs. Rather, the church capitalizes on vision, experimentation, and re-evaluation. Like a successful business, the leadership will cast a vision. They will experiment and see if this direction or program produces benefits. If a particular program does not produce growth, the leadership will evaluate the program and tweak it if possible. But if these adjustments do not create productive growth, the program is terminated. In fact, any program that merely subsists will be stopped even to the chagrin of those who are involved in it.

We will now extrapolate three values from this description of the seeker-sensitive movement. First, this movement seeks to mirror activities that the community values. Secondly, it values creative ways to attract people to the church. Lastly, it values experimentation to produce better results, for its focus is on growth. Let us now discuss these values before we turn our attention to the pluralistic emerging movement.

---

[241] Hamilton, "Willow Creek's Place in History," 62-3.
[242] Editorial, "Mega-Mirror: Mega Churches are not the answer or the problem," *Christianity Today* (August 2009): 20.

1. Mirror the community. The manner in which seeker-sensitive churches seek to be culturally inviting is by reflecting what is familiar outside of the church. For example, the architecture, music style, entertainment, technology, and other activities are indistinguishable from the community. Unlike a Gothic cathedral, for example, there is no novelty. In an effort to be non-threatening and shake the poor connotations many hold of the traditional church, the same message of old is repackaged with contemporary décor to reach greater numbers. The look, sound, and feel of these churches reflects what is seen, heard, and felt in other inviting, popular, and nonreligious places of the culture.

2. Commercialize the church. The seeker-sensitive church actively seeks to find the most creative, innovative, and irresistible ways to attract people to the church targeting felt-needs. These types of churches are "artful practitioners" of commerce.[243] David F. Wells puts it this way, "The marketing of the faith now seems so natural because the spiritual and the material markets have come to resemble one another."[244] In essence, the church as an institution is responding "to today's consumerist ethos."[245] Interestingly, the church will even "use branding to expand their market share: Willow Creek finished in the top 5 percent of one survey of 250 major American brands."[246]

3. Focus is on growth. The seeker-sensitive church continually experiments, evaluates, reflects, and strives to think "outside of the box" in order to achieve growth and generate benefits for both attendees and community. Thus, the seeker-sensitive church uses business theory, strategic planning, and visionary thinking to maximize its present ministry while anticipating and meeting future needs. In fact, Mick-

---

[243] David F. Wells, *Above All Earthly Pow'rs: Christ in a Postmodern World* (Grand Rapids, MI: 2005), 283.

[244] Idem. Wells notes:
The line between faith and retailing, business and belief, the Church and the world has been under steady assault in evangelicalism for many years. Examples of the blurring of the line can be found not only in these seeker churches but on all sides—in Christian music, in Christian bookstores, and in those Christian churches which are not only marketing the faith but also facilitating the sale of life insurance, vacation packages, and hair styling, to name but a few [Idem].

[245] Sargeant, *Seeker Churches*, 11; Wells, *Above All Earthly Pow'rs*, 281.

[246] Micklethwait and Wooldridge, *God is Back*, 188.

lethwait and Wooldridge discovered that even businesses are learning about marketing strategies from the religious sector. They write:

> The management thinker Peter Drucker used to point out that these churches are superb at motivating their employees and volunteers, and superb, also at transforming volunteers from well-meaning amateurs into disciplined professionals. The best churches have discovered the secret of low-cost and self-sustaining growth–transforming seekers into Evangelicals who will then go out and recruit more seekers. How many businesses could boast such committed customers?[247]

Interestingly, according to Thumma and Travis, in a 2005 survey of mega-churches like Willow Creek, only 15% of them have not changed their format or style in the past five years. In contrast, 60% said one or more of their weekend services have changed "somewhat" or "a lot."[248]

Having described how the seeker-sensitive movement seeks to bridge the culture gap and engage in aesthetic activities we will now direct our attention to a description of the emerging church movement(s) and its values. This pluralistic movement champions that which is experiential, pluralistic, and sensory. In fact, of all the churches we have examined, emerging churches are the most difficult to pin down given their emphasis on particular contextualization, creativity, spontaneity, and pluralistic practices in order to bridge the culture gap and offer a meaningful worship experience to their community each and every week.

A DESCRIPTION OF THE EMERGING/EMERGENT CHURCH

The emerging movement(s) is a mindset that strives for an "incarnational" way of "becoming." An incarnational mindset is seeking to specifically identify with Jesus Christ in word, action, and lifestyle. Emerging churches believe that imitating Christ is how the

---
[247] Ibid.,189.
[248] Ibid., 155.

church is to be, live, and have its becoming, especially because many emerging leaders declare that we live in a "post-Christian culture," that is, a society where the Christian consensus no longer remains in terms of values, customs, and habitual practices. As a result, emerging churches see themselves as being intentionally missional by means of nature and function. In other words, they consider the church to be a "verb," namely, "community in Christ-like action," and not a "noun," that is, a place where believers attend. To them, a church that is a "noun" is reflective of traditional and seeker-sensitive churches.[249]

Being "missionally minded" also involves particular contextualization, that is, adjusting to the interests, needs, and practices that is reflective of the church's specific cultural and social context. Given the amount of sub-cultures that exist in this pluralistic society, how each emerging church relates within its particular context may greatly differ. As a result, certain aesthetic practices and rituals may vary from one emerging church to another. For example, an emerging church may adapt its activities to reflect a neighborhood that is largely composed of Chinese-Americans.

Therefore, emerging churches are diverse because of the sensitivity to the particular contexts in which they are embedded. Because this is a recent expression in Christian thought and practice, these groups are developing as they learn about themselves in relation to the particular historical, situational, and social contexts. They are also experimental for each particular church may continually change its emphasis, worship experience, and activities. A general sense of openness to creative expressions of worship mark this movement, as it sees itself as an organic expression of the Christian life in a culture that continues to change.

Lastly, emerging churches value community in terms of authenticity and shared experience, whereby both "belief" and "belonging" are integrated together. In other words, they want to create contextualized communities of faith where honest questions may be asked, where interpersonal relationship are meaningfully constructed, and where presuppositions and pre-understandings may honestly be evaluated

---

[249] For the purposes of simplicity and coherency, I will continue to use "church" to mean an assembly in this and all later chapters.

within the context of genuine, humble dialogue. Presuppositions are fixed biases that do not change unless extreme pressure is applied and pre-understandings are moldable fluid-like influences that come and go. Dialogues or "conversations" of this sort occur with the recognition that we are within and not above culture. We are finite creatures within a larger universe and are real people, not mere products. Being made in the image of God involves such factors as personality (e.g., intellect, will, and emotion), stewardship, interpersonal relationships, and divine representation. In other words, like an ambassador representing the interests of his government in a foreign land, we are called to be God's representatives who represent His interests on earth. Thus, authenticity and evaluation all take place together in an experiential and incarnational context. These are all aspects of what may be described as community worship.

We will begin by defining the term "emerging" and how this sociological word became identified with a church movement. We will then consider the origins of the movement followed by the various types of emerging churches. Afterwards, we will synthesize some of these churches' aesthetic values.

1. The Meaning of "emerging." The term, "emerging," is both a difficult term to define and a very complex phenomenon. Hence, any description of this term is limiting because emerging churches are so diverse, and also because they are a recent development.[250] Notwithstanding these difficulties, three judgments stand out.

First, the term "emerging" finds sociological expression in the groundbreaking work of Jeffrey Jensen Arnett.[251] In essence, psychologist Arnett discovered a new and distinct period of human

---

[250] Eddie Gibbs and Ryan Bolger, *Emerging Churches: Creating Christian Community in Postmodern Cultures* (Grand Rapids, MI: Baker, 2005), offers a helpful definition of the emerging church:
Emerging churches are communities that practice the way of Jesus within postmodern cultures. This definition encompasses nine practices. Emerging churches (1) identify with the life of Jesus, (2) transform the secular realm (3) live highly communal lives. Because of these three activities, they (4) welcome the stranger, (5) serve with generosity (6) participate as producers (7) create as created beings, (8) lead as a body, and (9) take part in spiritual activities [Scot McKnight, "Five Streams of the Emerging Church," *Christianity Today* (February 2007) 35].

[251] See Jeffrey Jensen Arnett, *Emerging Adulthood: The Winding Road from the Late Teens through the Twenties* (Oxford, UK: Oxford University Press, 2004).

development in our culture that he identifies as "Emerging Adulthood." Too old to be described as adolescents, but not having accepted the responsibilities normative to adulthood, emerging adults are between the ages of 18-29. Arnett's conclusions are helpful in understanding the contemporary culture gap between churches and community. But his findings also explain why emerging churches are very critical of the internal structures, activities, goals, and interests of both traditional and seeker-sensitive churches.[252]

Reflective of Taylor's insights about the current trends in our culture, Arnett's empirical studies discovered that 22% of emerging adults embrace either atheism, that is, they plainly reject any belief in God, or agnosticism, meaning, they are unsure about what to believe about religious questions.[253] On the other hand, 28% of emerging adults embrace deism, 27% consider themselves to be liberal believers, and 23% claim they are conservative believers.[254]

Arnett also discovered a minimal connection to the religious beliefs emerging adults received when they were children and adolescents. In essence, emerging adults are determined to think for themselves. They want to make their own decisions about religious belief.[255] One reason

---

[252] In his book, *The Deep Church*, Jim Belcher concludes from his survey of emerging churches that this movement(s) is critical of traditional and seeker-sensitive churches' integration of the following seven outdated and abusive ideas: (1) captivity to Enlightenment (basing truth on natural reason and not revelation; championing individualism, rationalism, and pragmatism and the justification of their positions on the basis of the self-evident truth of reason and common sense); (2) poor emphasis on consistent and meaningful Christian living (sanctification); (3) theological belief before belonging, that is, a person must possess correct theology before one can be accepted and ministered to by the community; (4) un-contextualized worship that is, using music and practicing activities that do not speak to the particular culture in which churches are situated; (5) ineffective preaching, that is, didactic teaching from a singular authoritarian voice; (6) weak ecclesiology whereby the church is more concerned with its form than with its mission. In other words, the church is more of an institutional authority concerned more about protecting its assets and preserving its traditions; (7) sectarian position in community [*The Deep Church: A Third Way beyond Emerging and Traditional* (Downers Grove, IL: InterVarsity Press, 2009), 41-3]. The traditional church is "known for what it is against more than what it is for" [Ibid., 43].

[253] Arnett, *Emerging Adulthood*, 167.

[254] Arnett states that emerging adults are declare deism as a "general belief in god or a 'higher power' or 'spirituality,' but only in a general sense, not in the context of any religious tradition" [Ibid., 169]. Liberal believers, share the deist's skepticism of organized religion and accepting of different believes, yet describe themselves as members of a specific religious tradition such as Catholicism, Baptist, or Jewish [Ibid., 170]. In contrast, emerging adults who are conservative believers express beliefs in the doctrinal traditions of organized religion [Ibid].

[255] Ibid., 174-7.

why religious training in childhood and adolescence makes so little difference in their lives is that, "...in the course of growing up, people gradually become exposed to more and more influences and ideas outside of the family."[256]

Emerging adult religious beliefs are often diverse because the individuals value the notion of constructing or embracing their own set of religious beliefs instead of receiving dogma. In fact, for emerging adults, constructing a set of religious beliefs is a personal responsibility. Being skeptical of religious institutions, emerging adults "...tend to personalize their relationship with God in a way that makes participating in organized religion unnecessary or even an impediment to the expression of their beliefs."[257]

Even though, for many emerging adults, individual happiness means gaining a broad range of life experiences, Arnett also discerned many of them have life-goals that reflect collectivist values such as generosity, loyalty, and self-sacrifice with family and community in view.[258] In fact, both individualism and collectivistic notions are not assumed to be in conflict with one another.[259]

Second, associated with above, "emerging" refers to a generation of people who are born or raised in a culture, which considers the philosophical ideas of the Enlightenment (namely the emphasis upon reason and science alone to create better people and better society) to be philosophically and existentially bankrupt.[260] Instead, ideas are being cultivated having roots in Romanticism. The celebration of spirituality, the power of the imagination, the elimination of separate categories in favor of unity, and the largeness of reality are a few examples of this resurgence. These ideas stand in contrast to one who desires to "hold knowledge in the structures of human rationality (with or without

---

[256] Ibid., 176.
[257] Ibid., 173.
[258] Ibid., 180-7.
[259] Ibid., 183.
[260] For example, see Jean-François Lyotard, *The Postmodern Condition: A Report on Knowledge* (Minneapolis, MN: University of Minneapolis, 1984); Daniel Taylor, *The Myth of Certainty: The Reflective Christian and the Risk of Commitment* (Grand Rapids, MI: Zondervan, 1992). I have come to discover that this popular claim we are now living in a postmodern culture is an exaggeration. This is substantiated, for example, by the popularity of books written by naturalists like Richard Dawkins and Christopher Hitchens and the existence of communities that espouse foundationalism, namely, that all knowledge is ultimately supported on a basis or foundation of justified belief.

God)."[261] Though emerging churches differ greatly church-to-church, emerging adults share this Romantic mindset. Taylor describes them as "seekers."[262]

2. Emerging churches against "modernistic" evangelicalism. Emerging churches find themselves at odds with both seeker-sensitive and traditional churches. They are opposed to both because, in part, the framework, thought, and activities of these institutions are integrated with Enlightenment ideas, and thus, are considered to be foreign to Scripture. For example, the idea that theology can be built upon mind's rational ability to perceive totalizing knowledge with certainty outside of the historical process as unconditioned specialists are modernistic assumptions and need to be rejected. Not surprisingly, emerging churches have a distrust of modernistic claims of theological knowledge. But that does not mean emerging churches declare all interpretations are invalid. Stanley Grenz puts it this way:

> Ultimately the metanarrative we proclaim lies beyond the pale of reason to discover or to evaluate. Therefore, we agree that in this world we will witness and struggle among narratives and interpretations of reality. But we add that although all interpretations are in some sense invalid, they cannot be equally invalid.[263]

We have entered into a decisive era marked by a secular upheaval, replacing the values of the old civic order with a new one. The values generated in the 1960s are so strongly identified with dysfunction and cultural decadence, they are no longer considered viable for positive

---

[261] Following Os Guinness, a careful distinction needs to be made between "modernism" and "modernity." He understands modernism to be a philosophical idea whereas modernity refers to structural developments in areas such as technology and medicine [Mars Hill Interview, "Calling, Postmodernism, and Chastened Liberals: A Conversation with Os Guinness," *Mars Hill Review*, no. 8 (Summer 1997): 69-82].

[262] *Listening to the Beliefs of the Emerging Church*, 25.

[263] Stanley J. Grenz, *A Primer on Postmodernism* (Grand Rapids, MI: Eerdmans, 1996), 164-5. See also Stanley J. Grenz & John R. Franke, *Beyond Foundationalism: Shaping Theology in a Postmodern Context* (Philadelphia: Westminster John Knox, 2000); Stanley Grenz, *Revisioning Evangelical Theology: A Fresh Approach for the 21st Century* (Downers Grove, IL: InterVarsity, 1993; Brian D. Ingraffia, *Postmodern Theory and Biblical Theology* (Cambridge, UK: Cambridge University, 1995); Nancey Murphy, *Anglo-American Postmodernity: Philosophical Perspectives on Science, Religion, and Ethics* (Boulder, CO: Westview Press, 1997).

change. As a result, young generations of people, some even identifying themselves as "post-evangelical," are turning away from organized institutions that embody Enlightenment practices such as individualistic focus, systematic doctrinal formulations, and passive participation. Likewise, they are also rejecting seeker-oriented churches that focus on felt-need programs, are performance driven, or reduce personhood to commodities or numbers.[264]

Consider the following examples. In his book, *Divine Commodity*, Skye Jethani, captures this anti-sensitive-seeker sentiment well when he states:

> Not long ago I was attending a ministry conference at a very large church. The setting was impressive by any measure. The mammoth auditorium sat thousands in cushioned theater seats rising heavenward. Where I looked a dozen flat-panel displays crammed my field of vision with presenters flashing their high-definition smiles. And the stage was alike, a mechanical beast to behold. It was moving fluidly, breathing smoke, and shooting lasers through its digital chameleon skin. The band members were spread across the platform as jagged teeth in the beast's mouth, and the drummer was precariously suspended from the ceiling like a pagan offering. But even this spectacle could not hold me. In fact, with each passing minute I felt a growing need to escape.[265]

He then leaves the auditorium and walks out to the balcony to be by himself.

> It was dusk. The moon was low on the horizon and the first stars were appearing. With the beauty of creation unfurled before me,

---

[264] The descriptive term, "post-evangelical," is used to refer to their Christian faith after deconstructionism is applied to strip evangelicalism of it modernistic mindset and approaches to Christian theology and practice. How this is done is, in part, is by examining Christian theology and practice for prejudices, totalizing claims, and social structures of control. For example, the theological doctrine inerrancy does not sufficiently express the truth about the Bible [Scot McKnight, "The Ironic Faith of Emergents," *Christianity Today* (September 2008): 62.

[265] Skye Jethani, *Divine Commodity: Discovering a Christian Faith Beyond Consumer Christianity* (Grand Rapids: Zondervan, 2009), 9.

and the glitz of American Christianity behind me, I began to ponder: Is this what Jesus envisioned? Is this why he came, and suffered, and died? Is this why he conquered death and evil, so that we might congregate for multimedia worship extravaganzas in his name? On that balcony, taking the chilled air into my body and watching the stars appear, I met with God in silence-my questions filling the space between us.[266]

The second example flows out of a conversation I enjoyed with a former seeker-sensitive pastor. This dynamic, now emerging, leader explained to me that when he first planted a seeker-sensitive church outside of San Antonio, it was a tremendous success. The church dramatically grew and, within two years, had two services every Sunday morning. People's needs were met and God was glorified. But when he later attempted the same method in North Texas several years later, the church plant failed. Why? First, he did not take into account the particular context in which he sought to plant the church. And second, culture itself had changed. He eventually came to the conclusion that the seeker-sensitive approach reduces people to a product. Under a mechanical, modernistic machine, it not only offers a product, but people become a product. Once the product conforms, then it (he or she) will bring other people to the church to become products themselves. Having recognized these issues, he is now a pastor of an emerging ministry. Even now he is exploring how the church may implement practices of monasticism (e.g., The Benedictine Order) in a way that expresses a commitment to contemplation, community, and missions.

The traditional church, like the seeker-sensitive model, is also a target for criticism as it is an institutionalized construct of religion, captive to modernistic assumptions and practices. For example, in Doug Pagitt's *Preaching Re-Imagined: The Role of the Sermon in Communities of Faith*, the author contends that traditional preaching is not only generated from the Enlightenment ideas and practices, such as an overconfidence by the preacher to know absolute truth that transcends all contexts, but is both dogmatic and dehumanizing since it sets the

---

[266] Ibid., 8-9.

pastor above the people as the expert.[267] Instead, Pagitt contends that the pastor is just one of many voices in the Christian community since all Christians are "believer-priests," possess the Bible, and have the Holy Spirit to guide them.

In sum, emerging leaders believe these modernistic traditional churches champion privatized faith over authentic community. They disproportionally focused on doctrinal content over practical application. In fact, spiritual formation is reduced to head knowledge. As a result, needs of the whole person remains unmet and the community is not served. In order to even be welcomed into a church, one must first embrace "correct theology." They typically make no serious attempt to speak to the present culture. Rather traditional churches are opposed to culture, perhaps better known for what they stand against than what they stand for.

3. Emerging churches against traditional understanding of church community. Emerging churches find both the traditional church and seeker-sensitive church to be more concerned with form than mission. In other words, focus is directed more toward institutional authority and preservation than toward begin being an "incarnational witness" to culture.[268] Modernistic churches are only talking to themselves, unable to change anything or anyone by their own teachings while culture has changed. Willfully or non-willfully failing to adapt, what they offer does not minister the whole person.

Moreover, people are more than products. The hunger for rich experiences, opportunities for participation, and intimate connectivity. In his research, Wade Clark Roof discovered 40% of those who describe themselves as "born again believers" are open to a dialogical setting where questions and doubts are seriously discussed. He goes on to say, "A surprising number of them actually identify themselves as 'seekers,' saying they believe in God but are not sure about organized religion (meaning churches as they have known them), or raise serious questions about the truthfulness of Christianity itself."[269]

---

[267] Belcher, *The Deep Church*, 146-7.
[268] Ibid., 41-3.
[269] Wade Clark Roof, *Spiritual Marketplace: Baby Boomers and the Remaking of American Religion* (Princeton, NJ: Princeton University Press, 1999), 189.

Why are people hungering for such things as connectivity? In his work, *Post-Modern Pilgrims: First Century Passion for the 21st Century World*, emerging leader, Leonard Sweet, observes that technology (e.g., internet) is contributing to interpersonal alienation, disconnectedness, and sterility. He says:

> The more wired to the world our electronic cottages (castles?) become, the more the church will need to be a place that can form authentic community where individuals can be free to be themselves. The more connected we become electronically, the more disconnected we can become personally."[270]

While I do agree with Sweet's statement, I would also add that people like Christopher Lasch concluded two decades earlier the decline of family importance in our society also generated these same problems, both psychologically and socially (e.g., inauthenticity, inner emptiness).[271] Coupled with narcissistic issues such as an awareness of separation and helplessness, the need for belonging, and the source of gratification outside of us (a psychoanalysis idea), connectivity is an ongoing need and emphasis to this generation.[272]

---

[270] Leonard Sweet, *Post-Modern Pilgrims: First Century Passion for the 21st Century* (Nashville, TN: Broadman & Holman, 2000), 115.

[271] Christopher Lasch, *The Culture of Narcissism: American Life in an Age of Diminishing Expectations* (New York: W. W. Norton & Company, 1979), 239. Interestingly, Lasch writes:
Narcissists may have paid more attention to their own needs than to those of others, but self-love and self- aggrandizement did not impress me as their most important characteristics. These qualities implied a strong, stable sense of selfhood, whereas narcissists suffered from a feeling of inauthenticity and inner emptiness. They found it difficult to make connection with the world. At its most extreme, their condition approximated that of Kaspar Hauser, the nineteenth-century German foundling raised in solitary confinement, whose 'impoverished relations with his cultural environment,' according to the psychoanalysis Alexander Mitscherlich, left him with a feeling of being utterly at life's mercy [Ibid., 239-40].
After further reflection on Freud's insights on narcissism, Lasch goes on to say:
The best hope of emotional maturity, appears to lie in a recognition of our need for and dependence on people who nevertheless remain separate from ourselves and refuse to submit to our whims. It lies in a recognition of others not as projections of our own desires but as independent beings with desires of their own. More broadly, it lies in acceptance of our limits. The world does not exist to satisfy our desires; it is a world in which we can find pleasure and meaning, once we understand that others too have a right to these goods. Psychoanalysis confirms the ancient religious insight that the only way to achieve happiness is to accept limitations in a spirit of gratitude and contrition instead of attempting to annul those limitations or bitterly resenting them [Ibid., 242].

[272] Ibid., 241-2.

Therefore, emerging churches in North America contend that both seeker-sensitive churches and traditional churches are no longer effective in bridging the culture gap. To them, both types of churches do not recognize that our Western culture is now "post-Christian" and in many ways has rejected institutionalized religion and Enlightenment assumptions (e.g., that we can obtain neutral knowledge), considering them to be philosophically and existentially bankrupt. They are powerless to reach a new generation that has been born and raised, valuing such notions as authenticity, particular contextualization, spirituality, and tolerance.[273] Essentially, emerging churches are seeking to be pre-modern in thought and practice, that is, looking beyond rational knowledge for God and a meaningful life.[274]

As a result, emerging churches are advocating an "agents of Christ" approach to church, community, and culture at large, seeking to find relational ways in which authenticity, wholeness, and meaning may be expressed against the daily grind of alienation, disconnectedness,

---

[273] Interestingly, in her book, *Generation Me: Why Today's Young Americans Are More Confident, Assertive, Entitled-and More Miserable than Ever Before*, Jean Twenge, a sociology professor at San Diego State University, empirically concludes that our culture has so concentrated on "self-esteem" issues that children born in the 1970s, 1980s, and 1990s are a generation of people with narcissistic mindsets [(New York: Free Press, 2007), 1-15].

[274] Joseph Bottum's article, "Christians and Postmoderns" offers helpful insight in understanding the philosophical definitions of these overused and plastic terms, namely, "premodern," "modern," and "postmodern." He writes:

It is premodern to seek beyond rational knowledge for God; it is modern to desire to hold knowledge in the structures of human rationality (with or without God); it is postmodern to see the impossibility of such knowledge.... The premoderns said that without God there would be no knowledge, and the postmoderns said we have no God and have no knowledge. The premoderns said that without the purposefulness of final causation, all things would be equally valueless, and the postmoderns say there is no purpose and no value. The premoderns said that without an identity of reality and the Good, there would be no right or wrong, and the postmoderns say there is neither Good nor right and wrong. Though they disagree on whether God exists, premoderns and postmoderns share the major premise that knowing requires His existence. Only for a brief period in the history of the West 'the period of modern times' did anyone seriously suppose that human beings could knowledge without God ["Christians and Postmoderns," *First Things* (March 2010), 44].

But then Bottum goes on to claim:

By itself, this parallel between premodern and postmodern does us no good, for we cannot use it to return to the age of faith. Postmodernity is still in the line of modernity, as rebellion against rebellion is still rebellion, as an act on the constraints of grammar must still be written in grammatical senses, as a skeptical argument against the structures of rationality must still be put rationally. Our conceptions of the premodern and the postmodern turn equally on the modern project. Though the postmodern attack on modernity may move our historical imagination to a periphery from which to view the center, it does not remove us from the circle. The failure of the present age is not cured by recognizing it as failing. We need, rather, a different center in order to hold knowledge [Idem].

and oppression. Just as Jesus Christ ministered in a non-Christian, pluralistic culture, they seek to follow his example in a post-Christian, pluralist culture as participants in community, not merely as isolated individuals.

4. The origins of the emerging movement. The emerging church in the United States finds its origins in a Young Pastor's Conference in the late 1990s. Organized by Bob Buford and the Leadership Network, the goal was to bring young pastors together to discuss the cultural change and how churches might meet those changes. Mark Driscoll, founder and pastor of Mars Hill Church in Seattle, Washington from 1996-2014, gave a presentation about the cultural emergence of and identification with postmodernism among Generation X (a descriptive title to refer to the generation of people born between 1961 and 1981). From this conference of young pastors the emerging movement in the United States was conceived.[275] Even though Driscoll eventually distanced himself from the Leadership Network (later called the Young Leader Network) because other members of the group were contending for a theological agenda that troubled him (e.g., low view of Scripture), other dynamic leaders, such as Tony Jones, Dan Kimball, Brian McClaren, and Doug Pagitt, contributed to the movement's attractiveness, influence, and growth.

While the emerging movement offers a way of looking at the Christian faith, it is not centralized with an institutional focus. Instead, various "streams" of emerging movements exist, all discussing how Christian leaders should "do church" in a post-Christian culture. While the general desire is to bridge the culture gap and minister to the needs of post-Christian culture as Christ-centered Christians, emerging churches vary greatly in their given approach. Therefore, it is impossible to sufficiently categorize the activities of the emerging church because they are so contextually driven. Notwithstanding, Doug Pagitt offers a helpful tool of analysis. Emerging churches seek to minister to postmoderns, others with postmoderns, and others as postmoderns.[276]

---

[275] Mark Driscoll, *The Radical Reformission* (Grand Rapids, MI: Zondervan, 2004), 15-6.

[276] Scot McKnight, "Five Streams of the Emerging Church," 37. McKnight describes postmodernism this way:
Postmodernity cannot be reduced to the denial of truth. Instead, it is the collapse of inherited metanarratives (over-arching explanations of life) like those of science or Marxism. Why have they collapsed? Because of the impossibility of getting outside their assumptions

Worship as Experience

5. Three types of emerging churches. As we begin to explore these various types of emerging churches, we need to recognize not all emerging leaders and/or emerging churches are using the term "postmodernism" to refer to philosophical postmodernism, an aspect of continental philosophy.[277] Many of them use this term to literally mean "after-modernism." In other words, emerging from the cultural insolvency of modernism is a generation of people who tend to be experiential, inclusive, and pluralistic, following the intellectual bankruptcy of modernism. While this does not necessarily mean that modernism is dead, it does mean that the emerging adulthood generation questions or rejects this worldview and even blames it for some of the great ills of our society. So, the term, a "postmodern evangelical," may be a declaration against modernism without necessarily commitment to the postmodern ideas of people like Jacques Derrida.

Emerging churches question and challenge long-held assumptions, convictions, and human authorities and emphasize how our environment, biases, and influences affect the way one comes to, understands, and embraces a particular belief. Though emerging churches seek to dismantle the Enlightenment in Christian thought and practice, this does not necessarily mean every emerging church embedded in a particular community believes absolute truth does not exist or that people are determined by their subculture.

For example, a church worship experience may entail people sitting around a circle. The pastor offers a provocative message in order to provide an occasion to uncover fixed biases. He may encourage dialogical conversation, that is, teaching by discussion, or may even publicly share his own doubts or questions about a long-held belief and speculate whether this belief is truly biblical. At other times, this corporate activity may take place over a meal, coffee, or even a hooka. But what is important is to cause those in attendance to re-evaluate what they believe, why they believe it, and move them to look at truth in a different way.

[Ibid., 36].
[277] David West, *An Introduction to Continental Philosophy* (Cambridge, UK: Polity Press, 1996), 1.

The examination of the doctrinal statements, values, or instruction among emerging churches shows many of them openly proclaiming that the Bible is divine and special revelation, and redemption is the grand-meta-narrative of the Bible. They also whole heartily reject cultural and moral relativism. They are not opposed to transcendental truth and transcendental standpoints (e.g., Bible) and take seriously the history of Christian thought and practice with many emerging churches integrating ideas and activities from Patristic and Reformation eras. Moreover, emerging churches advocate the possibility of change, personal responsibility, as well as the social responsibility to make a significant difference in the lives of others. Therefore, it is a mistake to assert all emerging churches embrace philosophical postmodernism.[278] For example, Mark Driscoll states:

> No one is born with a clear comprehension of who God is… But God has chosen to lift the fog of human speculation with divine revelation. Whereas speculation is the human attempt to comprehend God, revelation is God's communication to humanity with clarity that is otherwise impossible.[279]

He later states:

> Scripture themselves teach that they are best understood by being in Christian community. Also, since the church includes all the saints from all ages, we are wise to study the Scripture by learning from the great legacy of teachers who have gone before us, such as Athanasius, Augustine, Calvin, and Wesley.…Therefore, the key to properly understanding Scripture is to come with a humility that is willing to repent of sin and reorient life toward God's commands.[280]

---

[278] Interestingly, in their work, *Why We're Not Emergent: By Two Guys Should Be*, Kevin DeYoung and Ted Cluck contend that the most radical stream of emerging churches, known as emergent, are not philosophically postmodern. Rather, their root problem is resistance to biblical authority. Instead, they are simply a new expression of modernism [(Chicago: Moody Press, 2008), 160-66]. They say, "many of the leading books display a familiar combination of social gospel liberalism, a neo-orthodox view of Scripture, a post-Enlightenment disdain for hell, the wrath of God, propositional revelation, propitiation, anything more than a vague, moralistic, warmhearted, adoctrinal Christianity" [Ibid., 160].
[279] *Listening to the Beliefs of Emerging Churches*, 22.
[280] Ibid., 26.

As we will see, Driscoll does not speak for all emerging churches, as some clearly incorporate some of the insights or tools from the philosophical critique of modernism by philosophical postmodernists. Moreover, one stream of the emerging movement embraces philosophical postmodernism, using the term "emergent" to describe its followers. Emergent leaders go as far as to, "impose on the text cultural meanings and desires that ignore or alter the meaning of the Scripture altogether."[281] As a result, emerging leaders like Mark Driscoll react by noting that the "interpreter is elevated in authority over the text of Scripture, no longer humbly coming under Scripture…"[282]

Emerging churches that "minister to postmoderns," perhaps known best as "relevants," seek to restructure the aesthetics of the worship experience and church leadership style. In other words, they seek to be "relevant" in their activities and leadership but not change their commitment to evangelical theology and the role of the local church as an institutional authority.[283] An example of this type of church is Mars Hill Church where Mark Driscoll served as pastor and founder.

How these types of churches seek to be relevant differ from one another. Some churches may involve changing the design of the auditorium or sanctuary altogether. Instead of pews facing a lectern, the church auditorium may look more like a coffee house with chairs and couches facing each other so that authenticity, interpersonal conversations, and community may be promoted. Pews facing a lectern, for example, promote disconnectedness, isolation, and instruction that is mindful of modernistic impulses that have dominated both traditional and seeker-sensitive churches (e.g., centralized authoritarianism, institutional authority, and instructional passivity). Other churches may have folding chairs facing a lectern, offer contemporary worship, use technology, and offer topics that are relevant by nature, speaking to the whole person.

Emerging churches that "minister with postmoderns" are "reconstructionists." They are not only interested in reaching out

---

[281] Idem.
[282] Idem.
[283] For instance, Doug Pagitt, *Spiritual Formation* (Grand Rapids, MI: Zondervan, 2003); Belcher, *The Deep Church*, 45.

to postmoderns, but they are also reconsidering the nature of the church and its structures. They often find that traditional and seeker churches are both unbiblical and irrelevant to address cultural change. For example, these two types of churches look more like hierarchical organizations, protective of their rights and privileges, and less like Jesus Christ as being servant-leaders to the community. Caught up in arbitrary social formalities and authority structures, these traditional churches do not embody the disposition of Jesus Christ whereby humility is exercised, the needs of others come first, and Christian practice is emphasized.[284]

Reconstructionist-type emerging churches often turn to other expressions of worship such as those practiced in the first three centuries of the Christian church (before Roman Emperor Constantine). As a result, Christian worship primarily revolves around house churches or monastic-type communities, but not centralized institutions. Following the examples of the early church or monastic orders (e.g., Benedictine; Franciscan) reconstructionists stress an incarnational (servant) lifestyle in community and advocate ancient liturgies and practices that speak to the whole person.

For example, in ancient Christian literature, such as Justin Martyr's *First Apology* and Tertullian's *Apologeticum*, we have records of ancient liturgical worship. The documents reveal the order of worship involved biblical readings, homilies, prayers of intercession, presentation of the bread and mixed cup of wine and water, Eucharistic prayer, reception of communion, collection for the support of widows and orphans, and taking communion to those unable to be present. Therefore, people like Robert E. Webber are advocating what he describes as "ancient-future worship."[285] This will be discussed in more length in the next chapter.

But what is central to reconstructionist-type churches is the observation that that there is no single prescriptive tradition of worship. For example, in his article, "The Apostolic Tradition," Maxwell E. Johnson observes:

---

[284] Belcher, *The Deep Church*, 46.
[285] Robert E. Webber, *Ancient-Future Christianity: Proclaiming and Enacting God's Narrative* (Grand Rapids, MI: Baker, 2008).

That is, the history of Christian worship in these centuries is not the history of a *single* [his italics] tradition of worship that undergirds the diversity of liturgical practices stemming from some pristine, unitive, or 'apostolic' core; rather, it is itself the history of a plurality of liturgical practices from the very beginning. There is no clearly deduced 'apostolic tradition' of Christian worship, but, as we have seen, a variety of tradition. ....What we see instead in these centuries is not a single tradition of Christian worship ready-made or fully formed in a tightly constructed package to be handed on unchanged to subsequent generations of the church. Rather, what is encountered here is what we might call various building blocks of that 'tradition' in development. And it is from these building blocks that the Church in subsequent generations throughout history, both through evolution in continuity with these centuries and by means of occasional revolution or reform in discontinuity, will pick and choose as it seeks to understand and express its ecclesial identity liturgically within changed historical, social, and cultural contexts in order to continue being faithful to the gospel.[286]

For example, in one reconstructionist-emerging church, the religious service integrates early church liturgy and provocative sermons. After the message, the pastor invites the attendees to go to stations that have been set up at different locations around the church. One station may be labyrinth where one can meditate. Another station may a place where people can write letters to God as an expression of worship. Another may be a foot washing station. Another may be a place where one can go to corporately confess sins using a computer screen and receive encouragement by others who appreciate the authenticity. In fact, after one particular message on the person and work of Christ, various prints of Rembrandt's depictions of Christ were stationed at various locations around the room. The pastor invited the participants to examine the works and relate them to his message. All of these stations are examples of creative interplay and expression of worship.

---

[286] *The Oxford History of Christian Worship*, edited by Geoffrey Wainwright and Karen B. Westerfield (Oxford, UK: Oxford University Press, 2006), 67.

Emerging churches that "minister as postmoderns" are the revisionists.[287] In order to separate from other emerging churches but still retain some association, many of them identify themselves as "emergent." They are the most controversial as they apply such tools as deconstructionism to central evangelical doctrine and practices, speculating whether these endeared and central doctrines and cherished activities are truly appropriate in a postmodern context. Moreover, like those who integrated modernism with theology, evangelical scholars are integrating postmodernism with theology. Others are advocating a nonfoundational theology.[288] For example, Philip Kennison claims that a commitment to both objective truth and the correspondence theory is merely "…an epistemic project [that] is funded by 'Cartesian anxiety,' a product of methodological doubt…"[289]

Traditional evangelical churches are criticized for integrating Enlightenment reason such as formulating systematic theological doctrines from a disinterested, objective point of view that is scientific in nature. The attitude that comes with such formulations tend to be certain or dogmatic, and triumphalistic.[290] Thus, "theological non-negotiables" such as the doctrine of inerrancy, the gospel, and substitutionary atonement are now being deconstructed.[291] Why? They argue that our theological assumptions and practices are embedded if not determined by a particular historical context.[292]

---

[287] Helpful introduction to postmodernism is Joseph Natoli's, *A Primer to Postmodernity* (Oxford: Blackwell, 1997).

[288] For example, see "How Firm a Foundation: Can Evangelicals Be NonFoundationalists?" in *Border Crossings: Christian Trespasses on Popular Culture and Public Affairs* by Rodney Clapp (Grand Rapids, MI: Brazos, 2000); Grenz and Franke, *Beyond Foundationalism: Shaping Theology in a Postmodern Context*; Nancey Murphy, *Anglo-American Postmodernity: Philosophical Perspectives on Science, Religion, and Ethics* (Boulder, CO: Westview, 1997).

[289] Phillip Kennison, 'There's No Such Thing as Objective truth, and It's a Good Thing, Too," in *Christian Apologetics in the Postmodern World* (ed. Timothy Philips and Dennis Okholm; Downers Grove: InterVarsity, 1995), 157.

[290] Jim Belcher, *The Deep Church*, 79. For example, In "Five Streams of the Emerging Church," Scot McKnight cites a comment made by theologian LeRon Shults:
From a theological perspective, this fixation with propositions [propositional truth] can easily lead to the attempt to use the finite tools of language on an absolute Presence that transcends and embraces all finite reality. Languages are culturally constructed symbol systems that enable humans to communicate by designating one finite reality in distinction from one another. The truly infinite God of Christian faith is beyond all our linguistic grasping, as all the great theologians from Irenaeus to Calvin have insisted, and so the struggle to capture God in our finite propositional structures is nothing short of linguistic idolatry [37].

[291] Ibid., 46.

[292] In 2004 the Evangelical Theology Society's annual conference was, "What Is Truth?" four

For example, emergent leaders like Doug Pagitt, contend theology is an expression of one's relationship with God, integrating both a person's story with God's story.[293] Theology is part and parcel of our lives, not an organized system of thought detached from living life. Theology is always contextual because theology is always human.[294] "It is people who create theology as a tool of our culture to explain reality as we see it."[295] Theology is also particular because we live in particular situations. Thus, the gospel must meet those particular situations.[296] In fact, in a response to Mark Driscoll's emphasis on the gospel message, Pagitt states:

> I think much of our difference comes from the fact that in many ways we are telling different stories of Christianity. We seem to be calling for different starting and ending points. This could be reason to just turn from one another and part ways, but I am not choosing that path. I feel that we need to engage with one another, even though the difficulty that accompanies such an effort.[297]

As a result of this view, emergent people are re-evaluating not only what is non-essential to Christian orthodoxy (e.g., Rapture of the Church), but central doctrines. For example, in his on-line article posted on the Emergent Village website, "A Time To Reconstruct," Jonathan Brink contends that the traditional way of seeing the Gospel story just didn't work for him anymore. Therefore, deconstructionism is necessary in order that new insights may be discovered. Moreover, conflicting historical views of the atonement (e.g., Ransom Theory;

---

plenary sessions were devoted to the relationship between truth, church, and postmodernism from biblical, theological, and philosophical perspectives in view of the postmodern impact on evangelicalism. See Andreas K. Köstenberger, "'What is Truth?' Pilate's Question in Its Johannine and Larger Biblical Context," *JETS* 48/1 (March 2005): 33-62; R. Albert Mohler, "What is Truth? Truth and Contemporary Culture," *JETS* 48/1 (March 2005): 63-75; J. P. Moreland, "Truth, Contemporary Philosophy, and the Postmodern Turn," *JETS* 48/1 (March 2005): 77-88; Kevin J. Vanhoozer, "Lost in Interpretation? Truth, Scripture, and Hermeneutics," *JETS* 48/1 (March 2005) 89-114.

[293] *Listening to the Beliefs of the Emerging Church*, 121-3.
[294] Ibid., 123-4.
[295] Ibid., 123.
[296] Ibid., 124.
[297] Ibid., 42.

Penal Substitution) could no longer be ignored. While wrestling with these theories is important, Brink came to the point whereby he stopped believing in the story people told him, while retaining his belief in Jesus Christ. In sum, he had reached a point as a Western evangelical that he could no longer accept the theological views that were handed down to him. Thus, as a result of a three-year period, he discovered that the gospel message could be framed as "ferocious love," an act of divine mercy. Brink writes:

> Seeing this new possibility changed everything. It informed both my sense of pain and suffering, justice, and reconciliation. It gave me new meaning to God's invitation to love my neighbor as myself. Salvation was no longer release from something out there, but from something within. Redemption was about me trading in my false judgment for God's.[298]

This posting is part of the Emergent Village, which is described as a "council of practitioners" who promote a network of organizers and participants engaged in revisionist-type dialogue and ministry. Conceived by Tony Jones, Brian McLaren, and Doug Pagitt on June 21, 2001, this organization has become a distinguishable branch of the emerging movement described as "emergent."

In Brian D. McLaren's groundbreaking book, *A New Kind of Christian*, the author shares his own personal story as a pastor about having a "crisis of faith."[299] He writes, "Sometime in 1994, at the age of thirty-eight, I got sick of being a pastor. Frankly, I was almost sick of being a Christian."[300] Though he only thought he had two alternatives, either continue practicing and promoting a type of Christianity about which he had deep reservations or leave the Christian ministry altogether, he came to a realization that there was a third alternative open to him, namely, "learn to be a Christian in a new way."[301]

---

[298] Jonathan Brink, A Time To Deconstruct," Emergent Village Webblog (July 18, 2010) at www.emergentvillage.com. Retrieval Date: July 20, 2010. http://www.emergentvillage.com/weblog/brink-reconstruct.

[299] Brian D. McLaren, *A New Kind of Christian: A Tale of Two Friends on A Spiritual Journey* (San Francisco: Jossey-Bass, 2001).

[300] Ibid., xii.

[301] Ibid., xiv. In, "McLaren Emerging," McKnight summarized McLaren's struggle with and recovery of Christianity this way:

In this personal story he refers to Alan Roxbourge, a fellow colleague of the Terranova Project, which is "an initiative to explore how Christian faith will reconfigure in the postmodern matrix."[302] Roxbourge instructs people how to deconstruct and reconstruct their lives, which McLaren describes as a process of paradigm change. This process, which he personally experienced as he gave up the former way of doing church to a new way that integrates philosophical postmodernism, normally involves five stages:

(a) The first stage is "stability." At this phase one holds to a paradigm or system of thought by which one perceives the world. Everything is adequately explained. But over time this way of seeing eventually gives way to feelings of entrapment or imprisonment.

(b) Stage two is "discontinuity." Here a high level of aggravation and dissatisfaction surfaces. The current paradigm is no longer as adequate. At this level one reacts and "can't stop talking about how wrong, inhumane, or insupportable it is."[303] One can be affected psychologically and physically.

(c) Stage three is "disembedding." Face with the knowledge that the current theories or systems are unsupportable, one begins the process of disconnecting from those beliefs. McClaren states, "In area 3, people gradually turn from deconstructing the past to constructing the future and begin the hard work of designing a new paradigm to take the place of the old."[304] This stage is filled with "creative exhilaration, challenge, and anxiety" in view of the lack of assurance that new paradigm will be superior to the old one and because it invites conflict with the defenders of the old paradigm.

(d) "Transition" is stage four. At this level one is still working through habituated patterns from the former theories or system. As a result, one has not "fully entered the new world."[305] Even though adjustment is in play, new freedoms and possibilities arise.

To use the words of fellow emergent thinker Peter Rollins, the Northern Irish philosopher at Ikon Community, McLaren experienced the 'fidelity of betrayal.' He had to betray the Jesus and the gospel and the church that nurtured him to become faithful to the Jesus of this kingdom vision [61].

[302] Ibid., xv.
[303] Idem.
[304] Idem.
[305] Idem.

(e) Stage five is "reformation." At this level one decides to experience this new world. Being invigorated with a hope and passion, he steps out into this new way of seeing.[306] McLaren adds, "Of course, one must anticipate a time when the new liberating paradigm itself becomes confining and old."[307]

In sum, emergent churches redefine "orthodoxy" as a way of being in the world rather than a set of fixed beliefs about the world; for theological doctrines and descriptive terms fail in sufficiently expressing totalizing truths, and theology itself is language-bound and shaped. Not only does the movement speak about the end of meta-narratives and express disapproval of those who make absolute truth claims, but also the adherents then recast theology as an on-going conversation about God.[308] As a result, the emergent leaders are calling for Christianity to "deconstruct itself" and "reconstruct itself" in order to reach a postmodern culture.[309]

6. An additional type of emerging church. While the emergent movement is one aspect of the larger emerging movement, another emerging expression has recently appeared in reaction to the emergent

---

[306] Idem.

[307] Idem.

[308] For example, Scot McNight observes:

...ironic faith grows out of emergents' realization that language plays a large role in our faith and our claims to know the truth. Even a first-year college course in literature or criticism exposes students to philosophers Michel Foucault, Jacques Derrida, Richard Rorty, or Stanley Fish, and few students are left unchanged and unchallenged. Emergents reason that theology is language-bound; language has its limits; the Bible is in language; that means the Bible, too, has the limits of language. The Christian faith, many emergents conclude, is language-shaped and that means it is culturally shaped. Why does one language-either ancient Middle Eastern or modern Western-get to tell the whole story? Emergents by and large plead for a multilingual approach to theology, which can lead to an ironic relationship to the language of the Bible and Western theology [Scot McKnight, "The Ironic Faith of Emergents," *Christianity Today* (September 2008): 63].

[309] Skye Jethani, *The Divine Commodity: Discovering a Faith Beyond Consumer Christianity* (Grand Rapids, MI: Zondervan, 2009), 9. Jethani recommends that Christians commend themselves to the process of deconstruction and reconstruction. For example, he states we need to deconstruct our commodified view of God and reconstruct a sense of wonder through silence; deconstruct our branded identities and reconstruct identities rooted in faith through love; deconstruct our attempts at transformation through external events, and reconstruct internal transformation through prayer; deconstruct our devotion to institutions as God's vessels, and reconstruct relationships with our brothers and sisters in Christ; deconstruct our unceasing pursuit of pleasure, and reconstruct the redemptive power of suffering through fasting; deconstruct our contentment with segregation, and reconstruct the unity of all people through the cross; deconstruct the individualism pushed by consumerism, and reconstruct our love for strangers through hospitality [Ibid., 170].

stream. There is a growing movement of emerging churches who are combining Reformed theology with the "relevants" in a very dynamic way. Known as the Acts 29 Network, like-minded Reformed emerging churches are dynamically growing, even among conservative students of Scripture. The Acts 29 Network is an association that not only offers a way to interact with fellow churches, but also promotes aggressive church planting.

Adherents' emphasis on Reformation theology stresses the heart cries of a past era to a future generation. Driscoll, for example, emphasizes Augustinian-Reformation themes including the sovereignty of God, depravity of man, Sola Scriptura, and the wonder of Calvary. Utilizing technology such as podcasts, plain-talking, and contemporary music, as well as promoting incarnational living, Mark Driscoll's influence alone cannot be ignored in contemporary evangelicalism. While agreeing with the emerging leaders that traditional churches have compromised in their integration of Enlightenment and are insensitive to the postmodern culture, he contends that the emergent leaders are promoting heresy.[310]

7. Six themes that encapsulate the emerging church movement(s). While these four types of emerging streams are able to summarize the various types of emerging churches, Scot McNight offers six themes that help us to collectively describe this diverse movement. Once again, each of these themes flows on a continuum, differing from one church to the next.[311]

---

[310] For example, Mark Driscoll writes:
What is at stake is nothing less than the gospel of Jesus Christ and people's eternal destinies. If in our day culture rises up in authority over Scripture in the church, any god rises up other than the Trinity, and any gospel is preached other than the death and resurrection of Jesus for our sins, then we literally have hell to pay for emerging into false teachers with false doctrines, false gods, and false gospels that assure false hope [*Listening to the Beliefs of Emerging Churches*, 35].

[311] Scot McKnight's insight is helpful:
The emerg*ing* movement, the larger movement of which emerg*ent* is a segment, remains more or less connected to the core of evangelicalism. It contains a variety of missional impulses; it remains concerned about the church; and its theological ideas will undoubtedly continue to impact evangelicalism. John Stott recently sketched three core practices of emerging churches: the way of Jesus, breaking down the sacred-secular divide, and community living. He says that, 'emerging churches are rediscovering [these core practices] and giving them a fresh emphasis' Rediscovering accurately describes what is doing on, but those in the emerging movement feel these core practices are a fresh discovery ["McLaren Emerging," 59].

First, emerging churches are provocative in rhetoric. Emerging leaders are not afraid to seriously question and address long-held beliefs and practices in a worship experience. For example, in one emerging church the pastor shares his personal fears and frustrations with non-negotiable doctrine such as inspiration of Scripture in an effort to promote sincere dialogue with those who are experiencing the same issues. "If there are so many views about the inspiration of Scripture, then how can we really know our view is really right?"

Second, while emerging churches react differently to philosophical postmodernism, all agree that postmodernism has opened opportunities of dialogue with various communities of the Christian faith, whether Catholic or Protestant and are interacting with non-Christian religions. Moreover, having rejected Enlightenment assumptions and using deconstructionism to critique their own ideas and practices, many are drawing from Christianity's heritage of thought and practice, reconstructing religious expressions or activities of worship in creative, pluralistic, experiential, and sensory ways.

Third, and perhaps the most important theme to emerging churches is the focus on living out the Christian faith. For instance, the focus on praxis is evident in how they restructure the worship service. The use of art, candles, incense, and sacred space are just a few examples. They may form a circle and pray in silence, study a Christian icon, meet social needs, or read Patristic prayers to one another. Moreover, they desire to practice "the way of Jesus" in order to meet needs in culture, for right thinking does not necessarily equate right living.[312] Fourth, emerging churches contend their focus is to be missional, or actively participating in the community where God's redemptive work takes place. McKnight writes:

> This holistic emphasis finds perfect expression in the ministry of Jesus, who went about doing good to bodies, spirits, families, and societies. He picked the marginalized up from the floor and put them back in their seats at the table; he attracted harlots and tax collectors; he made the lame walk and opened the ears of the

---

[312] Scot McKnight, "Five Streams of the Emerging Church" *Christianity Today* (February 2007): 34-9.

dead. He cared, in other words, not just about lost souls, but also about whole persons and whole societies.[313]

Therefore, emerging church see themselves as avenues by means of which God is working, demonstrating authentic living in action. For example, some own coffee houses and art galleries while others are constructing and participating, that is, literally living with those who are described by society as "homeless."

Fifth, because emerging churches are protesting against such things as the integration and reductionistic spirit of modernism in evangelical thought and practice, they often describe themselves as "post-evangelical." For example, systematic theologies that tend to be finalizing, formulistic, totalizing, and transcendental, are held with suspicion because they are scripted by the author's particular context, and because no language exists that is truly able to capture the person, nature, and activities of God. Thus, the Christian epistemology of emerging leaders is chastened by such ideas as contextualization, human finiteness, and the noetic effects of sin.

And sixth, since these churches emphasize an incarnational mindset, they are especially sensitive to the plight of the those who are alienated, oppressed, unfortunate, and victimized, and they tend to be proactively involved in what may described as the social gospel.[314] They are not committing themselves to addressing acts of injustice and the difficulties of those who are impoverished on the basis of promoting a postmillennial kingdom. Rather, they desire to truly reflect Christ to their neighbors.

8. Description of aesthetic activities. Given the diversity and fluid-like nature of emerging churches, it is impossible to evaluate the aesthetics of a given emerging church. However, underlying the specific activities, which may vary from week to week, and church to church, six themes stand out. While they often overlap one another, they provide valuable insight in examining the aesthetic practices of emerging churches.

---

[313] Idem.
[314] For example, Randall Balmer, *Thy Kingdom Come: How the Religious Right Distorts the Faith and Threatens America: An Evangelical's Lament* (New York: Basic Books, 2006); David Kuo, *Tempting Faith: An Inside Story of Political Seduction* (New York: Free Press, 2006).

First, aesthetic activities are contextualized. While they may draw upon various expressions of worship used elsewhere, emerging churches strive to promote aesthetic activities that reflect their own particular situational and historical context. For example, one emerging church is found in the Bohemian district of a metropolitan city; its church design is a functional coffee house. The coffee house becomes the center of worship on Sundays.

Second, the emerging churches embrace a "living aesthetic," that is, activities or expressions of worship are connected to a particular community's contextual situation. Instead of fixed observances of actions or procedures, aesthetic activities of worship are organic. For example, one pastor explained to me that the worship activities change depending upon the particular needs or climate of their community. "One week we may dance in celebration to the great things God has done and another week we may express our worship together in total silence."

Aesthetic activities are also tied to the actual ambiance of the community. In other words, the particular context and tone of the culture in which the church is embedded informs the manner and frame of mind in which the church will pursue its activities of worship. For example, if the greater community is distressed about a particular issue, the church designed to minister to that particular community is so "fluid-like" in its form that it is willing to take on a particular project as an expression of worship. If social injustice takes place, then the church may offer a candlelight vigil, focusing on how the Bible, practical experience, and Christian tradition inform the people of social injustice.

Third, emerging churches promote tension. Rather than merely focusing on knowledge (e.g., traditional churches) or skills (e.g., seeker-sensitive), they call people to free themselves from a blinded conformity of socially accepted beliefs or customs of behavior resulting from traditional conceptions of worship. Therefore, they attempt to create a worship experience that is secure or safe and challenging enough in order to deal people's underlying fears, prejudices, or problems. By challenging one's assumptions or fixed ways of doing something, using a conversational format, an attempt is made to move the person to consider truth in a different way. They are after qualitative growth in the lives of those who attend. For example, if one is struggling with a particular addition, then the church might have one who is recovered come to the church and share his or her story.

Fourth, aesthetic activities involve active engagement of the whole person. For example, one emerging pastor in Louisiana explained to me that by having various stations in a given worship service, he is able to touch on all the physical senses (touch, taste, sight, smell, and hearing), promoting inviting, challenging, and memorable experiences. In other words, various learning styles are taken into account to stress a particular theme, striving to impact the human mind, heart, and will.

For example, a service begins with music and prayer. Using Scripture, the pastor presents a frank discussion about temptation and sin in his own life. Afterwards, he invites the participants to silently and collectively walk through seven stations. The first station is a collection of statements from Oscar Wilde's *The Picture of Dorian Gray* and C. S. Lewis' *Screwtape Letters*, all creatively organized on the wall. The second station is a large reprint of Rembrandt's "Blinding of Sansom" from Judges 16:20-21. The significance is that no one is immune to sin. The third station is bitter herbs used in a Jewish Passover service. The fourth station involves a person offering testimony about his own destructive addiction, and how he found recovery, peace, and hope in God and accountability. The fifth station is an invitation to deal with one's sins by writing them down on a piece of paper. The sixth station involves nailing those papers to a large wooden cross, reflecting forgiveness. The seventh station is the celebration of the communion. The service ends with singing and dancing as they celebrate God's forgiveness. They leave with a sheet of paper with Wilde and Lewis quotes and Scripture passages about the consequences of sin and the promises of God's grace.

Fifth, emerging church offers "pluralistic" expressions of activities. Rather than exclusively revolving its worship around the exposition of Scripture, there are multiple ways one may participate in a given worship services given one's particular disposition, interest, or mood. For example, in one emerging church, there is an assortment of activities one may pursue at a given Sunday occasion during corporate worship.

One may choose to spend a Sunday morning studying the Scripture, silently meditating upon God in silence lit by candles by incense, or paint in response to what the pastor said. These activities may change from week to week. In fact, the entire design of the interior of the church may change from Sunday to Sunday. Furthermore, emerging churches will draw from various historical and cultural activities to enhance the worship experience. For example, a shofar, an ocarina, a harpsichord, a banjo, and an electric guitar may all be used. In one service, Latin jazz may be incorporated whereas in another service, the emphasis may be on the Eucharist. Emerging churches are not only acknowledging that various forms of worship are generated from particular communities, but also they are welcoming opportunities to interact and grow from multicultural expressions, practices, and rituals.

Sixth, aesthetics is experientially pluralistic. Because of its emphases on contextualization and experimentation, the emerging church inquires, invites, and pursues different ways to enhance the worship experience. Its justification is to enrich each other's lives intellectually, emotionally, and spiritually, as well as engage in expressions that continue to break biases. Thus, the interplay of history, foreign culture, and novelty will free people to worship God in new ways, spurring creativity, memorable meetings, and cultural connections that otherwise might be missed or neglected.[315]

CONCLUSION

We have examined two recent attempts to bridge the culture gap and offer meaningful religious activities, practices, and rituals: the seeker-sensitive movement and the emerging church movement(s). Both movements recognize problems and failures of the activities of traditional churches and believe that culture has changed to the extent that their practices are ineffective in bridging the culture gap. The seeker-sensitive church seeks to revolutionize the way the church is done, in part, by changing the church's presentation before the community. By mirroring community and targeting felt-needs, striving to be experimental, innovative, and self-examining, the leadership and members hope to bridge the culture gap and provide a memorable

---

[315] *Listening to the Beliefs of the Emerging Church*, 128-9.

worship experience. On the other hand, while the emerging churches vary in approaches to bridging the culture gap, they all embrace particular or situational contextualization and seek to practice incarnational living to a post-Christian society. Their practices are pluralistic, sensory, and experiential. Now we shall utilize our Deweyan tool to assess the strengths and weaknesses of these two movements.

> *"What if, as a I firmly believe,…that evangelicalism-out of fear or ignorance, or in its zeal to transform the world-has simply gotten modern art wrong; that in its eagerness to make modern culture safe for the gospel and Christian values (not often in that order) evangelicalism has distorted it? And if evangelicalism and the North American church has modern art wrong, then is it possible that other, more popular and perhaps more 'influential' cultural artifacts, like music, film, and television have suffered a similar fate? And if that is the case, which, again, I believe it is, then the North American church needs to completely rethink how it understands culture and creative cultural artifacts."*
>
> ~ Daniel A. Siedell [316]

---

[316] *"Afterward: So What?"* in *Modern Art and the Life of A Culture: The Religious Impulses of Modernism* by Jonathan A. Anderson and William A. Dyrness (Downers Grove, IL: InterVarsity, 2016), 331.

AESTHETIC ANALYSIS OF THE SEEKER-SENSITIVE CHURCH AND THE EMERGING CHURCH

"I sometimes wonder whether our churches--living as we do in American death-denying culture, relentlessly smiling through our praise choruses--are inadvertently helping people live not as much in hope as in denial."

~ Mark Galli

Using Dewey's aesthetics we will now evaluate the seeker-sensitive movement and the emerging church movement(s) in view of their striking attempts to bridge the culture gap between local churches and community and promote meaningful experiences to all involved. We will first examine the seeker-sensitive movement addressing both strengths and problems. We will then turn our attention to the emerging church movement(s). With each examination I will draw attention to particular issues contributing to non-aesthetic experiences. Different details will be included with both examinations. However, the understanding these churches have gained on the ways to bridge the culture gap and offer fulfilling religious activities, practices, and rituals will be taken into account in each analysis. Afterwards, I will discuss why both recent movements fail to adequately address the culture gap. I will then offer four Deweyan insights to better equip local churches to be relevant to each and every generation.

STRENGTHS OF THE SEEKER-SENSITIVE MOVEMENT

The seeker-sensitive movement is to be extolled for embracing experimentation, offering opportunities where aesthetic experience can occur, and exercising artistic engagement in religious activities in order to bridge the culture gap and offer a memorable worship experience. Let us take a closer look at these commendable qualities.

1. The value of experimentation. The seeker-sensitive church is willing to experiment in order to know how to best engage culture. Unlike the elite, broken, and humdrum, the seeker-sensitive church

purposefully continually experiments, striving to adapt to the cultural context in relevant ways. Experimentation is a value and a tool embraced by the seeker-sensitive church. Seeker-sensitive churches will experiment even if it means reengineering the church's visible structures and religious activities. An activity becomes stagnant or is not as effective as the leadership expects, the leadership is willing to investigate and modify. If the adjustments do not work, a seeker-sensitive church like Willow Creek will likely terminate the program and make inquiries elsewhere. Thus, it is the expectation of a seeker-sensitive church to experiment, adjust, assess, and even cut off any activity that achieves nothing or performs mechanically.

Experimentation is critically important given the neglect of such activities by the elite, broken, and humdrum churches which struggle with activities that fail to generate beneficial ends (e.g., bridge the culture gap). Though it is difficult to end some of these ministries for reasons such as tradition, habituated expectations, or hurting people's feelings, traditional churches fail to realize non-aesthetic experiences are forgettable and do not feed the soul. Being unwilling to change makes a church a slave to its traditions or other stifling factors and, even worse, prevents growth and can lead one to irritation if not existential dissatisfaction with not only local churches, but also the very idea of institutional religion.

Consider the testimony of Brian McLaren, a pastor who became terribly frustrated with the traditional church. His confession reveals how the mechanical routine led him to a vacuous disposition, hungering for something more, but also how the routine became the normative experience and fixed expectation of his audience. To introduce something different in church worship was not perceived as a potential opportunity. Rather, it was seen as a threat to traditional churchgoers. He writes:

> I preach sermons that earn the approving nods of the lifelong churchgoers, because they repeat the expected vocabulary and formulations, words that generally convey little actual meaning after hearing them fifty-two times a year, year after year, but work like fingers, massaging the weary souls of

earnest people. Meanwhile, as the initiated relax under this massage of familiar words, as they emit an almost audible 'ahhh' to hear their cherished vocabulary again, these very massaging messages leave the uninitiated furrowing their brows, shaking their heads, and shifting in their seats. They do this sometimes because they don't understand but even more when they do understand-because the very formulations that sound so good and familiar to the 'saved' sound downright weird or even wicked to the 'seekers' and the skeptics. These people come to me and ask questions, and I give my best answers, my best defenses, and by the time they leave my office, I have convinced myself that their questions are better than my answers.[317]

Then he goes on to say:

I do the reverse: I preach sermons that turn the lights on for spiritual seekers but earn me critical letters and phone calls from the 'veterans' of the church often because the expected fingers didn't reach through my message to massage them as expected.[318]

This above account by McLaren not only revealed the pastor's hunger for aesthetic experiences, but also supports an important point Dewey makes in his discussion about having an experience. Dewey notes:

There exists so much of one and the other of these two kinds of experience [non-aesthetic extremes of either randomness or routine] that unconsciously they come to be taken as norms of all experience. Thus, when the esthetic appears, it so sharply contrasts with the picture that has been formed of experience, that it is impossible to combine its special qualities with the features of the picture and the esthetic is given an outside place and status.[319]

---

[317] McLaren, *A New Kind of Christian*, xvii.
[318] Idem.
[319] Dewey, *Art as Experience*, 41-2.

Ironically, members who attend a local church that demands a non-aesthetic routine may relish new and exciting aesthetic experiences in their daily lives. Why should churches be excluded from such opportunities? Once again, this irony is reminiscent of Van Gogh's "Starry Night" where beauty is found outside but not inside the church. This is in stark contrast to the Jewish accounts of God's Shekinah glory inhabiting the tabernacle and later the temple. In the midst of an organized and detailed religion that was governed by laws and precepts, aesthetic experiences were seen, felt, heard, and tasted among the people as they sacrificed, celebrated, grieved, and exalted their God together as a community. Experimentation is a refreshing quality to have in any church and the seeker-sensitive movement has proven its benefits.

2. Value creativity and innovation. The seeker-sensitive church is ever willing to inquire into new possibilities of communicating with its attendees and reaching out to the community. Unlike the elite and humdrum church, the seeker-sensitive church is willing to draw from its own resources in order to discover and ideas.

Unfortunately, criticisms abound about the seeker-sensitive church turning to "secular" resources to help a church become effective. But what these critics fail to understand is the church looks upon these resources (e.g., using business theories to structure church authority) as tools, that is, as instruments to generate better ends. Therefore using a tool that was created in spheres of life such as business and marketing, does not mean that the church is no longer "sacred." Rather, intelligence is being displayed by assimilating amoral resources in order to better minister to people. No one can doubt the incredible response churches like Willow Creek have received from the utilization of varied tools and the moving results provided for both the church and community.

3. Focus on community. Opportunities such as fixing cars to give away to people in need or washing and styling the hair of a mother who is both homeless and battered, enrich all involved and provide opportunities to properly engage in experience as a participant and not a passive spectator.[320] When this occurs, the

---

[320] Ibid., 54.

possibility for the emergence of an aesthetic experience is created. To be sure, the experience must move from inception, maturation, and ultimately to fulfillment. Of course, at each point the doing and undergoing must appropriately respond to each other, for the doing gives movement and variety and the undergoing, which is the corresponding element in the rhythm, supplies unity. This relationship between the doing and undergoing is remarkable, for the doing prevents monotony and useless repetitions whereas the undergoing saves the work from the "aimlessness of a mere succession of excitations."[321] But what follows from this continuous developing integral experience is something enjoyable, exciting, and memorable: an inclusive and fulfilling close! The experience of fixing the car or styling hair can be an experience "lifted high above threshold of perception and is made manifest for its own sake."[322]

Granted, opportunities to be involved will inevitably lead to problems for the local leadership such as handling stubborn personalities and opinions or sorting the ones who truly need help more than others. Nevertheless, opportunities are offered for people to actively participate and "take in" an experience. When we are able to take in a moment, we experience an "aliveness" that we do not receive when we are merely passive spectators in a church pew.[323] Thus, when a person is actively involved in a ministry project, not only will tension occur (since one is beginning with an indeterminate situation), but the possibility of closure or the completion of an experience, can also occur. As a result of the meaningful feeling of satisfaction from completion of serving others in an aesthetic experience, the participant may desire additional service-oriented experiences that lead to moments of intense continuity. "The moment of passage from harmony is that of intensest life."[324]

But we must not forget about the individual or persons receiving the gifts of the ministry (the car, the hairstyle, etc.). They too are part of that experience. Thus, there is the possibility for them to

---

[321] Ibid., 58.
[322] Idem.
[323] Ibid. 54-5.
[324] Ibid., 16.

be enriched as well. An aesthetic experience will be meaningful to them and can also lead to important changes in their lives. People hunger for aesthetic experiences. "The time of consummation is also one of beginning anew."[325]

4. Value artistic engagement. From the audio-visual technicians to the musicians, attentive care, engagement, and intense interest in doing well is typically exhibited. These are aesthetic qualities. Thus, the architecture in the auditorium, the choice of music and performance of, the use of cutting edge technology, and the messages given are thoughtfully planned, carefully designed, and creatively displayed to arrest the mind, provoke the heart, and stimulate the will to action. Talent, architecture, and technology are integral with human excellence. On-going critical reflection and adjustments are central to the activities as they continually improve week to week.[326]

WEAKNESSES OF THE SEEKER-SENSITIVE MOVEMENT

In spite of all of these remarkable strengths, a number of significant problems need to be addressed in seeker-sensitive churches. To be sure, not every seeker-sensitive church is alike. But the following problems seem to be common: efficiency, focus, imbalance, exploitation, reductionism, amusement, and consumerism.

1. Problem of efficiency. While Dewey values experimentation, he would give a word of caution to the seeker-sensitive church about becoming too practical or mechanically efficient. Dewey states:

> It is possible to be efficient in action and yet not have a conscious experience. The activity is too automatic to permit of a sense of what it is about and where it is going. It comes to an end but not to a close or consummation in consciousness. Obstacles are overcome by shrewd skill, but they do not feed experience.[327]

---

[325] Idem.
[326] Ibid., 4.
[327] Ibid., 40.

In contrast, between the poles of mechanical efficiency and aimlessness there "lie those courses of action in which through successive deeds there runs a sense of growing meaning conserved and accumulating toward an end that is felt as accomplishment as a process."[328]

2. Problem of focus. While the seeker-sensitive church should be commended for imagining, planning, and preparing in order to achieve beneficial ends, the church should be warned in its "visioneering," that is, projecting where the church should or will be in the future. The community in which the church is embedded is very precarious in nature. Moreover, because of the bilateral relationship between the church and community, the church itself changes and is affected by the culture. Allow space for the unpredictable.

But more importantly, if the church focuses too much on the future, people may lose where they are, who they are, and what they have in the present. In other words, we can become so preoccupied with the future that we neglect the opportunity to see our present experience. Dewey invites us to be "all there in the present," that is, to "take in" the actual moment in which we find ourselves with all that we are. Dewey writes:

> To the being fully alive the future is not ominous but a promise; it surrounds the present as a halo. It consists of possibilities that are felt as a possession of what is now and here. In life, that is truly life, everything overlaps and merges. But all too often we exist in apprehensions of what the future may bring, and are divided within ourselves. Even when not overanxious, we do not enjoy the present because we are subordinate it to that which is absent.[329]

This is also applicable if a church focuses too much on the past. Dewey notes, "our past is perceived as an oppressive burden rather than storehouses of resources by which to move confidently

---
[328] Idem.
[329] Ibid., 17.

forward."³³⁰ But Dewey also claims, "Only when the past ceases to trouble and anticipations of the future are not perturbing is a being wholly united with his environment and therefore fully alive."³³¹ I would personally add that our reflections upon the past moments of continuity and discontinuity and the precarious aspects of our future could be used to properly motivate us to seize the "now" with every aspect of our being.

3. Problem of imbalance. Strangely, in both cases of the elite church and the seeker-sensitive church, which offer two polarized ways of doing church, a struggle with passivity in corporate gatherings of worship surfaces. The seeker-sensitive church's worship experience is aesthetically imbalanced in several ways. Though the didactic teaching has been replaced with entertainment, visual and auditory stimuli, colorful use of lights, and conversational-style speaking, the attendees are passive recipients of the experience. While aesthetic qualities exist in those moments when musical instruments are played with brilliance, when songs are performed with skill, and powerful images emerge on the giant screens, the audience is still only the spectator, not the participant. There is excessive doing from the worship team and excessive receiving experienced by the congregation. Likewise, there is deficient receiving from the few participants and deficient doing by the congregation. As a result, all miss opportunities to dynamically learn, reflect, and grow together. The results of this aesthetic imbalance include personal and collective malnourishment.

Now it might be argued that the church is sensitive to issues related to aesthetic balance. If one were to stand back and look at the sum-total of the church's activities, it is clear that the church purposefully directs its attendees to extensive programs of ministry and outreach unlike the practices of the elite, broken, and humdrum churches and their small group ministries. To be sure, the seeker-sensitive church goes beyond the traditional churches we have examined, emphasizing active service to the community. This is a very commendable quality because the spectator becomes

---
³³⁰ Idem.
³³¹ Idem.

a participant in service to others. Notwithstanding, the concern is whether the audience is a participant or a spectator in the religious activity of corporate worship. If the audience is a spectator, then an imbalance results because the agent is passive in the worship experience. Therefore, in order to make the experience more enriching, passivity must go beyond recognition to engagement. Dewey writes:

> Recognition is perception arrested before it has a chance to develop freely. In recognition there is a beginning of an act of perception. But this beginning is not allowed to serve the development of a full perception of the thing recognized. It is arrested at the point where it will serve some other purpose, as we recognize a man on the street in order to greet or to avoid him, not so as to see him for the sake of seeing what is there.[332]

4. Problem of exploitation. Similar to the sensational church, the worship experience can easily tilt to the excessive with its technology and assorted stimuli. The ever-present danger exists that a seeker-sensitive church may turn from using entertainment as a tool to enrich, to a means of exploiting the audience. One can be so saturated or overwhelmed with stimuli that critical thinking is ignored. Intoxication breeds impulsive and irrational decisions. If the church measures success by how many attend church, how many decisions are made to become a Christian, how many attend small groups, and how many baptisms take place, then I suspect the possibility becomes even more acute. Quality is exchanged for quantity.

Again, like the sensational church, the potential imbalance exists of imposing an experience upon a group rather than allowing an experience to organically and integrally develop within the activity of worship. How do we balance technology, stimuli, and entertainment whereby an aesthetic experience might occur without forcing an aesthetic simulation upon people? These instruments contribute to our experience when there is an organic "aliveness,"

---

[332] Ibid., 54.

where everything fits together, and organic consummation occurs. But if the experience goes beyond its natural course of fulfillment, we have reason to believe these instruments are being used to enforce or continue something that goes beyond its natural limitations. Aesthetic consummation leads to release. While aesthetic experience may prove difficult to measure in a theater-like environment where these instruments abound and can simulate an experience, the question we must ask ourselves is that which Jonathan Edwards asked of the experiences he witnessed during the First Great Awakening, namely, have our lives authentically and qualitatively improved for the better from that worship service?

5. Problem of reductionism. The church also promotes historical and methodological reductionism. While advocating experimentation in order to improve lives, Dewey contends that we are never to ignore our past. Rather, Dewey calls us to take our past experiences, our lessons, and our heritage and engage the present.

> But the live creature adopts its past; it can make friends with even its stupidities, using them as warnings that increase present wariness. Instead of trying to live upon whatever may have been achieved in the past, it uses past successes to inform the present.[333]

We should look at our past, such as events, ideas, and implications as a "storehouse of resources by which to move confidently forward," and then use the past, such as our stupidities as "warning signs" and our "past successes" to help us inquire, engage, and take in the present.[334]
In particular, by breaking away from their past in an effort to become relevant to culture, seeker-sensitive churches neglect their own theological, biblical, and philosophical heritage. This is unfortunate because it is in our past that we have a record of the consequences of ideas.[335] Moreover, the Christianity stands on the

---

[333] Ibid., 17.
[334] Idem.
[335] Joseph Bottum, "Christians and Postmoderns," *First Things* 201 (March 2010): 45.

shoulders of many historical figures, and it is only to our detriment to ignore and move past their contributions to the faith. Like those who relegate art-products to museums, seeker-sensitive churches rob their attendees of the rich benefits church history offers to a context.

The exposition of Scripture, doctrinal teachings, and liturgy can be done in a manner that is not mechanical or routine. In fact, the exposition of Scripture can be strength for a church as indicated in our analysis of the elite, broken, and humdrum church. This singular strength in the elite church continues to draw both the young and the old to its services. In those inductive teaching opportunities, interests can be aroused, creativity exercised, and attention fixed upon the riches of the past to inform us of our present condition and future possibilities.

Reductionism also finds expression in the area of religious art-products. If everything is directed to satisfying "me" in view of entertainment, where is the mystery to inquire, ponder, and reflect? For example, when one enters the Notre Dame Cathedral in France, the symbols and imagery can move the person to not merely look at the object, but to follow it along to an idea, historical event, person, or theme. The artwork serves as much more than an element to impress the eyes. An interest is stirred to investigate, to reach beyond impressions, and reflect. Art-products can engender those types of interactions. But in seeker-sensitive churches where the auditorium reflects a contemporary theater devoid of art-products, especially enduring art-products (e.g., certain images like the crucifix), reductionism is introduced because the focus is entirely on performance.

The sacred symbols, the stained glass, and the iconic arrangements can provoke one's interest, move one's affections, and add intellectual and historical depth to a religious activity, especially if it memorializes past events. In fact, if one explores the various world religions and their people-groups, imagery tends to naturally emerge, develop, and contribute to religious experience. In other words, imagery, whether religious or civic, seems to be part of our human experience and can be used to incite the best in us (e.g., our nation's flag).

Now one might argue that the music, entertainment, skits, and visual stimuli are the icons of today's worship experience. While that might be true, using these avenues of expression exclusively neglects other historical and material mediums that connect the past to the present (e.g., the cross). It is doubtful icons like the crucifix will ever be transient art-products. Certain ancient icons have historically stood the test of time and they have cross-culturally and generationally contributed to aesthetic experiences.

Interestingly, the removal of sacred symbols from the worship experience and the construction of buildings that are more reflective of a convention center than a church introduces aesthetic barrenness, not novelty in common life. Like the Parthenon or the Notre Dame Cathedral, certain architectural designs and art-products such as the Rose Window stir our interests, generate community pride, and add "richness," not "sterility" to an urban or suburban landscape. More importantly, this connection between the past to the present becomes critical for another important reason. In the words of John J. McDermott:

> The human body is neither a container nor a box in a world of boxes. To the contrary, our bodies are present in the world as diaphanous [almost transparent] and permeable. The world, in its activities as the affairs of nature and the affairs of things, penetrates us by flooding our consciousness, our skin, and our liver with the press of the environment. We respond with our marvelous capacity to arrange, relate, reject, and, above all, symbolize these transactions.[336]

I do not want to neglect the idea that certain art-products may indeed be barriers to those who have been deeply hurt or alienated by a church. Yet the question must be asked, is viewing them as an obstacle, an obstacle in itself? The use of art-products links the past to the present and offers opportunities of aesthetic engagement that go beyond the sights and sounds of contemporary music, digital imagery, and inspirational words.

---

[336] John J. McDermott, "Glass without Feet: Dimensions of Urban Aesthetics," in *The Drama of Possibility: Experience as Philosophy of Culture*, 205.

6. Problem of amusement. In his work, *Amusing Ourselves to Death*, Neil Postman observes: There is no doubt, in other words, that religion can be made entertaining. The question is, by doing so, do we destroy it as an 'authentic object of culture'? And does the popularity of a religion that employs the full resources of vaudeville [popular entertainment] drive more traditional religious conceptions into manic and trivial displays?[337]

His basis for these two questions not only follows his analysis of the relationship between religion and entertainment, but is also built around an observation made by Hannah Arendt. She writes:

> This state of affairs, which indeed is equalled nowhere else in the world, can properly be called mass culture; its promoters are neither the masses nor their entertainers, but are those who try to entertain the masses with what once was an authentic object of culture, or to persuade them that Hamlet can be as entertaining as My Fair Lady, and educational as well. The danger of mass education is precisely that it may become very entertaining indeed; there are many great authors of the past who have survived centuries of oblivion and neglect, but it is still an open question whether they will be able to survive an entertaining version of what they have to say.[338]

Thus, the danger is not in the Christian faith becoming the content of entertainment, but entertainment becoming the content of seeker-sensitive churches. Is non-religious architecture a potential foreshadowing of non-religious activities? In *Technopoly: The Surrender of Culture to Technology*, Postman writes:

> Here, I am merely making the point that religious tradition serves as a mechanism for the regulation and valuation of information. When religion loses much or all its binding power—if it is reduced to mere rhetorical ash—then confusion

---

[337] Neil Postman, *Amusing Ourselves to Death: Public Discourse in the Age of Show Business*, 20th anniversary edition (New York: Penguin Press, 1985, 2005), 124.
[338] Ibid., 123-4.

inevitably follows about what to attend to and how to assign it significance.[339]

Similarly, I suggest we ask ourselves whether excessive entertainment introduces genuine perspective, inflames our intelligence and creativity into action, and generates practical benefits for all involved.[340] If entertainment replaces the content of any church, will the church serve, as an instrument that directs us toward something beyond our consumer needs? Will communities be qualitatively enriched? Will "enduring art-products" be created from such an environment?[341] Is there a "better adjustment in life and its conditions"?[342] Since excessive entertainment is non-aesthetic, I suspect Dewey would contend if this warning is ignored and entertainment becomes the content of religious activity, the church will not make the world a better place, no matter how well intentioned it may be.[343]

7. Problem of consumerism. While I sincerely applaud targeting the community in order to meet genuine needs and involving marketing experts to assist in that effort, there is the real possibility that people have been or will be reduced to "consumers" and not treated as persons.[344] Combined with excessive entertainment, the following

[339] Neil Postman, *Technopoly: The Surrender of Culture to Technology* (New York: Vintage Books, 1993), 80.
[340] "From A Common Faith," *James & Dewey on Belief and Experience*, eds. John M. Capps and Donald Capps (Urbana, IL: University of Illinois Press, 2005), 237.
[341] Ibid., 235.
[342] Ibid., 233.
[343] Ibid., 220.
[344] Consider Walt Kallestad's *Entertainment Evangelism: Taking the Church Public* (Nashville, TN: Abingdon Press, 1996), 8-9. This author observes:
Perhaps the most important effect of the United State's production, consumption, and exportation of entertainment products are the distinctions between entertainment, information, communications, and education is becoming less clear. Right now the average American spends forty hours and thirty dollars a week on entertainment. Entertainment is the most used medium in the world [Ibid., 8].
He then goes on to say:
If entertainment is such a force in our world, why don't we utilize this human and cultural vehicle and redeem it for the proclamation of the gospel? Why should we allow our churches to become empty and sterile? Empty cathedrals and sterile church life do little to glorify God When I see the kind of entertainment that America is exporting all over the world, I find it much of it disturbing. I can envision something different. Why could we not become the center for exporting positive images and values around the world? Do we need to allow destructive entertainment to dominate the culture? Why should not the church develop a style of engaging worship, music, and entertainment that can compete

concerns can easily become real problems.

First, Willow Creek emphasizes a dependence model of the church. Its ministry model is, "Figure out what you think everyone needs and then provide it through a program or an activity."[345] By focusing on people as consumers, the church as an institution reconfirms its audience that life is self-oriented. As a result, individualism is affirmed over and against other aspects of life such as community.

But we are more than just individuals. We are participants in community. When we are preoccupied with ourselves, we become insensitive to our citizenship in community. For example, I have seen people neglect the opportunity to foster meaningful relationships in community even though they participate in community-centered programs because they perceive everything revolving around themselves. Will we be able to think beyond ourselves and inquire beyond the satisfaction of our desires, inclinations, and preferences to address and enrich the lives of others in a manner that is endearing, heroic, and perhaps even altruistic?

Targeting people as consumers also undervalues the benefits of tension. Like the humdrum church, seeker-sensitive churches fail to appreciate the benefits of tension found in experience. Consumerism values the acquisition of goods. Thus, by satisfying those tensions for people, not only are they placating the opportunity for them to experience self-discovery, but also creativity, ingenuity, and progress. As a result, dependence upon the church and unrealistic expectations begin to develop. In contrast, it is the conversion of resistance and tensions that help move us toward an aesthetic experience. Dewey states, "That which distinguishes an experience as esthetic is conversion of resistance and tensions, of excitations that in themselves are temptations to diversion, into a movement toward an inclusive and fulfilling close."[346]

---

with anything on the market in terms of quality, yet springs from far different values and theological commitments? [Ibid., 8-9].

[345] Hawkins, Greg, Cally Parkinson, & Eric Arnson, *Reveal: Where Are You?* (Barrington, IL: Willow Creek Resources, 2007), 65.

[346] Dewey, *Art as Experience*, 58.

If we combine consumer approach with entertainment, then we face the legitimate concern that the novelty of church in common life will become irrelevant. Why go to church when one can be entertained elsewhere in community? What nutritious activities, events, and practices are offered if entertainment is the driving force of the worship service?

Using marketing tactics to target consumer needs in people can also lead to exploitation and constraint of both freedom and intelligence if diligent care is not applied. Not only can the value of people be reduced to a "number," especially considering the church's focus on quantitative growth, but the combination of consumerism and marketing strategies based on psychological and sociological habituations and responses can be used to manipulate people. For example, Dewey writes:

> We seem to be approaching a state of government by hired promoters of opinion called publicity agents. But the more serious enemy is deeply concealed in hidden entrenchments. Emotional habituations and intellectual habitudes on the part of men create the conditions of which the exploiters of sentiment and opinion only take advantage.[347]

But the problem of entertainment and consumerism goes beyond exploitation, for it can also result in decadence. When members are in a passive posture of receiving, dependency upon the church become normal, the self-motivation to actively face our discontinuity with the environment and intelligently, creatively, and resourcefully work through the problems ourselves is stifled. Unfortunately, when our consumer needs are met for us, opportunities for the experience of personal discovery and enrichment that results from working through problems, overcoming obstacles, and exchanging ideas are displaced.[348] Dewey put it this way, "...freedom in its practical and moral sense (whatever is to be said about it in some metaphysical sense) is connected with the possibility of growth, learning, and modification of

---

[347] Pappas, *John Dewey's Ethics*, 222 cf. LW 2:341.

[348] Ibid. Colin Campbell's *The Romantic Ethic and the Spirit of Modern Consumerism* (Oxford, UK: Blackwell, 1987) and Don Slater's *Consumer Culture and Modernity* (Cambridge, UK: Polity Press, 1997) offer helpful analyses of the origins and nature, and impact of consumerism.

character, just as is responsibility."[349] When we lose our freedom, we lose the possibility to grow.

Church decadence also takes it toil on pastors and their families. In his *New York Times* editorial, "Congregations Gone Wild," G. Jeffrey MacDonald contends that American pastors are suffering from burnout because of congregational pressure to "soothe and entertain them."[350] MacDonald writes:

> In the early 2000s, the advisory committee of my small congregation in Massachusetts told me to keep my sermons to 10 minutes, tell funny stories and leave people feeling great about themselves. The unspoken message in such instructions is clear: give us the comforting, amusing fare we want or we'll get our spiritual leadership from someone else.[351]

He concludes his argument by stating, "As religion becomes a consumer experience, the clergy become more unhappy and unhealthy."[352] I could not agree more.

Therefore, everyone involved must continually ask whether targeting consumer-oriented goals enrich and improve lives, contributing to values such as freedom and health? While seeker-sensitive churches are "others-directed" in terms of small groups and community-driven programs, the idea is not just to serve others and experience a sense of belonging and purpose, but hopefully meet

---

[349] John Dewey, *Theory of the Moral Life* (New York: Holt, Reinhard and Winston, 1908, 1932, 1960), 171.

[350] G. Jeffrey MacDonald, "Congregations Gone Wild," *The New York Times* (August 8, 2010): WK9.

[351] Ibid.

[352] MacDonald goes on to say:
Congregations that make such demands seem not to realize that most clergy don't sign up to be soothsayers or entertainers. Pastors believe they're called to shape lives for the better, and that involves helping people learn to do what's right in life, even when what's right is also difficult. When they're being true to their calling, pastors urge Christians to do the hard work of reconciliation with one another before receiving communion. They lead people to share in the suffering of others, including people they would rather ignore, by experiencing tough circumstances — say, in a shelter, a prison or a nursing home — and seeking relief together with those in need. At their courageous best, clergy lead where people aren't asking to go, because that's how the range of issues that concern them expands, and how a holy community gets formed. Ministry is a profession in which the greatest rewards include meaningfulness and integrity. When those fade under pressure from churchgoers who don't want to be challenged or edified, pastors become candidates for stress and depression [Ibid].

practical needs in a way that inspires greatness as individuals and as active participants in community. We have analyzed the aesthetics of the seeker-sensitive church from a Deweyan perspective and uncovered four areas of strengths and seven problems. But because of Willow Creek's emphasis on constant experimentation, review, and research, interesting discoveries were made that led to a shift in this megachurch's paradigm.

In 2007 Willow Creek made a public announcement, shocking both seeker-sensitive churches and traditional churches alike. After hiring one of the nation's foremost marketing experts, Greg Hawkins, to survey church members in 1991, the leadership discovered disturbing information in the scientific research of church members. Hybels writes, "Among the findings: nearly one out of every four people at Willow Creek were stalled in their spiritual growth or dissatisfied with the church-and many of them were considering leaving."[353] He goes on to say, "When I first heard these results, the pain of knowing was almost unbearable. Upon reflection, I realized that the pain of not knowing could be catastrophic."[354]

Since experimentation is one of the church's core values, a new strategic plan was revealed to the congregation in April 2007. The leadership stated:

> We are convinced of one thing as we move forward: we don't know if our plans will work, but we are committed to learning as we go. We might head in a wrong direction, but we would rather make a move than stand still, because we believe God is challenging us to act on what we've learned so far.[355]

Therefore, Bill Hybels told his congregation that Willow Creek's message, "We know what you need and we can meet those needs for you" is wrong.[356] The leadership discovered that this message created unhealthy dependence and inappropriate levels of expectations. Hybels states, "We have been wrong. We need to rethink the coaching we

---

[353] Hawkins, Parkinson, & Arnson, *Reveal: Where Are You?*, 4.
[354] Ibid., 4.
[355] Ibid., 64.
[356] Idem.

give you as you pursue your spiritual growth."[357] The leadership made the decision that they "want to move people from dependence on the church to a growing interdependent partnership with the church."[358] In other words, the congregation needs to learn how to "feed themselves." Hybels declared that the church must also transition from being a "spiritual parent to a spiritual coach."[359] As a result, the church has rejected the idea of one program or plan that fits all, and it is creating assessment tools and customized directions to meet individual needs.[360]

Lastly, the church realized the excessive receiving of those who attended its religious services. Therefore, the leaders want to extend the impact of the weekly services. Though they are still brainstorming, one idea attempted was during "a five-week series on the book of James, we distributed a free journal that was designed to help people take next steps wherever they were along the spiritual continuum."[361] The journal had pages for note-taking, week long study questions in view of the passage examined, study questions for those in small groups, and insights from a biblical commentary for those who want to dig deeper independently.

In sum, the church is now encouraging other seeker-sensitive churches in its association to (1) Ask more than "How many?" (2) Go beyond "How are you?" and (3) Ask "How does that help someone grow?" Thus, with renewed excitement, Willow Creek's team of leaders contends that this research forced them to ask questions, continue to try new things, and keep reassessing in order to help people grow.[362]

Before we move to our analysis of the emerging church, one additional comment is needed regarding a recent criticism of the seeker church. This will serve as a transitional point to our analysis of the emerging church and reveals a common problem among many of the churches in this study. Some scholars are claiming the seeker-sensitive church has already failed to adjust to culture. Eddie Gibbs and Ryan Bolger of Fuller Seminary believe these churches are unable to reach our culture.[363] Why? They contend we are turning into a "post-

---

[357] Idem.
[358] Ibid., 65.
[359] Idem.
[360] Ibid., 65-6.
[361] Ibid., 66.
[362] Ibid., 73.
[363] Belcher, *The Deep Church*, 36-7.

consumeristic culture," that is, we are no longer embracing the belief that value is determined by economic factors. Values such as personal identity, purpose, and goals are separated from material objects people own, possess, pursue, or consume (vanity). Thus, for post-consumers, the seeker-sensitive approach of using marketing tactics to bridge the culture gap generates personal alienation, a lack of authenticity, and genuine interest in the well being of others. Ironically, the seeker-sensitive church feeds our narcissistic appetites. Additionally, they symbolize authoritarian institutions no matter how performance driven they may be. Church polity and proclamations from the pulpit still reside in the pastor or leadership staff.

I reject Gibbs and Bolger's meta-narrative claim that our culture is transitioning to a post-consumeristic culture because we are embedded in culture and do not stand above it with a God-like viewpoint. But what we can say is there is a growing interest in ideas that find historical expression in Romanticism (e.g., the hostility toward reason and expansiveness of reality).[364] We have inherited history from previous experiences. As a result, people turn to past ideas, expressions, and events to better understand and deal with the present and prepare for future possibilities.

In his work, *A Secular Age*, Charles Taylor contends that, in response to modernism, authoritarianism, material success, and consumerism, a resurgence of Romanticism is finding contemporary expression.[365] Taylor observes young people who are seeking "a kind of unity and wholeness of the self, a reclaiming of the place of feeling, against the one-sided pre-eminence of reason, and a reclaiming of the body and its pleasures from the inferior and often guilt-ridden place it has been allowed in the disciplined, instrumental identity."[366] In *Spiritual*

---

[364] W. T. Jones, *Kant and the Nineteenth Century: A History of Western Philosophy*, 2nd ed., rev (Belmont, CA: Wadsworth, 1975), 101-08.

[365] Charles Taylor, *A Secular Age* (Cambridge, MA: Belknap Press, 2007), 507. See also, Paul Heelas, Linda Woodhead, Benjamin Seel, & Bronislaw Szersynski *Spiritualities of Life: New Age Romanticism and Consumptive Capitalism* (Oxford, UK: Blackwell, 2008).

[366] Taylor, *A Secular Age*, 507. In the National Study of Youth and Religion, funded by the Lily Endowment, Sociologist Christian Smith recently concluded from his comprehensive study among contemporary teenagers (ages 13-17), that their "religion" is moralistic, therapeutic, and deistic [*Soul Searching: The Religious and Spiritual Lives of American Teenagers* (Oxford, UK: Oxford University Press, 2009)]. In fact, he defines their religion as "Moralistic Therapeutic Deism." While institutional religion may be helpful, teenagers do not believe it is necessary. Historic, orthodox Christianity has little bearing upon these findings.

Marketplace, Wade Clark Roof asserts there is a growing amount of people who are "looking for a more direct experience of the sacred, for greater immediacy, spontaneity, and spiritual depth."[367] In fact, Clark contends that three aspects of our present situation particularly stand out. "Large sectors" of the American population today are interested in "deepening their spirituality," emphasizing "self-understanding and self-reflexivity" (e.g., quest, seeking, and searching, and have 'spiritual yearnings').[368] Those who are appealing to Romantic ideas emphasize themes such as holism, individuality, integrity, and unity. Words often used include balance, flow, harmony, integration, and being at one, that is, centered.[369] Moreover, they are in pursuit of what may be described as an "ethic of authenticity." Taylor's description of this ethic is helpful:

> I have to discover my route to wholeness and spiritual depth. The focus is on the individual, and on his/her experience. Spirituality must speak to this experience. The mode of spiritual life is thus the quest…It is a quest which can't start with a priori exclusions or inescapable starting points, which could pre-empt this experience.[370]

As a result, these scholars are noting among many young people who exhibit a desire for "spirituality" but not "institutionalized religion."Once again, reminiscent of Vincent Van Gogh's "Starry Night" with his contrast of cosmos offering light whereas the church does not, many are turning away from "institutional religion" with all of its authority and rules, and are more inclined to consider subjective aspects of spirituality with an emphasis on self, wholeness, health, and feelings.

In sum, what we are able to say is there are people who are point-

---

[367] Wade Clark Roof, *Spiritual Marketplace: Baby Boomers and the Remaking of American Religion* (Princeton, NJ: Princeton University Press, 1999), 86. Interestingly, he contends that the Baby Boomers are emerging into five sub-cultures: dogmatists (religious but not spiritual), born-again Christians, mainstream believers, metaphysical believers and seekers (e.g., Zen Buddhists; Wiccans; New-Agers), and secularists (areligious).

[368] Ibid., 9

[369] Heelas, Woodhead, Seel, Zzerszynski, & Tusting, *The Spiritual Revolution* (Oxford, UK: Blackwell, 2004), 26.

[370] Taylor, *A Secular Age*, 507-8.

ing to what we have inherited from history and are using that to inform their present experience. While no one can say from a bird's eye perspective that our culture is universally "post-modern" or "Romantic," or "narcissistic," the lesson for us is as our culture continually changes, old ideas, expressions, and events are inevitably considered and are used to inform people's present conditions, shed light upon previous experiences, and anticipate and prepare for new experiences. Therefore, exclusively using one approach to bridge the culture gap only aggravates the discontinuity between church and community. Instead, a church should appeal to a plethora of tools to achieve temporary continuity. Appealing to history is one of those tools.

STRENGTHS OF THE EMERGING CHURCH MOVEMENT (S)

One recent attempt that certainly appeals to the past while not ignoring the present is the pluralistic emerging church movement. We will now direct our attention to analyzing this complex phenomenon. We will discover the emerging church is more aligned with Dewey's aesthetic insights than any other church we have examined. Yet, ironically, the emerging church struggles with some of the same issues that the elite, sensational, and seeker-sensitive churches face.

Emerging churches are to be commended for attention to contextualization, diversity, creative spontaneity, dialogical teaching, and the willingness to use historical resources as tools to enrich present experience. Moreover, emerging churches are sensitive that they are in culture, not above it. Let us now explore these strengths before we turn to the problems this church movement has or will inevitably face.

1. Embrace contextualization. In order to bridge the culture gap, emerging churches embrace contextualization. Presupposing that our contemporary society is pluralistic and post-Christian, they contend that the church needs to return to the ways in which it originally spread in first few centuries of Christianity's existence in order to bridge the culture gap. Thus, the subculture should be allowed to penetrate and inform how the church goes about its activities. Direct experience comes from the ongoing interaction of the community and the church together.[371]

---

[371] Dewey, *Art as Experience*, 15.

Contextualization involves "exegeting the community" and examining how other successful churches in similar contexts are reaching out to their particular communities.[372] "Exegeting the community" means asking the community about its needs, preferences, and values, and discovering what the local objections are regarding church, life, and other relevant issues.[373] The emerging church realizes its own existence and mission are bound to the community in the most intimate way. This is seen in such ways as how the church is designed and how activities, practices, and rituals of worship are conducted.

The benefit of contextualization resonates with Dewey's understanding of our relationship to our environment. Emerging churches claim the traditional and seeker ways of doing church are already irrelevant. Churches, like organisms, continually fall out of step with the "march of surrounding things." Thus emerging churches realize they must reach out to the culture by means of contextualization. So the music, the food, and the way a pastor teaches will conform to the subculture. One emerging church, for example, actually meets in a gay bar every Sunday morning right in the center of the gay district in a metropolitan city. That does not mean this emerging church is advocating the practice of homosexuality. In fact, this particular church, since it is a member of the Acts 29 Network, embraces Reformation theology. But it does mean a church can contextualize even in the most unlikely places and in the most malleable ways. Thus, for them, church and culture overlaps and merges in various ways. They are always becoming, never fixed in their attitude toward culture and themselves, recognizing the pluralistic differences and changes that occur in culture and even within them.

Emerging churches' sensitivity to contextualization illuminates the importance of diversity. There is no single prescriptive way in which worship and other activities are to be done. As evidenced in the practices of the early church (pre-Constantine), each church contextualized according to its setting. While some streams of the emerging church have differing perspectives on the authorities and relationship of Scripture, tradition, and experience, they all value

---

[372] Ed Stetzer & David Putnman, *Breaking the Missional Code: Your Church Can Become a Missionary in the Community* (Nashville, TN: Broadman & Holman, 2006), 21.
[373] Ibid., 24.

diversity. While emerging churches may question the way orthodoxy has been constructed, they remain committed to the core beliefs of the Christian faith as expressed in certain historical creeds of the church. For example, Robert Webber writes, "Stop doing ministry shaped by this or that cultural narrative and go back to the story of the triune God in history, authoritatively recorded in Scripture and summarized in the Nicene Creed (AD 325)."[374] Emerging pastor John Burke puts it this way, "We must let our culture's questions help us better conform to truth and God's revelation."[375] Thus, the typical emerging church contends for both contextualization and orthodoxy.

2. Spontaneous expressions of creativity. For emerging churches, creativity is a gift from God that needs and deserves to be exercised in corporate worship. In fact, the use of creativity contributes to the church's context and on-going conversation about such issues as God, the human condition, and living life in a broken world. Unlike the elite church, these followers promote the active use of creativity to think about or investigate a particular biblical, philosophical, or theological idea, question, or theme. In fact, they affirm the sensory without being sensational. They recognize expressions of creativity are often able to communicate apart from words.

For example, in an emerging church in Houston, while the pastor speaks, artists are painting. From my observation the artists are interacting with the message, the conditions of the worship service, and the particular situation. Emerging churches recognize what Dewey said many years ago: "There are values and meaning that can be expressed only by immediately visible and audible qualities, and to ask what they mean in the sense of something that can be put into words is to deny their distinctive existence."[376]

The churches' "spontaneity of expression" is admirable. They are organic expressions, taken up in present experience, contributing to the experience of the moment and with each other. Why is this spontaneity of expression important? Consider the words of Dewey:

---

[374] *Listening to the Beliefs of the Emerging Churches*, 199.
[375] Ibid., 54.
[376] Dewey, *Art as Experience*, 77.

Staleness of matter and obtrusion of calculation are the two enemies of spontaneity of expression.... But an expression will, nevertheless, manifest spontaneity if that matter has been vitally taken up into a present experience. The inevitable self-movement of a poem or drama is compatible with any amount of prior labor provided the results of that labor emerge in complete fusion with an emotion that is fresh.[377]

As a result of the use of creativity, the worship experience may be different and memorable each and every Sunday.

How local churches treat or react to the spontaneity of expression reveals a lot about their habituated way of seeing and doing and the standard employed by which they measure a successful worship experience. In fact, no test surely reveals the one-sidedness of their ecclesiology as its treatment of creativity.[378] For example, by only affirming one prescriptive way of doing church and not allowing the spontaneity of expression to take place within the context of worship, traditional churches are acting out modernistic biases. In fact, because of the traditional church's incorporation of modernism into theology, polity, and practice, emerging churches contend that traditional and seeker-sensitive churches are not able to bridge the culture gap; for they put up unnecessary barriers in the way they communicate the Christian faith (e.g., centralized authority, reason, logic). But spontaneity of expression breaks down barriers as people creatively engage each other using words, art-products, and dialogical teaching in the context of corporate worship. Here's why.

From the insights we have gained about the generations of people since the baby boomers, described as the "emerging adulthood," the "seekers," and the "me-generation," people born in the 1970s, 1980s, and 1990s are skeptic about dogmatic claims, are cynical about organized religion, see religious belief as a preference, have a deep appreciation for creativity, and hunger for spirituality that speaks to the whole person, not merely the mind. While churches are unnecessary to them, these younger generations are looking for a context in which

---
[377] Ibid., 73.
[378] Ibid., 286.

to ask and probe into spiritual questions, engage in diversity, and experience creativity in all of its forms. Obviously, emerging churches provide those opportunities.

3. The value of dialogical instruction. Teaching by conversation in corporate worship provides the opportunity for the spontaneity of expression to emerge, and more importantly, affords the opportunity to ask the hard questions and probe into an experience with God that transcends into mystery. In contrast to all of the previous churches in our study, emerging churches that use this approach are promoting opportunity to actively participate in the learning experience. No longer is the congregation merely a spectator observing worship. Individuals are able to critically engage with each other on an equal footing in a way that honors tolerance, values people, exposes biases, and promotes the evaluation and justification for assumptions and ideas. Conclusions are tested by group discussion.

The informality of the worship experience promotes accessibility, authenticity, and transparency in a setting where intellectual, moral, and spiritual struggles of the soul are taken seriously and without animosity. One can quietly discover deep questions are not isolated to one person, but perhaps common to many. In fact, no particular theological doctrine is forbidden from discussion. Why? Like Dewey, emerging churches recognize people are in culture, not above it, and are influenced by context, though not necessarily determined by it. For example, Robert Webber notes:

> Theology is an 'adventurous exploration of new horizons.' Theology is more like a 'mysterious adventure than a mathematical puzzle.'[379] Or consider the insights of emerging pastor John Burke who writes:

> Because most people I interact with assume religious belief is a preference thing—like preferring blue over green—for them, arguing that blue is better than green (or Christianity is right and other religions are wrong) feels like foolishness. For that reason,

---

[379] *Listening to the Beliefs of the Emerging Churches*, 199.

we must avoid arguments about religion and get back to the basics of knowing God.[380]

Burke, who contends that our "knowledge is really biased by our cultural upbringing," wonders if modern systems of theology have blinded us to somehow think that since we have Scripture systematized, we have God figured out.[381] Burke goes on to say:

> Postmodern relativism creates a wonderful theological bridge from our culture to the amazing revelation of God. Because in many respects, the Jain parable nails it—we are all blind. And on our own, none of us can accurately describe God beyond a blind guess. So the moral fundamental question is, 'Has God revealed his identity?' Now we're on level ground with all the world's religions.[382]

Therefore, incorporating conversation as an aspect of worship rather than didactic teaching allows for the doing and undergoing to occur for all involved, that is, the pastor and the congregation. Each worship service is an opportunity to be enriched by other's insights and experiences.

4. Using history as tools for worship. Emerging churches utilize historical expressions, practices, and rituals from the past, incorporating them in the present activities of worship. For example, rejecting either/or practices, Robert Webber promotes an idea that has been largely popular in emerging churches: Ancient-Future faith. Webber writes, "An Ancient-Future faith calls upon us all to embrace a both/and future."[383] An Ancient-Future faith involves three major ideas: affirming the ancient roots of faith, a connection to the universal church in all times and everywhere, and a commitment to an authentic engagement with culture."[384] Let us briefly explore these three ideas and relate them to the worship experience.

---
[380] Ibid., 59.
[381] Ibid., 60.
[382] Idem.
[383] Ibid., 213.
[384] Ibid., 215.

Worship as Experience

First, this movement calls for a return to the ancient roots of Christianity where early followers emerged from a culture that was religious, spiritual, secular, and pagan. These Christians were able to bridge the culture gap because they affirmed truth and practiced particular contextualization. These factors predate the splits between the Catholic, Orthodox, and the Protestants.

Second, an Ancient-Future faith involves seeking understanding in the particulars while affirming unity in the common tradition. Webber states, "While there is a common tradition that defines us all, there are particular traditions that characterize the diversity we experience within our unity."[385] Thus, this approach affirms the differing ways of expressing the Christian faith while remaining faithful to its core beliefs.

Third, Ancient-Future faith takes on the ever-present challenge of bridging the culture gap, recognizing that culture itself continually changes. Authenticity and personal transformation are central to facing these cultural changes. But what changes all the time is how the Christian faith is articulated and defended. Webber claims:

> The shift in science, from a mechanistic view of the world to the world as a web of interconnections; in philosophy, from rationalism to mystery; in globalization, from monoculture to multiculture; in historical consciousness, from anti-historical to nostalgia for the past; in language, from propositional to performative; in communication, from monologue to dialogue; in technology, from word to image; in society, from individualism to community; and in the rise of terror that moves us from a state of stability to personal vulnerability. Christians can and do affirm these new cultural realities and speak an unchanging faith through them.[386]

Webber goes on to say, "Indeed, what lies before us is an arduous task, a journey through perilous waters that must be navigated with great care and embraced with anticipatory joy."[387]

As a result of ideas such as "Ancient-Future Christianity," emerging churches are utilizing ancient, medieval, and Reformation Church

---
[385] Ibid., 214.
[386] Ibid., 214-5.
[387] Ibid., 215.

activities, practices, and rituals in contemporary activities of worship. For example, emerging leader Karen Ward uses the *Revised Common Lectionary* (Scripture readings from the Consultation on Common Texts) in her weekly services described as a "Mass gathering."[388] She desires to provide the church a "scriptural diet that is rich and varied enough to prevent anemia, and one that allows for solid spiritual growth over the long haul in the grace and love of God."[389] The church she leads emphasizes the narratives of Scripture rather than didactic teaching in order to "walk in" that is, participate in the stories of faith and God-encounters.[390] Her church also welcome's people into their community using "an organic and free-range form of the ancient process which the early church called the 'catechumenate' [Greek word, "catecheo" which means to "sound in the ear.]"[391] They use an experience-based pattern, following the pattern used by Christ and his apostles, by inviting people to join them on their journey. Rather than using a didactic style of simply teaching them doctrine, this church desires to come alongside "seekers" and be a community to them as they embark on a life-altering journey. She states:

> We come together as children to be gathered around and taken up into the Big Story told by our Father, which we are invited to hear, touch, taste, smell, and see through the life of Jesus. Then we are provided time and open space to talk and share at the table, to eat by the warmth of the Spirit's fire.[392]

She goes on to say

> At apostles we call our reflections on the Word the 'reverb.' Reverb may or may not be a sermon, as a sermon is just one way to break open the Word among many other ways we might use (drama, art, music, discussion, poetry…).[393]

---

[388] Ibid., 167.
[389] Idem.
[390] Ibid., 168.
[391] Ibid., 170.
[392] Ibid., 167.
[393] Idem.

This church also incorporates ancient and medieval icons in its worship activities allowing people the opportunity to meditate or reflect upon these depictions. Lastly, Ward reports they are just beginning to investigate how the church community may express itself as a monastic order.[394] The willingness to utilize historical resources in an effort to engage and enrich the worship experience and church community resonates with Dewey's task of removing barriers where art-products, ancient rituals, and activities have been relegated to separate realms.[395] Many emerging churches are striving to restore the continuity between art-products such as icons that have long been extinguished in many traditional churches since the rise of iconoclasm and religious reductionism in worship. Iconoclasm is the willful removal and even the destruction of religious icons, statues, and symbols for reasons such as idolatry or perceiving them as violations of the Second Commandment, namely, the precept that there shall be no "graven image." This is unfortunate because these art-products (e.g., icons) emerged from the development of religious activities.[396] Like Dewey states:

> The collective life that was manifested in war, worship, the forum, knew no division between what was characteristic of these places and operations, and the arts that brought color, grace, and dignity, into them. Painting and sculpture were organically one with architecture, as that was one with the social purpose that buildings served. Music and song were intimate parts of the rites and ceremonies in which the meaning of group life was consummated. Drama was a vital reënactment of the legends and history of group life.[397]

Religious reductionism is committed when the nature of worship is identified with only one activity of worship. Thus, many emerging churches are describing themselves as "post-evangelical."

---

[394] Ibid., 177.
[395] Dewey, *Art as Experience*, 2.
[396] Ibid., 10.
[397] Ibid., 5-6.

WEAKNESSES OF THE EMERGING CHURCH MOVEMENT (S)

Now having highlighted four particular strengths of the emerging movement(s), a Deweyan analysis reveals six problems. Since emerging churches value particular contextualization within a certain community, there may be exceptions. Nevertheless, Dewey's insights might prove helpful as this pluralistic movement continues to develop.

1. Problem of dependency. So much of the creative activities of the worship experience rely upon the pastor or pastoral team in churches where spontaneity of expression does not occur among those gathered. Ironically, like the elite church, the activities are dependent upon the pastor's supply of creativity or aesthetic experience in preparation. If the leadership falls short of a regular dose of inspiration for creativity, the worship experience that particular week will fall short as well. As a result, the worship experience may not necessarily be organic, but imposed.

2. Overuse of tension. Unlike the humdrum church, corporate worship in emerging churches welcome tension. For example, the use of deconstruction in dialogue, the spontaneity of expression, and the use of unfamiliar historical methods all invoke tension in order to challenge worldviews and move congregants to look at the beliefs and practices in different ways. There is value in this approach. Like Dewey states:

> Struggle and conflict may be themselves enjoyed, although they are painful, when they are experienced as a means of developing an experience; members in that they carry it forward, not just because they are. There is, as will appear later, an element of undergoing, of suffering, in its large sense, in every experience. Otherwise there would be no taking in of what preceded. For 'taking in' in any vital experience is something more than placing something on the top of consciousness over what was previously known. It involves reconstruction, which may be painful.[398]

---

[398] Ibid., 42.

Notwithstanding, tension can be so great that people are not able to overcome it. When the tension is ongoing, the participants can become weary. For people who have attended any of the churches previously mentioned in chapter 3, this lack of familiarity adds to the tension and can make the experience too foreign. Like visiting another country, the novel ideas and sights and sounds are intriguing. But once the time of vacation has passed, or when we face a crisis or long for a place of continuity, we would not find where tension is emphasized to be a haven. To the movements' defense, the lifetime churchgoers and those between the ages of 40 to 80 are not the targeted audience. But the concern regarding the tension that the emergents especially enjoy remains valid. We will long for continuity and will leave in order to find it. Discussions do not always answer questions fully. Thought-provoking contemporary topics may not give adequate comfort. An ever-changing context can make us long to hold onto a place that feels like home. For example, John Newton's masterpiece, "Amazing Grace" has become a staple of comfort to many throughout the world. Though styles of music have changed immensely since it was written, it is still played whenever people are hurting and need to hear a sound of the familiar. A church that offers deconstruction of ideas and assumptions will likely have a few losses of people who found that the tension was too much.

3. *Unbeneficial dialogical instruction*. There is a serious concern about the importance of conversation of the participants. The conversation will only be as strong as the crowd is alert, educated, comfortable, and informed on the particular topic. It can easily become an unprofitable time of shared ignorance with minimal growth. If the congregants have been raised to question everything, pursue relative truth, tolerate others' opinions at all costs, and spurn harsh authority figures, then a multitude of ideas will come forth. Furthermore, a pastor who is in a position to lead a discussion where his views, no matter how well formulated, are on an equal plane as his peers in the room, will inevitably struggle in an effort to move forward. As a result, there can be too much emphasis on plural and free participation but not enough on listening or on the quality of discourse. Qualitative instruction will take a great deal of time if it occurs at all because

of the time spent listening to all of the other opinions. Finally, it is not unthinkable to foresee one of those opinions, expressed strongly enough, easily leading the church in a direction entirely unorthodox.

4. Problem of Novelty. While so much effort is spent on contextualization and being anti-traditional, anti-evangelical, or anti-modern evangelical, many of these churches neglect the strengths or beneficial values of the traditional and seeker-sensitive churches. This becomes all the more interesting when they draw from resources of ancient, medieval, and Reformation practices. Emerging leaders are too quick to assume traditional churches are irrelevant and not meaningful to baby boomers, emerging adulthood, and other younger people. So, as pluralistic as they say they claim to be, emerging churches fail to consider the accomplishment of the church of the modernistic age. Thus, they over-emphasize novelty over and against the benefits and values traditional churches and seeker-sensitive churches have to offer.

For example, approximately forty percent of the local traditional church where I attend is comprised of people who are part of Generation X and emerging adulthood. What is the draw? For one, they find that inductive teaching, which is the one of the greatest strengths of this traditional church, to be profitable. They find the worship experience to be meaningful and practical. Some also find singing the traditional songs and hearing familiar words to be nostalgic and comforting.

Therefore, if emerging churches really value pluralism and contextualization, any cynicism toward traditional expressions of worship should be displaced. As discussed with the elite church, aesthetic experiences can occur in an inductive setting. Moreover, some of these traditional churches are operating within a cultural or sub-cultural context that values the strengths of certain modernist assumptions.

The problem of novelty also generates reductionism. Reductionism finds expression when the value of systematic formulations of theology, inductive study of Scripture, and modern philosophy are displaced in favor of provocative rhetoric, dialogical teaching, and creative and sensory expressions of worship. However, these tools should not be marginalized or rejected for the following three reasons.

First, systematic theology, inductive study of Scripture, and modern philosophy should be considered, as with other historical resources, as tools to help us engage in the task before us. Our culture is too precarious to dismiss their usefulness. Like Dewey states, "... the blundering ineptness of much that calls itself judicial criticism has called out a reaction to the opposite extreme."[399] Moreover, "The critic who is not intimately aware of a variety of traditions is of necessity limited and his criticisms will be one-sided to the point of distortion."[400] These tools help us adopt our past, value our mistakes, and serve as warnings as we inquire, engage, and commit ourselves to certain directions within an unpredictable environment.[401]

Second, these ideas, methods, and expressions emerged out human creativity, need, and purpose. Creativity, intellect, collective thought and interaction, and tension and recovery were used to bring forth such activities such as the systematizing of Scripture into a coherent system of thought. Activities, rituals, practices, and art-products were created out of a context of need, intelligent inquiry, and curiosity.[402] They are a part of our history, that is, who we are.

And third, we are foolish not to draw from those resources in order to prepare us for the future. Depth of study may be compromised to creative experience, thus resulting in groups of people whose faith is "a mile wide and an inch deep." In the name of novelty, answers for which the adherents are searching may never be found. Emerging leader John Burke for example, states he is fearful that the emerging church will "cut loose from the authority Scripture in an effort to relate to culture."[403] Just as the "power of 'story' in authentic emerging churches is huge," the tools of systematic theology, biblical exegesis, and modern philosophy are also beneficial to our situation, the way we direct our inquiries, and our goals.[404]

5. Aesthetic problem of disorganization. Dialogical instruction, the spontaneity of expression, the exercise of creativity, and pluralistic activities can become disconnected, disorganized, incoherent, and

---

[399] Dewey, *Art as Experience*, 317.
[400] Ibid., 323.
[401] Ibid., 17.
[402] Ibid., 240.
[403] *Listening to the Beliefs of Emerging Churches*, 61.
[404] Dewey, *Art as Experience*, 79.

aimless. When an activity is marked by disorganization, an aesthetic experience will not occur. The one place where experience should not fall apart into disorganization is in the church since the activities are meant to tell a larger story. If this occurs often enough, the people gathered for corporate worship will not only be deeply affected negatively by the experience, but will also become aesthetically anemic.

6. The problem of narcissism. Empirical sociological studies are revealing that while these recent generations are open to spirituality and relish creativity; these same "seekers" are also embracing narcissism. For example, in their book, *The Narcissism Epidemic: Living in the Age of Entitlement*, Jean Twenge and Keith Campbell contend that the distinction between self-admiration and narcissism appears to be significantly blurred among Americans. Just as the Greek character Narcissus was frozen by his own self-admiration, unable to intimately connect with anyone outside himself, these recent generations are doing the same.[405] Young people are not just confident they are overconfident, with an over-inflated view of one's own abilities.[406] Twenge and Campbell write:

> The central feature of narcissism is a very positive and inflated view of the self. People with high levels of narcissism—whom we refer to as 'narcissists'—think they are better than others in social status, good looks, intelligence, and creativity. However, they are not. Measured objectively, narcissists are just like everyone else. Nevertheless, narcissists see themselves as fundamentally superior—they are special, entitled, and unique. Narcissists also lack emotionally warm, caring, and loving relationships with other people. That is a main difference between a narcissist and someone who merely high in self-esteem: the high self-esteem person who's not narcissistic values relationships, but the narcissist does not. The result is a fundamentally imbalanced self–a grandiose, inflated self-image and a lack of deep connection to others.[407]

---

[405] Jean M. Twenge and Keith W. Campbell, *The Narcissism Epidemic: Living in the Age of Entitlement* (New York: Free Press, 2009), 18. Their empirical research on the origins of narcissism is worth examining. See chapter 4, "How Did We Get Here? Origins of the Epidemic," 57-69.
[406] Ibid.
[407] Ibid., 19.

As a result, overemphasizing themes such as "self-esteem," and "loving yourself," have generated narcissistic values in terms of personal entitlement and self-expression. Unfortunately, these values are leading them to damaging consequences such as doing what benefits the self even if that means others will have to bear the cost.[408] And though a drive to bridge the culture is admirable, a culture that is self-absorbed is gong to be a special challenge for any church, since all churches in this examination agree on the one point that the church's foremost purpose is to worship God, not ourselves.

While emerging churches seek to contextualize their worship to the community, relish opportunity for creativity, the question becomes how different is the emerging church from the culture it mirrors? Is the call for "relevance" a cloak to further inflame narcissistic tendencies? Creative expression, dialogical instruction, and the desire for community can so easily be used as platforms to further contribute to narcissistic behavior such as believing that "they are better than others in social status, good looks, intelligence, and creativity."[409]

How the church addresses narcissism in a context that values self-expression demands regular attention. Why? Because the "actual world, that in which we live, is a combination of movement and culmination, of breaks and re-unions..."[410] We have to show them that such things as self-admiration is costly and entitlements such as success is not guaranteed in this life.[411] Life itself is too precarious, too fragile.

THE FAILURE TO BRIDGE THE CULTURE GAP

Our analysis has revealed two recent reactions to the problems of the traditional church. The seeker-sensitive church and the pluralistic emerging movement have sought to bridge the culture and offer relevant corporate worship. The seeker-sensitive church restructured and reinvented the church to become culturally inviting. Thus, in the name of an open invitation, the architecture was redesigned and anything was removed that might prove to be a barrier to the

---

[408] Ibid., 55.
[409] Ibid., 19.
[410] Dewey, *Art as Experience*, 16.
[411] Twenge and Campbell, *The Narcissism Epidemic*, 54-6.

"unchurched," and performance-drive corporate worship became the focal point. On the other hand, the emerging movements sought to contextualize themselves to particular communities like a missionary would to a foreign culture in order to bridge the culture gap with an incarnational mindset. Moreover, in response to the influences of modern philosophy and the attitudes and interests of the emerging adulthood, the "seekers," have sought to create a corporate worship experience utilizing past expressions of faith, pluralistic activities (e.g., stations), and community living in order to integrate both belief and belonging. But I contend while each of these approaches have a number of strengths, they fail to adequately address three underlying and commonsensical issues, namely, the gap itself, the need for adaptation as a core aesthetic value, and aesthetic experience.

1. Commit reductionism. While these two movements recognize a gap, they assume it is only a culture gap, thus committing reductionism. For example, the leaders clamor to say that our society is "consumeristic," "postmodern," "post-consumeristic," "relativistic," or "post-Christian." Thus, the seeker-sensitive church seeks to appear attractive as possible, competing with other options of entertainment in the community. Then it uses marketing theories to target felt-needs such as "Seven Steps on How to Be Successful at Work." On the other hand, the emerging church movements appeal to the attitudes and interests of people who are identified with "generation-me." These "seekers" express the "language of the self as their native tongue."[412] Good feelings about themselves are the prized virtue. They are filled with "soaring expectations" and are experiencing "crushing realities" for "the gap between what they have and what they want has never been greater."[413] But by addressing their attitudes and expectations, allowing them to have more sensory-filled experiences, these churches still do not address the underlying problem.

2. Fail to adequately understand the biological aspects of reality. The gap is much more than avant-garde ideas becoming mainstream,

---

[412] Jean M. Twenge, *Generation Me: Why Today's Young Americans Are More Confident, Assertive, Entitled-and More Miserable Than Ever Before* (New York: Free Press, 2006), 2.
[413] Idem.

ideological and cultural paradigm shifts, or even consumer trends among the masses. Instead, life itself, that is, the biological aspects of reality, is one that involves discontinuity with our environment.[414] In other words, we are constantly experiencing separation from continuity, fulfillment, and balance. At the same time we have an unconquerable impulse to have ordered relations with our environment.[415]

Evidence for discontinuity is seen and felt when we examine our real human needs. According to Dewey, every real need we have is an authentic lack. For example, the need for food or water demonstrates a lack of it. Thus, every need denotes at least a "temporary absence of adequate adjustment with surroundings."[416] But this need is also a demand. A demand is a "reaching out into the environment to make good the lack and to restore adjustment by building at least a temporary equilibrium."[417] In other words, we are reaching out to fulfill that need. Dewey writes:

> Life itself consists of phases in which the organism falls out of step with the march of surrounding things and then recovers unison with it—either through effort or by some happy chance. And, in a growing life, the recovery is never mere return to a prior state, for it is enriched by the state of disparity and resistance through which it has successfully passed. If the gap between organism and environment is too wide, the creature dies. If its activity is not enhanced by temporary alienation, it merely subsists. Life itself grows when a temporary falling out is a transition to a more extensive balance of the energies of the organism with those of the condition under which it lives.[418]

When a person is able to make terms with his environment in a particular setting at a specific point in time, then one secures temporary continuity, stability, or fulfillment. Let us now turn to four aspects of how we might bridge the gap between churches and community.

---

[414] Dewey, *Art as Experience*, 12.
[415] Ibid., 4.
[416] Ibid., 12.
[417] Idem.
[418] Ibid., 12-3.

HOW TO BRIDGE THE CULTURE GAP

1. Acknowledge that discontinuity with our environment is inevitable. The first step in bridging the gap between churches and community is to accept that discontinuity with our surroundings is inescapable and certain while we tarry on this earth. Dewey states, "Nature is the mother and the habitat of man, even if sometimes a stepmother and an unfriendly home."[419] As a result, people have real and deep needs.

2. Target deep needs. A second and very important step is meeting people's real needs, that is, existent physical, existential, and spiritual needs they have living this life. In doing this, the local church will always be relevant to an ever-changing community. For example, we have physical needs such as food, water, and good health. We have existential needs such as meaning, purpose, identity, and fulfillment. And we also have spiritual needs such as absolution, forgiveness, mercy, and redemption.

While providing a criteria for real needs versus felt-needs may prove to be difficult and further inquiry would be needed, we may at least say that real needs go beyond our conscious desires and preferences. Felt-needs are what we consciously desire and change throughout our life. For example, a mother in her mid-twenties is looking for a "mother's day out" program. A man in his seventies is looking for friends with whom he can golf. On the other hand, deep needs are more general, common to our human plight. Dewey writes:

> The first great consideration is that life goes on an environment; not merely in it but because of it, through interaction with it. No creature lives merely under its skin; its subcutaneous organs are means of connection with what lies beyond its bodily frame, and to which, in order to live, it must adjust itself, by accommodation and defense but also by conquest. At every moment, the living creature is exposed to dangers from its surroundings to satisfy its needs. The career and destiny of a living being are bound up with its interchanges and with its environment, not externally but in the most intimate way.[420]

---
[419] Ibid., 28.
[420] Ibid., 12.

Thus, the church will be in a better position to bridge the reoccurring gap by meeting the real needs people possess and not merely targeting felt-needs, even though there may be times whereby both types of needs overlap such as our need for relationships and purpose.

Sure, both seeker-sensitive and emerging churches target needs but they do not adequately understand the nature of discontinuity and continuity as an aspect of reality. This is demonstrated, for example, in the seeker-sensitive church's realization that its experiment targeting felt-needs failed. The people were not qualitatively growing. They were becoming discontent. On the other hand, the emerging church's focus is how to "speak" to this younger generation, to "form a new evangelical identity marked by new insights, new concerns, and new patterns of theological application, worship, spirituality, and ministry."[421] The danger here is that an emerging church can be so ambitious in forming a new identity in an attempt to break away from the old, that it neglects the needs that are presently before it. Moreover, the solutions suggested by emerging churches to bridge the gap is only temporary because it is only offering a new way to do the same things again. If they are only aiming for a new identity they will themselves, once again, be caught up in the same trap as evidenced by the elite, broken, humdrum, sensational, and seeker-sensitive churches.

3. Embrace adjustment as a core condition for aesthetic value. The third step is for the church to embrace adjustment as a core aesthetic value. On-going adjustment, that is, continual fine-tuning of activities in corporate worship, should be a central value that will assist the church in engaging the desires, inclinations, and interests of each generation. Interestingly, adjustment affects both our churches and our situational context; it is bilateral.[422] Marriage is an

---

[421] *Listening to the Beliefs of Emerging Churches*, 16.

[422] In *A Common Faith*, Dewey elaborates on what he means by "adjustment." He writes: But there are also changes in ourselves in relation to the world in which we live that are much more inclusive and deep seated. They relate not to this and that want in relation to this and that condition of our surroundings, but pertain to our being in its entirety. Because of their scope, this modification of ourselves is enduring. It lasts through any amount of vicissitude of circumstances, internal and external. There is a composing and harmonization of the various elements of our being such that, I spite of changes in the special conditions that surround us, these conditions are also arranged, settled, in relation to us. This attitude includes a note of submission. But it is voluntary it is something more than a mere Stoical resolution to endure unperturbed throughout the buffetings of fortune.

excellent example of adjustment because it changes us as individuals and the conditions of our environment (e.g., each season of our marriage will bring different looks to our home).

In particular, the emergent movement, the most radical stream among emerging movements, is most problematic because it, like modern theologians did in a previous century (modern theology) is integrating the worldview of postmodernism to the extent that many followers describe themselves as "soft postmodernists." By embracing a theoretical paradigm like postmodernism, the gap between the local church and ever-changing culture will inevitably reappear or remain. The emergent movement does not adequately consider its constructs, too, will become outdated as the desires and interests of people and culture change. Therefore, if the local church would continually aesthetically adjust to culture, then it will be in a better position to offer an experience that is personally meaningful to each generation. Further, the church will also be in a position to contribute to the community as well.

4. Value aesthetic experience. Lastly, the church needs to adequately grasp and value the conditions of aesthetic experience. These two movements fail to adequately address aesthetics in the local church, giving too much attention is given to the conditions that are needed to set the mood to worship God (e.g., use of technology, ambiance, icons, performance) to the detriment of the nature and conditions of aesthetic experience itself. This area of neglect is evident not only in the literature of contemporary church health and growth, but from ecclesiological discourse altogether. There is too much dependency on the pastoral team, technology, or environment. All too easily can these factors, whether intentional or not, impose upon and simulate an aesthetic experience. But the end result is that people have not been adequately fed. If these movements were to understand what it means to "take it all in" and what activity counts as non-aesthetic, then more attention would be given to artistic

---

It is more outgoing, more ready and glad, than the latter attitude, and it is more active than the former. And in calling it voluntary, it is not meant that it depends upon a particular resolve or volition. It is a change *of* will conceived as the organic plenitude of our being, rather than any special change *in* will [John Dewey, *A Common Faith* (New Haven, CT: Yale University Press, 1934), 16-7].

engagement and aesthetic moments would occur without being artificial or forced.

In the final chapter, we will take a look at all of the investigated churches and movements together, drawing from their strengths and addressing issues in aesthetic terms. We will imagine a new church that incorporates the best of aesthetics to touch the lives of those involved and ultimately bridge the gap and impact the ever-changing life of the community for generations to come.

> *"If the community of artists is truly to make a contribution to human welfare, however, they cannot each take a poll of what certain people say they like in art and then deliberately shape their work so as to satisfy them. Some, at least, must be an advance guard striking off in new directions, trusting that if they find something new in which they themselves can take aesthetic delight, others among their fellows will find this delight as well-but never really knowing, taking the risk. If a new land is to be discovered, some there must be who in stubborn integrity and unwarranted confidence sail westward. If human fulfillment is to be served and and shalom established, artists cannot all be obedient followers and timid calculators. Explorers are needed too.*
> - Nicholas Wolterstorff, *Art in Action, 169.*

THE LIVE CHURCH

"The whole world is a theatre for the display of the divine goodness, wisdom, justice, and power, but the Church is the orchestra, as it were-the most conspicuous part of it; and the nearer the approaches are that God makes us, the more intimate and condescending the communication of his benefits, the more attentively are we called to consider them."
~ John Calvin, *Commentary on Psalms*, Volume 5

"Worship is the believer's response of all that they are-mind, emotions, will, body-to what God is and says and does."
~ Warren Wiersbe

Three primary lessons may be gleaned from our examination of aesthetic problems in local churches. The first lesson is churches fail to adequately understand the nature of aesthetic experience. They focus more on end-results and not on process. The second lesson is if we integrate the strengths of these churches examined, then local churches will be in a better position to achieve authentic aesthetic experiences, "to take in" the moment, and experience an immediate delight, a heightened vitality that will point us to the God of the Bible afresh, qualitatively enriching, and worshipful. The third lesson is if churches want to contribute to society, as they once did in generations past, then they should seek to generate art-products and participate in activities that will benefit all involved. We will now consider these three lessons more closely.

AESTHETIC LESSONS LEARNED

1. The nature of aesthetic experience. What we have discovered in our examination of problem churches is that many do not adequately understand the nature of aesthetic experience. Their willful or non-willful ignorance or their misunderstanding of aesthetic experience has generated aesthetic malnourishment. This is ironic because outside of the church walls people have aesthetic experiences as

they go about their daily lives in such areas as cooking, employment, gardening, hobbies, recreation, and sporting events. This neglect has been seen in three different ways.

First, in many of the churches we have examined, for example, the elite, broken, and humdrum, we find that church leadership and its congregation are not typically concerned about what connects one moment of experience with another.[423] They go from one activity to another without any integral momentum. Each activity in the order of the service does not contribute to the whole experience. In other words, there is no significant movement of experience to aesthetic completion. There is no pervading unity that captures the activity.

What they do count as aesthetic experience is typically cognitive. For example, the exposition of Scripture is considered serious worship. While a pastor may have studied the passage and delivered it with artistic engagement, the music, prayers, and singing are delivered in a manner that is routine and mechanical. No interest is shown in doing well (e.g., music), finding satisfaction in the particular activity (e.g., prayers), or caring for the details or materials with genuine affection (e.g., singing).[424] In sum, the means is not fused with the ends, the medium is set apart from meaning, and the part is disconnected from the whole. Therefore, the experience falls short of what it could be.

These same churches do not deeply consider relationships of experience that link past experiences to present experience. In other words, how does the past contribute to the present engagement in experience? Each experience is disconnected from the week before. Unfortunately, these types of experiences are forgettable.[425] For example, the church leadership does not review what event or activity was fruitful and what was not. Little or no substantive "fine tuning" in the religious practices is applied.

No intelligent creativity is employed to recognize, modify, or guide the service. How does one aspect of the service connect, contribute, and integrally relate to another? While the leadership may attempt to provide some "thematic connection" such as ensuring

---
[423] Dewey, *Art as Experience*, 41.
[424] Ibid., 4.
[425] Idem.

the theme or title of certain songs match the central homiletic point of the sermon, aesthetic connectivity and integral momentum are neglected. People walk into the sanctuary. The church goes through the program and they leave. As a result, the worship experience is dead by routine. These churches drift along as the culture continues to change.[426]

Second, we have learned that in sensational and seeker-sensitive churches, imagery, music, performances, inspiring rhetoric, and timed arrangements are all unified to create a memorable experience. Appealing to our interests and desires, these churches are competing with culture or offering something that is counter to culture. But these problem churches focus on our emotions and passion, exalting our sensations to the point that this indulgent experience is equated with having a genuine aesthetic experience. But at the end we discover the spectacle, no matter how emotionally moving or indulgent, leaves us aesthetically malnourished. In other words, we have not been qualitatively changed for the better. Willow Creek Church, for example, discovered this to be the case in its recent statistical research.

Lastly, emerging churches seek to contextualize with their particular context. As a result, many are given to activities that are pluralistic. They are also sensitive to various learning styles and seek to be experiential. But in their focus to contextualize and offer worship that is sensory, experiential, and pluralistic, they still neglect what is before them, namely, the nature and value of aesthetic experience. They are reactionary against traditional and seeker-sensitive models, and their quest for creativity, self-expression, and pluralistic activities falls short of completion when they fail to relate those activities to experience in its integrity. In other words, like the traditional church, if no heightened vitality marks the experience whereby everything is properly related, then it will not reach completion. Every part of the service must contribute to the whole like each brush stroke applied to a canvas contributes to a portrait.

In each of these three cases, namely, churches absorbed by routine activities, indulgent activities, or reactionary activities, they

---

[426] Idem.

fail to absorb what is before them and move it forward. As a result, people are numbed. In his article, "Dewey and Art," Irwin Edman's insights about society can be applied to many of our churches:

> In our ordinary activities distortions and dislocations, made for practical or personal, or sentimental or dialectical reasons, mark experience. Passion drives us to exalt these senses as the chief quality of experience; on the other hand to the intellectual analyst all experience is essentially cognitive. There are in our society occasional orgies of sense without meaning. Among intellectuals there are orgies of abstraction without the vividness of the senses. In ordinary experience or in experience not quite fulfilled there seems to be conflict between the individual and universal, between feeling and thought.[427]

As a result we drift along while ironically enjoying aesthetic experiences in other aspects of life with artistic engagement, earnest zeal, and immediate delight.

When we go about in the hustle and bustle of our daily lives, pause, and look around, often times the ordinary becomes extraordinary. In this world filled with brokenness, loneliness, impoverishment, and replete with serious needs, people are reaching out, hungering for and finding temporary moments of continuity, fulfillment, and completion. For example, the housewife decorates her home using her imagination, resources, and energy. Each color is studied with keen interest, joy, and delight. The cook prepares the dish he loves. The fellow takes pleasure in his vegetable and fruit garden in the hot sun. The sage who smokes his pipe-weed with sheer delight before the roaring fire takes in the moment, absorbing the various parts into the total experience. But in those cases, namely, the cook, gardener, and sage, we see artistic engagement. Skill, finesse, and proper balance between doing and undergoing culminate in an experiential moment of meaningful joy. They are earnestly involved, appropriately engaging, and using lessons acquired from the past to engage the present.

---

[427] John Dewey: *Philosopher of Science & Freedom: A Symposium*, ed. Sidney Hook (New York: Dial Press, 1950), 64.

To be sure, some of those aesthetic experiences are so intense that it is forever imprinted on our mind such as the sight of the Grand Canyon, the children in a third world village tasting clean water for the first time in their lives, or the birth of one's own child. Nevertheless, in so many of local churches, which for many people is the focal point or heartbeat of their community or the lives of their family, worship is so forgettable, lacking rich aesthetic sustenance that could authentically contribute to or feed their lives.

Therefore, while there can be "aliveness" in the events and activities we experience in common life, problem churches typically neglect, displace, or ignore aesthetic experience. Churches can habituate themselves to the extent that non-aesthetic experiences are normative. Long-time attendees do not even expect a life-changing experience. But the irony is the one place where we should be aesthetically fed in community is in our churches. Why? Because many of our churches' core values involve a congregational commitment to exalt God, meet each other's practical needs, establish endearing relationships, and behave like "salt" and "light" in community (Matthew chapters 5-7). But if the religious activities of the worship experience seem anemic, aesthetic hunger may to lead people to activities that contradict the church's values.[428] But if the religious activities of the worship experience seem anemic, aesthetic hunger may lead to activities that contradict the church's values.

But another reason why aesthetic experiences in problem churches fall short is the philosophical and theological study of aesthetic experience is absent from ecclesiastical discourse. To be sure, theological aesthetics is becoming a growing field in recent times, but what is an aesthetic experience and why aesthetic experience is valuable lacks any significant discussion in the study of ecclesiology. Perhaps we are so concerned about bridging or not bridging the culture gap that we ignore the dichotomy in our lives, that is, having aesthetic experiences outside but not inside of church. We fail to consider the immense value aesthetic experience has in bridging the gap and generating meaning in the lives of people if aesthetic experience is appropriately valued in church activities.

---

[428] Dewey, *Art as Experience*, 4.

In summary, what we have discovered in our examination of these problem churches is they fall short of what may be described as the "live church." In other words, unlike the activities of the fox, the cat, or the bird in the wild, these problem churches fail to be "fully present," that is, all there, in all of activities. Instead, imbalance toward indulgence or mechanical routine results, generating non-aesthetic extremes.

SEVEN ASPECTS OF A LIVE CHURCH

But if we synthesize the strengths of all the churches in this examination and artistically and appropriately employ them in the worship experience with appropriate doing and undergoing, ever so careful to avoid imbalance (e.g., excessive/deficient; mechanical/disorganized), then I suggest that the aesthetic activities, practices, and rituals are likely to come "alive" and be very meaningful for those involved on a horizontal level. This "experience of aliveness" may be equated to an evening spent among musicians when they begin to play and soon discover that their instruments, voices, disposition, and surroundings all seem to fit together. The musicians find themselves responding to another. An inter-play develops between them and the energy from their actions and reactions gathers until it climaxes. Afterwards, the musicians say that the jam session was "on fire." Let us explore these strengths more closely.

First, the live church retains its rich history. Unlike the seeker-sensitive or emerging church, it uses the resources of previous experiences as tools to engage its present condition. In other words, the church leadership uses the past lessons, no matter how negative or positive, and applies them appropriately in the present experience in order to cultivate benefits for all involved. Therefore, the live church will never abandon or forsake its own past even if a certain era of history becomes unpopular (e.g., modernism).

Second, unlike the elite, broken, and humdrum church, the live church is very observant about its context and relationship to its surroundings. The church watches what stirs about, and the church, too, is stirred.[429] The church looks and listens, consciously engages

---

[429] Ibid., 18.

and appropriately withdraws when in danger. The live church does not hide, run away from, or separate itself from culture. Realizing it is a part of culture it will seek to appropriately adapt its aesthetics to the changes of society. In essence, the live church recognizes a bilateral relationship between itself and its environment without crossing over the contours of biblical orthodoxy.

Third, unlike the humdrum church, the live church does not placate tension. Rather, tension is welcomed as a catalyst to church development and changed lives. Emerging churches' use of dialogical instruction is very helpful in cultivating and addressing tension. When the live church experiences unforeseen tension, it utilizes the historical tools of the past, creativity, technology, and a wide range of resources and experiments, constantly seeking moments of continuity.

Fourth, the live church does not separate one activity from another or emphasize one against the others. Rather, the architecture, fellowship, liturgy, preaching, music, prayer, and all other activities are related to one another. All aspects are carefully examined to see how they might organically relate to the sum-total of the worship experience. Moreover, unlike the elite and seeker-sensitive church, people are not seen as observers, but as participants in that experience. Therefore, the church is ever so careful not to commit reductionism by neglecting one area of activity in favor of another.[430] How we worship is related to who we worship and this active (not passive), activity has the dramatic possibility to enrich the very spiritual formation of our worship, our disposition, our relationships, and even our situational setting. Adapting one of the major themes of Søren Kierkegaard's philosophy namely, to "live in existence," the live church "worships in existence." In other words, be all there!

Fifth, the art-products such as the architecture, candles, communion table, flowers, digital imagery, icons, pulpit, etc. are not merely studied or thought of as physical objects. Rather they are studied in relationship to their contribution to having a meaningful experience. In other words, the live church does not merely look at an art-product. Art-products are studied in their relationship to their

---

[430] Ibid., 11.

contribution to present experience. Thus, the live church continually examines how art-products function in experience. If it is discovered that certain art-products no longer contribute to the momentum of experience (e.g., decorative shag tapestries on the side of church walls), then an inquiry will be made. Do the art-products expand our lives in beneficial ways?[431] Experimentation with art-products is a core value of the live church. On the vertical plane, the live church acknowledges how the art-products can be utilized to point people to the God of the Bible.

Sixth, because the live church recognizes that the biological aspects of life oscillate between discontinuity and continuity in this sensible realm, it is especially sensitive to the deep struggles people continually face.[432] The mission is not merely to satisfy people's desires, inclinations, and preferences. Rather, a mindset is adopted that can be described as "incarnational." Realizing that every lack is also a demand, a reaching out for continuity, the live church seeks to focus on those deep needs in order to be relevant in any given generation.

Seventh, adjustment is also a core aesthetic value of the live church. Therefore, like the seeker-sensitive church, the live church will continue to examine, review, and critique its aesthetic results. As a result of constant inquiry, the live church will always strive to fine-tune its aesthetic activities, knowing that these adjustments will affect both the church and the community. Therefore, the live church will be in a better position to offer an experience that is personally meaningful to each generation, as well as contribute to the community as well. Like Dewey writes:

> The fact that civilization endures and culture continues—and some times advances—is evidence that human hopes and purposes find a basis and support in nature. As the developing growth of an individual from an embryo to maturity is the product not of efforts of men put forth in a void or just upon them, but of prolonged and cumulative interaction with the environment.[433]

---
[431] Ibid., 26.
[432] Ibid., 16.
[433] Ibid., 28.

Therefore, like a potter shapes his clay with attentive care, insight, and creativity, taking what he has learned in the past and applying into the present situation with a certain anticipation and hope in mind, churches should involve their attendees in the processes of the church whereby they take ownership. In those activities where appropriate energetic doing and undergoing is able to take place and both relate to each other in an integral way unto completion, the experiences for all involved will be marked by "aliveness."[434]

CULTIVATE AN AESTHETIC LEGACY:

The opportunity is before us to create a rich aesthetic legacy that will benefit the community and the church for both the present and the future. A rich legacy generated by the live church will be able to hopefully bridge the culture gap between the community and the church. How? Consider the following five axioms the live church will follow.

First, seek to understand our present moral, philosophical, and social landscape. We have now entered into a post-Christian sensate society that is divided by philosophical dualisms and fact/value splits, dehumanized by reductionistic worldviews, and disfigured by the celebration of the profane. In particular, reductionistic worldviews center their assumptions on one piece of reality while denying or ignoring all other related aspects of reality. The results involve cognitive and existential tension and a loss of our humanity. In his forward to Nancy Pearcey's *Finding Truth*, J. Richard Pearcey explains what we are facing quite well:

> Materialists thereby deny the reality of the mind (while they use their minds to advance materialism, determinists deny the reality of human choice (while they choose determinism), and relativists deny the fact of right and wrong (while they judge you if you disagree). These unfortunate theories do more harm than good. They undercut mind and reasoning, choice and freedom, truth and moral ideals. Inevitably, then, people who place their trust in such solutions begin to order their lives in ways that are

---

[434] Ibid., 55.

less than humane. Likewise, cultures in the grip of inadequate worldviews begin to actualize societies that are less than humane. Ideologues advance their idols under politically correct banners of tolerance, diversity, and fairness, but the actual impact is regress, not progress, fragmentation, not wholeness. People are crushed. The human being necessarily revolts against gods that fail.[435]

Coupled with the wounds of wickedness, the lack of personal integrity among our leaders, and the loss of civility in social discourse, our situation is made worse. But cultivating an aesthetic legacy offers a visual and auditory witness of truth, goodness, and beauty and intimations of authentic hope, transcendence, and wholeness.

Unprecedented in human history we have new mediums from which art products can be created (e.g., the use of clear acrylic resin for sculptors by artist Frederick Hart). New technologies are being invented, giving us access to distinctive people groups whose arts can engage, enrich, and inform our own traditions. Thus, the visual, the sounds, the techniques, and the words expressed can serve as beneficial catalysts for conversations to help people think critically. In our contemporary society, serious analysis, argumentation, and sound justification may not be the best starting point for conversation with certain people. But the arts have proven to open doors that are otherwise closed to us. They can be used to help us in the most dynamic ways to engage the mind, restore the heart, and feed the soul. Thus, understanding our present society will enable to us to best reach people where they are. The arts can help bridge our present and even future landscape-if they are done with excellence, rooted in what is true, good, and beautiful.

Second, learn from history. Consider this historical lesson from John Dewey:

> The Church, even more than the Roman Empire, served as the focus of unity amid the disintegration that followed the fall

---

[435] Nancy Pearcey, *Finding Truth*, 18-19.

of Rome. The historian of intellectual life will emphasize the dogmas of the Church; the historian of political institutions, the development of law and authority by means of the ecclesiastic institution. But the influence that counted in the daily life of the mass of the people and that gave them a sense of unity was constituted, it is safe to surmise, by sacraments, by songs and pictures, by rite and ceremony, all having an esthetic strand, more than by any other one thing. Sculpture, painting, music, letters were found in place where worship was performed. These objects and acts were much more than works of art to the worshippers who gathered in the temple. They were in all probability much less works of art to them than they are today to believers and unbelievers. But because of the esthetic strand, religious teachings were the more readily conveyed and their effect was more lasting. But the art in them, they were changed from doctrines into living experiences.[436]

There was a time Christians encouraged and produced art-products that had very powerful effects on society. History has also shown when art-products are done poorly, aesthetic impoverishment results. If enduring art-pieces are isolated from common life, aesthetic hunger in people and are likely to lead people to embrace art-products that contribute to cultural degeneration. But if local churches will realize the bilateral relationship they have with or to the communities in which they are embedded, the opportunity lies before them to create art-products that will not only contribute to the present society, but also leave an aesthetic legacy for generations to come.

Philosopher Nicholas Wolterstorff (1932-) puts it this way:

> Relatively few have as their dominant purpose to give delight upon aesthetic contemplation. But the rest do not simply escape our attention. With infinite gradation of degrees they lure our awareness, or force themselves upon it. And the aesthetic merits

---
[436] Dewey, *Art as Experience*, 342.

in them produce their effects on us whether or not we submit them to aesthetic contemplation. There is no such thing as a good artifact-a *good* shovel, a *good* wheelbarrow, a *good* house-which is aesthetically poor. Or to put it more cautiously, and more accurately: If an artifact occupies a significant place in our perceptual field, then, it is a better artifact if it is an aesthetically better artifact. Perhaps the ugly concrete-block flats in lower-class housing developments serve rather effectively the housing needs of those who live in them. Yet they are not *good* houses-not as good as they could be. Something is missing, something of the joy that rightfully belongs in human life, something of the satisfaction that aesthetically good housing would produce in those who dwell there. [437]

In the next paragraph, Wolterstorff goes on to say:

> Just as fundamental as our contemplation to promote the cause of art for aesthetic contemplation is our responsibility to promote aesthetic excellence in all of our surroundings, in the knowledge that even merely noticed and not explicitly contemplated, it works on us for joy and peace. [438]

Therefore, do not pursue art for art's sake alone. Connect them with other modes of activity whereby the architectural, educative, practical, moral, social, and spiritual are integrated together, introducing qualitative values into the life of the community. Since all people are equally made in God's image, our capacities to reflect God's glory in the arts we create, the community we carefully care for, the interpersonal relationships we make, the values we embrace, and even the pleasures we pursue, can be great. Integrating these modes together is necessary if the church is to generate an aesthetic legacy worth having.

---

[437] Wolterstorff, *Art in Action*, 170.
[438] Idem.

Third, intentionally invest in opportunities of aesthetics that will bridge the culture gap. Consider church facilities. Though there are significant costs, inconveniences, and risks, when we isolate church facilities from the greater community, citizens will miss out on the experiential aesthetic potentialities that could flow from the interplay between activities, art products, and their personhood within the context of the local church. Consequently, the culture gap widens between the community and the local church. While discernment, prudence, and wisdom is necessary, as in other spaces where other people groups meet, opportunities for aesthetic and spiritual enrichment as a ministry of missions to the community are forfeited when we reserve the facilities for its members (hence, broken church). The problem becomes more acute if the community in everyday living is deprived of enduring art products or if the church is competing against the community.

When the greater community enters into our churches, what do they hear, see, touch, and smell? Do the sacred spaces, art products, and activities create a viable setting where aesthetic qualities can abound? Do they point the community to something or someone greater than themselves? Is functionality valued over and against aesthetics? Are emotional responses valued over skill and technical excellence? Is beauty separated from what is true and good? Are feelings promoted to the neglect of biblical truths? Have hard earned skills, determination, and patience been displaced for expedience? Why do we tolerate mediocrity when it comes to the arts in the church? Is our aesthetic vision limited to the immediate range?

Look around. Does your church prize, cultivate, practice, and reinforce a hard work ethic, skill, technical excellence, and patience when it comes to generating aesthetic activities, products, and spaces? Or does it art products that are cliché or kitsch? Mediocre? Like the sensational church, the "wow" factor may be expressed repeatedly, but if church aesthetics are at best mediocre they will contribute to the anemic conditions many people are experiencing. Subsequently, the culture gap broadens between the community and the church.

In particular, we should not only be concerned about the lack of attention given to acquiring skills in favor of expedience, but also leery when Christians create sentimental art products. What is meant by sentimental art? Following the insight of Anthony Savile, sentimentality is not merely having an emotional response that is "full of feeling" to a particular art piece, song, movement, etc. No, sentimental art is a type of deception that flows from a false picture of the world "under the guidance of a desire for gratification and reassurance."[439] "We want to feel in certain ways, so we selectively and deliberately (though not necessarily consciously) misrepresent the world to ourselves so that we can feel in those ways."[440] In order to leave a rich aesthetic legacy, we must be careful of sentimentality that creates a mindset, an outlook, or sends a message that does not correspond to the way things actually or conflicts with biblical truths.

While it may be argued that financial funds should not be spent on aesthetics and the skilled artists who can create them to meet other church needs, that particular mindset, while well-intentioned, may be short-sided; arts in excellence can speak cross-culturally and cross-generationally as evidenced in Christianity's past with the arts and very churches they created. Art is in us; we are in art. We can be living art. Like Andrew Fletcher once stated, "Let me make the songs of a nation, and I care not who makes its laws."

We certainly need to invest in evangelism, humanitarian agencies, and missionary support. But we also need to invest in talented local artists who can contribute to both the church and the community. In fact, investment in local artists who seek to embody what is true, good, and beautiful not merely in their arts, but as a way of life, can be a strategic way to fulfill our cultural mandate. In his forward to *Western Culture at the American Crossroads*, John Carroll observed:

> ...when art no longer serves the pursuit of truth-as it did for the Old Masters, who saw their mission as the revealing of the important truths-then it will inevitably become subversive. Modern art is one long howl against the beautiful, the true, and the good, with shock tactics replacing virtuosity, and obscenity replacing insight.[441]

---

[439] *Arguing About Art: Contemporary Philosophical Debates*, eds. Alex Neill and Aaron Ridley (New York: McGraw-Hill, 1995), 221.

[440] Idem.

[441] Arthur Pontynen and Rod Miller, *Western Culture at the American Crossroads: Conflicts*

Following Dutch art critic, scholar, and jazz critic Hans Rookmaaker (1922-1777), we should invest in artists whose art harmonizes technical excellence with appropriate form or content whereby the form coheres with meaning, the art-form corresponds to the way things actually are, all within the unity of that true, good, and beautiful, which is reflective of the artists' true beliefs.[442] As a result, we will offer an aesthetic point of contact for aesthetic experiences involving the true, good, and beautiful. If these art products can be experienced in the daily life of the organized community, then the true, good, and beautiful can become an experiential union that speaks to our human condition in the midst of ever-changing cultural shifts and social changes. In fact, aesthetic excellence can awaken us, foster Godward longings, communicate God's timeless truths, promote the union of what is true, good, and beautiful, and bring forth intimations that are reflective of being made in God's image. Perhaps these art products can engender a respite from or even counter the subversive, the cheap, the mediocre, and the vulgar.

Fourth, seek integration. A rich aesthetic legacy must resist all forms of reduction. Instead, the local church proactively pursues, examines, and assesses integration of the material and immaterial, the physical and the spiritual, the one and the many, and the horizontal and the vertical dimensions of aesthetics. Consider the bilateral relationship between sacred space (material) and spiritual formation immaterial (material). Consider this observation made by James K. A. Smith (1970-):

> A cathedral is an intentional complex space for the people of God to engage in worship and discipleship. The way it is organized (in the shape of a cross) not only says something; it also does something to those who frequent its spaces. [443]

Over the Nature of Science and Reason (Wilmington, DE: ISI Books, 2011), xiv.
[442] "Norms for Art and Entertainment" in *The Complete Works of Hans Rookmaaker*, ed. Marleen Hengelaar-Rookmaaker (Pinquant Publishing, 2002): 3:76-9.

[443] James K. A. Smith, *Desiring the Kingdom: Worship, Worldview, and Cultural Formation* (Grand Rapids, Baker, 2009), 213.

Church architecture, the altar, bodily movements, instruments, hymns and spiritual songs, liturgy, physical nature and ecological landscape, Scripture, teaching, and use of artificial and natural lighting are fitted together with the material and immaterial aspects of our unique individuality as the unified local body of Christ. From out of our deep-seated affections (heart), our conscious thought life (soul), our ability to think, discern, and reflect (mind), and our emotional and physical bodily powers (strength), we, the many, come together as a unified body of Christ, the one. Thus, within the sacred space we have diversity and unity, the physical and the spiritual, as we worship the God of the Bible (Psalm 95: 6-7):

> [6]Oh come, let us worship and bow down;
> let us kneel before the Lord, our Maker!
> [7]For he is our God,
> and we are the people of his pasture,
> and the sheep of his hand (ESV)

We praise. We give thanksgiving. We confess. We intercede. We offer supplications. We serve one another using our giftedness, recourses, spiritual gifts, and time, anticipating, meeting, and exceeding each other's needs with what God has given us (1 John 3:16-17).

Flowing from this anti-reductionistic nexus, we are to displace every activity that is mechanical and mindless, chaotic and random, in favor of that which is balanced, creative, holistic, and organized. Aesthetic qualities emerge in the means and the ends that will not only create a viable setting of unabated worship that enriches and molds the whole person unto the glory of God, but will also offer an unmistakable beauty, a witness, an invitation, a relief, a release, a restoration. Aesthetic integration will offer something that is unique, powerful, and necessary for our humanity, namely, hope.

Consider our intellectual and existential landscape. Business, consumerism, fragmentation, incompleteness, isolation, and our place in the rhythm of machines and technology are so pervasive in everyday living that we are losing ourselves. We don't know who we are, what we are, and where we are going. Our individuality is reduced to a number, from an "I" to an "it." Against this age of cultural captivity of trivial diversions and non-sensical amusement, intoxicating pleasures have become addictive means to help us recover from our dehumanization, ease our angst over the fragility of life, soothe our disillusionment, and placate the pain from long-held dreams that will never be realized. These "fun-filled" distractions, which are also used to exploit us for economic gain, keep us from thinking about the larger questions of life:

> What is real?
> What is true?
> What is good?
> What is beautiful?
> What is wrong with this world?
> How can we fix what is wrong in this world?
> Who am I?
> Why am I here?
> How can I truly be happy?

To be sure, aesthetic experiences offer punctuated moments of fulfillment, meaning, and significance, a respite from the drudgery, the monotony, and the grind, and an excitement that stirs the whole person. They can generate remarkable creativity, nourish us, and aid us as we deal with significant personal and social problems. Ultimately, they are gifts from God, a grace given to humanity in in view of those oscillating moments of adversity and monotony. While they foster a textured richness of creativity, industry, possibilities, and cultural embodiment and unity, these aesthetic experiences do not possess staying power. The experience comes to an end. New problems arise. New solutions have to be imagined. But all physical things come to an end. Eventually, failure is inevitable for brokenness, loss, and suffering are also aspects of physical reality. Everything that flourishes will one day die. In fact, physical death is inevitable. Blaise Pascal puts it this way:

> Let us imagine a number of men in chains and all condemned to death, where some are killed each day in the sight of the others, and those who remain see their own fate in that of their fellows and wait their turn, looking at each other sorrowfully and without hope. It is an image of the condition of man.

Our human condition also reflects a deep existential human need for hope. Albert Camus (1913-1960) expresses our human need this way when he states, "Where there is no hope, it is incumbent on us to invent it." But we do not have to invent hope. If the local church is willing to create an aesthetic legacy that bridges the culture gap, then we are able to offer sacred space to the community whereby we are able to go beyond the horizontal dimensions of aesthetics (e.g., music) to the vertical dimensions of aesthetics (e.g., unabated worship). Within that intersection of the horizontal and vertical dimensions of worship beauty transcends from the one and only Triune God himself, the sum-total of His infinite perfections, who is the absolute, the true, the good, and the beautiful. Flowing from His divine disclosure by means of special and natural revelation, authentic and reasonable hope within is generated (Psalm 19:1-11). Our humanity will one day be fully restored and all will be made right for an infinite-personal God exists, and He is good and sovereign. Whenever God seems mysterious, study the person and work of Jesus Christ as recorded in the Gospels of the New Testament.

We can sort out the distinctive but related differences between the horizontal and vertical dimensions of worship by appealing to an event C. S. Lewis recorded in "Meditation of a Toolshed."

> I was standing today in the dark toolshed. The sun was shining outside and through the crack at the top of the door there came a sunbeam. From where I stood that beam of light, with the specks of dust floating in it, was the most striking thing in the place. Everything else was almost pitch-black. I was seeing the beam, not seeing things by it. Then I moved, so that the beam fell on my eyes. Instantly the whole previous picture vanished. I saw no toolshed, and (above all) no beam. Instead I saw, framed

in the irregular cranny at the top of the door, green leaves moving on the branches of a tree outside and beyond that, 90 odd million miles away, the sun. Looking along the beam, and looking at the beam are very different experiences. [444]

Likewise, the integration of the material and immaterial, the physical and the spiritual, the one and the many, are expressions of the vertical and horizontal in dimensions of worship. They go from looking at the movements, sights, sounds, smells to the vertical, transcendental dimensions of worship.

Lastly, worship in existence. There is a dynamic interplay of spiritual formation that takes place before, during, and following salvation. In essence, exposure to the Trinity changes us; the person of Jesus Christ changes us by uniting Himself to us (Romans 6:4-5); God's undeserved grace covers us; the Holy Spirit completes us. Because of what the Trinity did on our behalf, we now have the capacities to worship in existence, which means to actively, consciously, and qualitatively worship God in moment-by-moment living. Instead of a lifestyle of worship that is characterized by inactivity, mindless routine, and passivity, consciously strive to reflect his glory from a disposition that actively promotes intellectual and moral excellence (virtue). The true, the good, and beautiful are to be unified together in thought and life. In essence, to worship in existence is to worship in God in all life, introducing people to a real transcendent hope by our integrity, our words, and our presence. Consequently, we are able to offer a rich aesthetic way of living that meets people where they are, creating a bridge of credibility via excellent listening skills, personal integrity in alignment with the precepts and principles of Scripture, and anticipating, meeting, and exceeding people's practical needs.

Therefore, in order to leave a rich legacy, live out the following: Understand the assumptions and practices of our contemporary society. Listen. Ask good questions. Listen more. Speak less. Actively learn from history. But don't merely understand how the local church impacted the community that best reflected the words and works

---

[444] C. S. Lewis, *God in the Dock* (Grand Rapids: Eerdmans, 1970), 212.

of Jesus Christ; follow hard after Jesus Christ in thought, outlook, and relationships. Intentionally invest in aesthetic excellence and the artists who care for technical excellence and earnestly share in the belief and practice of what is true, good, and beautiful. Don't merely invest in them as a ministry of missions for the benefit of the community and the church, but also integrate the material and immaterial, the physical and the spiritual, the one and the many, and the horizontal and vertical dimensions of aesthetics on every level. Consequently, the live church will offer transcendent hope via aesthetics to the community. Lastly, worship in existence by the active manner in which you live in your local community as a living representative of God's image. His reflective glory in and through your life can be great as you abide in Christ, serving Him and those He loves (Philippians 2:12-13).

> "Ultimately, of course, the colorizers will lose this battle. If not immediately then future generations will surely discard these cheesy, artificial symbols of one society's greed. They will, of course, go back to the great originals. And if we are foolish enough to permit this monstrous practice to continue one can easily picture young men and women someday discussing us with disgust saying, 'They did this and nobody stopped them?'
>
> 'Well, there was a lot of money involved.'
>
> 'But surely the people could see the deeper value to America of its film treasury, of its image among civilizations. Surely they understood the immorality of defacing an artist's work against his will. Don't tell me it was the kind of nation that adored profit at any cost and humiliation.'
>
> Here I will finish because it's too early to know how it turns out, but I hope dearly that I will not be part of a culture that is one day ridiculed and reviled.'"
>
> ~ Woody Allen, "True Colors," *New York Review of Books*, August 31, 1987.[445]

---

[445] *Arguing About Art*, 35.

APPENDIX ONE:

THE AESTHETIC VALUE OF NATURE IN EVERYDAY LIVING

"Man does not like to remain alone; and as he loves, he must look elsewhere for an object for his love. He can find it only in beauty. Since, however, he is himself the most beautiful creature that God has created, he must find within himself a model for the beauty he seeks beyond himself."
~ Blaise Pascal

LOST IN OBSCURITY

As I interact with students in private, public, religious, secular and spheres of academia I come across young people who are experiencing a peculiar problem. Their lives seem incoherent, out of place, and ultimately unintelligible. Even those who are completely dedicated to their faith have experienced this same sort of problem. As one student confessed to me a few years, "I feel like I am living in a dream. Doc, this isn't fun. I need help. Can you help me?" As I probe their lives, trying to discover the root cause (s) or web-like issues in which they are entangled, I have discovered a common theme, namely, a disconnection with reality as it is. In other words, they are "lost in obscurity."

Unlike any previous generation, the situational setting in which these young people have been raised lacked rich exposure to nature. I am broadly defining "nature" as the physical world, natural phenomena, living things, and the processes that control them independent of our human will (e.g., ecological forces). Their place of habitation is the virtual world, the digital sphere. Victim to the pleasures and plight of the digital age, they live inside their dwelling places with the command center of technology at their fingertips. Fun, knowledge, conversations, and relationships take place with a screen in front of them in the comfort of their home, their school, and their vehicles. They do not have memories of playing games in the woods, long hours turning over limbs and rocks to see what lies underneath, swimming in a nearby pond or lake, or building tree houses or forts with their childhood friends. They have not experienced the blessing of spending hours lying on the grass, watching the birds and clouds above as they use their imagination and dream big. Gazing upon the myriads of stars above is a rarity. Because of poor exposure to working hard outside, they lack contact with dirt; their hands are smooth; their fingernails are ever clean. From their perspective, nature is not in their midst. Instead, nature is found at a zoo, a farm outside of the community, a state park, a national forest. Coupled with business, parental demands for success, and indoor activities, young people lack qualitative experiences with the "outside world."

I was first exposed to this growing problem when I attended a L'Abri conference many years ago at Asbury Seminary in Kentucky. A staff worker reported that unlike Francis A. Schaeffer's years of ministry in Switzerland, they are discovering that before they can minister to those who seem to be confused and out of touch with reality as it is they have to put them to work outside. While they are cultivating the ground with their hands for the very first time, nature is cultivating them, "sanding down" virtual barriers that have been placed all around in this "sensate age." As a result of qualitative exposure to physical nature, these prisoners in "Plato's cave" begin to break from their virtual chains and come to discover an intelligible world beyond shadowy images and imaginary beliefs.

What is needed? As argued by Dewey's *Art as Experience*, and in this work, *Worship as Experience*, we need to recover the continuity of aesthetics with the normal processes of living life. This recovery is perhaps more important than ever before because of the powerful impact the digital age is having on new generations. We have to realize that the metaphysical obscurity and existential tension these younger generations are experiencing can involve a lack of qualitative exposure or physical contact with nature. Failure to understand the real world, given the virtual, digital context in which they move, live, and have their becoming, they confuse these two categories. Flowing from such confusion of categories, namely, their digital habitation vs. reality as it is, the presuppositions they believe or even create about reality (and all that follows by means of application, namely, epistemology, morality, and aesthetics) do not correspond with reality. It is as if they are ignorantly or even willfully choosing to live in Plato's Cave. Yet while the chains are off, apps at the fingertips are designed to addict. Moreover, the comfort of one's dwelling space is difficult to leave given their access to information, products purchased, delivered, and consumed, the projection of self on social media, and social connections made and maintained via technology.

Thus, when exposed to nature as it is, cognitive dissonance finds expression. Their interaction with nature is inconsistent with their understanding of the world and all its structure, their belief structure, their habituated way of seeing and doing, and perhaps even their own virtual identity. Thus, it is very problematic and painful when their thought and practice, reflective of their digital habitation, does not harmonize with the external world and its form. Reminiscent of Francis A. Schaeffer's critique of twentieth century man:

> "No matter what a man may believe, he cannot deny reality as it is….Man cannot make his own universe and then live in it."

Following the trajectory of religious and philosophical thought from St. Augustine, Thomas Aquinas, Blaise Pascal, C. S. Lewis, Francis A. Schaeffer and J. Budziszewski, I contend God uses the witness of creation and human design to compliment our Godward longings to reach people where they are and take them where they need to be. For example, the design and beauty of God's creation or even certain raw forces of nature such as the impact of a hurricane can dredge up certain divine truths we want to suppress or ignore. I suspect this problem will only become more acute as our comforts and our technologies continue to advance and our face-to-face interactions with each other in this physical world decrease.

Presupposing the infinite-personal God who is the Creator of nature (a clear Creator-creature distinction), people are able to not only look at nature as "art" but are also able to follow the design, the movements, and functions of nature to God himself (a posteriori; going from "design" to the Author of the design). Thus, when we isolate nature from the daily life of a community by relegating it to a state park, putting it on a pedestal, or allowing nature to achieve some status apart from everyday life, we build walls that divide and deprive us of aesthetic experiences that point us to God. I think of nature as God's art just as we are His handiwork (Psalm 139). Moreover, these virtual barriers generate existential disconnections, distortions, emptiness, and even exhaustion because they become less normative in daily experience. I fear that since we hunger for beauty, we will find ourselves feasting on what is anemic. Therefore, understanding aesthetic experience to be a facet of common grace with both a vertical and horizontal dimension, nature provides a context for rich aesthetic experiences to occur in everyday life, especially in a world filled with loss, pain, tragedy (Genesis 3) and the machinations of our modernity whereby we easily become ensnared as appendages to cubicles, monitors, and assembly lines.

Borrowing from John Dewey's commonsensical insight, I am defining an aesthetic experience as a heightened process of continuity that is intense, memorable, involving active participation, perception and appreciation. Because non-aesthetic activities are so common, when we encounter an aesthetic event or moment, all too often we categorize the aesthetic experience outside of our normative activities. Moreover, we promote the fallacy of reductionism when we value experiences in nature divorced from the facts about nature.

When we isolate nature from everyday life, three sets of aesthetic problems emerge: (1) the problem of origin and use, (2) the problem of enrichment and poverty, and (3) the problem of division and emptiness. Therefore, adapting these Deweyan insights, the greater the isolation of nature from human experience the larger the need to fill it. As a result, not only do we miss out on opportunities to have aesthetic experiences in daily living that both enrich our lives in and ultimately point us to God in daily living, but we also develop an appetite for the cheap and vulgar (artificial & counterfeit). So, I will examine these three sets of problems and offer conclusion with some brief recommendations. But before we examine our first problem, namely, the problem of origin and use, let me offer three clarifications about the nature of dynamic interplay, the value of preserving nature, and the correspondence between nature and ordinary living.

There is as dynamic interplay that exists between our environment and us. Since we are in nature and nature is in us, or better yet, we are part of nature since we are an aspect of God's creation, a dynamic interplay exists for we feed on the environment and our environment feeds on us. Consider these two examples: We affect our environment and our environment affects us in the context of filthy living. If we surround ourselves with trash, we become trashy. Or as discussed in chapter 2 of *Worship as Experience*, our connection to our environment may be likened to the relationship between an unborn baby and mother. The baby's health affects the mother and the mother's health affects the baby. Thus, a symbiotic relationship exists between our environment and us. Though we are not determined by our surroundings, there is no doubt that we influence our environment just as our environment influences us.

Because of this dynamic interplay, the problem is not with parks, nature reserves, and master plan communities where natural landscaping finds pertinent expression. I recognize both the need and value of preserving nature and its various ecological systems. In fact, I am very appreciative of private charities, private landowners, government institutions, and research centers that protect these places. But when we think of nature outside of the community, elevate nature on pedestal, or support opportunities whereby "nature" achieves some status apart from everyday life, we construct barriers that limit aesthetic experiences with nature that can take place in the ordinary daily life of the organized community.

I contend that the witness of God's handiwork of creation is powerful (Psalm 19:1-6; Romans 1). Nature opens eyes, stir affections, slow down business, foster possibilities of personal inquiry and introspection, and are sources of meaning. Nature possesses aesthetic qualities in abundance. In order to visit nature, see wildlife, and experience the phenomena of the natural physical world, if we are led to believe that we have to travel outside the community to experience these aesthetic riches, especially in urban settings, we miss out 4 on the beauty and wonder God has created which give evidence of His existence, His creativity, and His genius in our daily lives. May we encourage our communities in a balanced away to support opportunities for physical nature to thrive within the commonplaces of life, where God's art may be dynamically experienced and collectively shared in ordinary living. Thus, in people's daily lives, in the comings and goings of work, home, study, and play, people are able to see, hear, touch, taste, and smell nature; the witness of God's creation is at work within and with each other.

Now having briefly addressed these three preliminary issues, our inquiry will now turn to the isolation of nature from everyday life by probing the problems of origin and use, enrichment and poverty, and division and need as applied to nature. All three sets of problems are interrelated. So we will examine these concerns like we might assess a multifaceted diamond. Afterwards, I will make some brief suggestions how we might bring about greater continuity between people in the life of the organized community and nature as God's art.

THE PROBLEM OF ORIGIN AND USE

The isolation of nature from ordinary living is tragic because nature possesses a quality of activity. Nature pulsates with and magnifies life, creativity, movement, color, intricate form, intelligence, purpose, relationships, communication, habituations, reproduction, power, tragedy, stability, instability, and even death itself. For example, when we watch a butterfly break out of it cocoon our attention is arrested. Aesthetic qualities abound in view of the colors, movements, and instinctual desires we observe. Thus, when we fail to recognize the fact that all of nature, including us, was created by our Creator and that humanity was placed within the context of physical nature and all of these aesthetic activities and images, we marginalize the aesthetic experiences we can have between nature and day-to-day living. God created Adam and Eve in the context of physical nature. Since God did not choose a different context to plant the creation of humanity, we commit the fallacy of selective emphasis when nature is isolated from daily living. While God created nature from where we ultimately draw our nourishment, clothing, shelter, and medicine, it is reasonable to infer that physical nature is also a magnificent source for aesthetic experiences that not only enrich our lives, but also move us to contemplate the ultimate Artist of it all.

For example, the beauty we see around us and the aesthetic experiences we have can lead us to seriously ponder God's existence. Consider the following arguments and evidences:[446]

Example 1:

1. Beauty implies a mind of beauty.
2. There is objective beauty.
3. Therefore, there is an objective Mind of Beauty.

---

[446] These arguments are translated from moral law arguments by C. S. Lewis, G. E. Moore, Hastings Randall, W. R. Sorley, Elton Trueblood, and Linda Zagzebeski [Norman Geisler, *Baker's Enyclopedia of Christian Apologetics* (Grand Rapids: Baker, 1999), 498-500].

In his article, "Argument from Design," Christian philosopher Richard Swinburne offers this analytical insight about aesthetics:

We saw that God has reason, apparently overriding reason, for making, not merely any orderly world (which we have been considering so far) but a beautiful world-at any rate to the extent to which it lies outside the control of creatures. (And he has reason too, I would suggest, even in whatever respects the world does lie within the control of creatures, to give them experience of beauty to develop, and perhaps also some ugliness to annihilate.) So God has reason to make a basically beautiful world, although also reason to leave some of the beauty or ugliness of the world within the power of creatures to determine; but he would seem to have overriding reason not to make a basically ugly world beyond the powers of creatures to improve. Hence, if there is a God there is more reason to expect a basically beautiful world than a basically ugly one-.... A priori, however, there is no particular reason for expecting a basically beautiful rather than a basically ugly world. In consequence, if the world is beautiful, that fact would be evidence for God's existence. For, in this case, if we let k be 'there is an orderly physical universe', e be 'there is a beautiful universe', and h be 'there is a God', P(e/ h.k) will be greater than P(e/ k); and so by our previous principles the argument from e to h will be another good C-inductive argument [A C inductive argument is one in which the premises contribute to the probability of the conclusion]. Few, however, would deny that our universe (apart from its animal and human inhabitants, and aspects subject to their immediate control) has that beauty. Poets and painters and ordinary men down the centuries have long admired the beauty of the orderly procession of the heavenly bodies, the scattering of the galaxies through the heavens (in some ways random, in some ways orderly), and the rocks, sea, and wind interacting on earth, 'The spacious firmament on high, and all the blue ethereal sky', the water lapping against 'the old eternal rocks', and the plants of the jungle and of temperate climates, contrasting with the desert and the Arctic wastes. Who in his senses would deny that here is beauty in abundance? If we confine ourselves to the argument from the beauty of the inanimate and plant worlds, the argument surely works [Richard Swinburne, "Argument from Design." www.orthodoxytoday.org. Accessed 10/15/2017. http://www.orthodoxytoday.org/articles2/SwinburnDesign.php].

Example 2:

1. It appears to human beings that normative (transcultural) aesthetic experiences occur.
2. The best explanation for aesthetic normative experiences (transcultural) is that it is grounded in God.
3. Therefore, God exists.

Example 3:

1. Universal signatures of beauty exists (e.g., symmetry, proportion, unity, complexity, intensity, and rhythm).
2. Universal signatures have the properties of being objective.
3. The best explanation for the existence of universal signatures of beauty is provided by theism.
4. Therefore, the existence of universal signatures of beauty provides good grounds for thinking theism is true.

Example 4:

1 Beauty is a rational enterprise.
2. Beauty would not be a rational enterprise if there were no aesthetic "order" in the world (e.g., unity, intensity, and complexity).
3. Only the existence of God traditionally conceived could support the hypothesis that there is an aesthetic order in the world.
4. Therefore, God exists.

Example 5:

1. Certain aesthetic norms of beauty have authority (e.g., imitation, representation, depiction, proportion, unity, complexity, intensity)
2. If they have authority, there must be a reliable motive for human beings to strive to follow these norms of beauty
3. No such motive could exist, unless there is a God to attach sanctions to behavior under aesthetic norms of beauty.
4. There is a God.

Example 6:

1. There must be objective beauty, otherwise:
    (a) There would not be such great agreement on its meaning.
    (b) No real disagreements of beauty would ever have occurred, each person being right from his own perspective.

(c) No value judgment of beauty would ever have been wrong, each being subjectively right.

(d) No question of beauty could ever be discussed, there being no objective understanding of beauty

(e) Contradictory views would both be right, since opposites could be equally correct.

2. Objective beauty is beyond individual persons and beyond humanity as a whole:

(a) It is beyond individual persons, since they often sense a conflict with beauty/ugliness;

(b) It is beyond humanity as a whole, for they measure the progress of civilization by its art-products in terms of beauty.

3. Objective beauty must come from an objective Mind of beauty because:

(a) Beauty has no meaning unless it comes from a mind; only minds emit meaning.

(b) Beauty is meaningless unless it is a meeting of mind with mind, yet people inherently desire to experience beauty

(c) Hence, discovery of and desire for beauty make sense only if there is a Mind or Person behind it.

4. Therefore, God exists.

Example 7:

1. Beauty is an un-analyzable property intuited by the human mind
2. The best explanation for this objective un-analyzable property intuited by the human mind is that it is grounded in God.
3. Therefore, God exists.

Example 8:

1. An absolutely perfect ideal of beauty exists (at least psychologically in our minds).
2. An absolutely perfect idea of beauty can exist only if there is an absolutely perfect Mind of beauty

(a) Ideas can exist only if there are minds (thoughts depend on thinkers)

(b) Absolute ideas depend on an absolute Mind (not an individual finite mind like ours)

3. Hence, it is rationally necessary to postulate an absolute Mind as the basis for the absolutely perfect idea of beauty.

Example 9:

1. Aesthetic value judgments are a rational enterprise.
2. Value judgments would not be rational if skepticism were true.
3. There is too much unresolved disagreement for us to suppose that skepticism can be avoided if human sources of aesthetic value judgments are all that we have.
4. Therefore, we must assume that there is an extra-human, divine source for aesthetic value judgments.

Example 10:

1. There is the music of Pink Floyd
2. Therefore, God must exist.

Adapting C. S. Lewis' moral law argument from *Mere Christianity*[447] we could translate the standard of validity in aesthetics this way: "How had I got this idea of beauty and ugliness? One does not call a line crooked unless one has some straight line. What was I comparing this art product with when I called it ugly?"

Evidences for objective beauty that point us to a God of beauty would include:[448] (1) We know what is beauty and what is ugly by the manner we react to what we observe; (2) We wouldn't know what is ugly if there was no absolute sense of what is beautiful. We only know something is ugly by comparing it to an unchanging standard of what is beautiful. (3) Real disagreements over what is beautiful would not be possible without some reference to objective beauty. In fact, every disagreement of beauty would merely be a matter of opinion. (4) While not disagreeing with subjective appetites for certain things, claiming they are beautiful, beauty cannot be strictly subjective. An independent standard must exist. Otherwise, no one can criticize an aesthetic claim of beauty; there would really be no substance to one's argument. (5) We would not make excuses for producing an ugly art product if we didn't have some conception of what is objectively beautiful. In fact, it is naturally difficult to desire to produce something ugly whether it is a flower garden, a painting, or a musical medley. (6) One can't extensively listen to poor music as compared to music of excellence. I could stare

---

[447] C. S. Lewis, *Mere Christianity* (New York: Macmillan, 1952), 45.
[448] Norman L. Geisler & Frank Turek, *I Don't Have Enough Faith to be an Atheist* (Wheaton: Crossway Publishers, 2004), 169-193.

at Michelangelo's David for a significant amount of time compared to a toddler's drawing of a bug-even though some creations take on a particular significance to us because of their subjective, personal meaning to our lives. But we recognize the difference between those types of works. (7) We would not substantively know if an artist's work is getting worse or better if there was no objective standard of beauty. It could be that this standard for what is beautiful and ugly is so transculturally evident that no defense for objective beauty is really needed. Like belief in God is "properly basic" the masses intuitively believe in a clear distinction between what is absolutely beautiful and what is absolutely ugly; this intuition transcends cultural and generational boundaries. This position is not only substantiated by timeless art products that are venerated across time and space, but also of the "aesthetic universals" evidenced by Denis Dutton (e.g., expertise or virtuosity; non-utilitarian pleasure; style; criticism; imitation; special focus; imaginative experience).[449]

Combined with other philosophy of religion arguments (e.g., cosmological; kalam cosmological; teleological; ontological; objective moral law; conscience; religious need; consciousness; innate), evidences (e.g., anthropic principle; specified complexity; irreducible complexity; information); religious experiences, and existential longings for God's existence (e.g., significance, meaning, purpose, love, joy, and identity), we have good reasons to believe God exists and He is the Creator of space-time reality. It is less likely that the universe and biological life forms, systems, and processes we observe from the telescope to the microscope, with all of the designs, order, complexity, fine-tuning, systems, DNA information/instruction, and beauty we empirically detect, not only came about by the undirected processes of time, energy, irrationality, and chaos, but ultimately from nothing, non-personality (mind), non-being, non-life, and non-beautiful. .[450]

If physical nature is expressed in ordinary living, then the quality of activity (both positively and negatively), the images, and the scenes of beauty and ugliness become a storehouse of memories, places of inspiration, and catalysts to stir our imagination, our intellect, our

---

[449] "Aesthetic Universals" in *Routledge Companion to Aesthetics*, edited by Berys Gaut and Dominic McIver Lopes (New York: Routledge, 2001), 203-214.

[450] Robert A. Morey, *The New Atheism and the Erosion of Freedom* (Minneapolis: Bethany House Publishers, 1986), 98.

creativity, our human condition, and longings to know God. Nature is a continual embodiment of meaning. Because of the transactional activities we enjoy with nature and recoil from, new meaningful experiences and relationships are made. Nature continually inspires new realizations individually and collectively on both a horizontal and vertical level. Nature, in both its beauty and horror, arouses us to make new inquiries, discover new connections, and create things that will benefit other.

Nature also dredges up the existential struggles of our soul with all of its beauty, its fragility, and its brutality. The precarious aspects of nature, for example, cause us to question our significance, our meaning, our purpose. Thus, nature with all of its constructions, patterns, and movements mark an experiential way of human envisioning, visualizing, imagining, contemplating, and soul-searching. The decay and death we observe in nature also moves us in powerful ways to consider our finitude and our frailties. Like Blaise Pascal claimed, "The eternal silence of these infinite spaces terrifies me." Nature reminds us that at any moment that what he hold dear may be snatched from us.

But the changes we witness outside of us and within us create deep and earnest longings for permanence. Since Adam's rebellion in Genesis 3, the beautiful and the horrific go hand-in-hand. Experiences such as witnessing the birth of a baby produce unspeakable joy while the death of a loved one generates unspeakable sorrow. The taint of brokenness is everywhere. The suffering and wickedness that abounds in nature not only stirs the angst within, but it also generates, at least for some, a deep longing or yearning for something more, namely, a place and state where permanent joy and peace may be found and where redemption from ruin will be realized.

This bi-relationship between nature and us is "pregnant" with new and open possibilities, developments, processes, relationships, questions, and introspection. Potentialities unfold and we change as we encounter, engage, and absorb these images, movements, and scenes within a spatio-temporal context. Stated differently, the dynamic transactional interplays between ourselves and the stable and precarious, unstable aspects of nature not only feed the human genius, but also bring to surface the ultimate questions of life such as, "Who are we?" "What are we?" "Where did we come from?" Unlike art-products that evoke these existential questions and ultimate issues, nature is invasive and is ultimately beyond our control (e.g., hurricanes). We can walk away from certain art pieces, music, and images that dredge up the larger questions of our human condition and the answers we willfully suppress, but we cannot with nature.

The power of dredging up of these issues and the natural facilitators that point us to God is not merely the material, efficient, formal, and final causes we observe in nature, but are also found when our experiences with nature become emotionally charged, both negatively and positively. Moments like these can come about suddenly when are introduced to spring plants in bloom or a coral reef abounding with marine life.

These moments can be overwhelming, fix our gaze, and delight us in the most marvelous ways. These experiences can be intense, are memorialized, and are set apart from the mundane moments in daily living. Experiences such of these do not have to be only found outside of the community in parks and nature reserves, but can also be found in greater abundance in daily living when we look out our window, step into our garden, or walk through our neighborhood. But these experiences can also be emotionally charged negatively when we observe a tragic misstep when young life is crushed or when forces of nature destroy what we cherish as individuals and members of a particular community.

As stated earlier, we also have to recognize that nature itself is invasive. While virtual shells within our indoor living distort our contact with the world and generate obscurity within, natural calamities have been used to wake many of us up from our virtual stupor. But in the most startling way, destruction, pain, and tragedy often bring us together, putting us into contact with the actual world in ways we have previously ignored. While some of us may not be able to respond to the deprivation and loss that the forces of nature can bring about, others of us do and are the better for it. Altruism and benevolence find expression and relationships with long-time neighbors are made. Adversity can move us in the most dramatic and beneficial ways whereas false pleasures, for example, immobilize us from making our lives count for something great personally and collectively.

THE PROBLEM OF ENRICHMENT AND POVERTY

When we marginalize nature from the daily life of an organized community, enriching opportunities of its apologetic witness, aesthetic experiences, and delightful perceptions are diminished both personally and collectively. In fact, the problem of isolation of nature from daily living, affects the moral, the creative, and human qualities and conditions of civilization itself. This will involve examining aesthetic experiences and the aesthetic functionality of nature. Isolation of nature from common life deprives people of potential aesthetic experiences in at least two compounding ways. First, isolation diminishes opportunities to have aesthetic experiences in ways that stir our mind, inflame affections, spark our imagination, and dredge up our existential longings. And second, isolation impoverishes the community as a whole because members of the community are not able to share and celebrate these experiences with one another in daily activities. Not only are we impoverished because we are not only impacted by the abounding presence, activities, and movements of physical nature, but also because of nature's practical ability to serve and inspire creativity, experimentation, and intelligence. Since we are affected by our surroundings, physical nature provides a context that does not inspire us to feast on the "cheap and the vulgar." Rather, physical nature motivates us to enjoy, produce, and replicate in art forms what empirically observe. But when there is a general loss of civic consciousness of physical nature in all of its aesthetic signs, we miss out on the creative impact nature has upon us to qualitatively enrich our lives and point us to God. I am fearful that where this occurs, the greater the possibility for people to turn to theories of art, language, and arbitrary authorities that are divorced from sound metaphysics and epistemology. Even our own kids, who go from screen to screen and game to game, inundated with interactions all day long within walls, vehicles, and buildings, are extremely deprived of possibilities, enrichment, and interactions with the power of nature as God's art. Interestingly, when we encounter a small piece of nature in the midst of business, mundane living, and closed settings, our hearts melt, our attention to it can easily become exaggerated, and longings for more are stirred. The excitement can be infectious.

In contrast, when physical nature connects with common life a sense of unity, a bond is constituted in the daily lives of the community where sources of meaning are embodied, significance is attached, and creativity finds new expressions in people as the drama of the physical unfolds, moves, changes, dies, and reappears. Wildlife finds a haven. Lives are enriched. Because of the wide array of colors and designs, the stable and precarious aspects of nature, and the beauty and brutal force of nature with all of its abilities are able to penetrate the deepest aspects of individuality as well as collectively over time and space and in spite of change. Stated differently, physical nature is able to impact the young and the old, the uneducated and educated, the tribal and the most sophisticated. Unlike certain art-products, aesthetic qualities of nature such as color, design, and purpose do not rob the best parts from us or lead us to moral degeneracy. Rather, a single flower, the sound of a bird, the grace of a swan can bring about a moment of serenity to a troubled soul, woo a romantic heart, or usher in delight to a rather uneventful day. Even an encounter with decay and death in nature can bring about the best in us, leading us to make beneficial contribution and investments in the lives of others. Tragedies that result from forces of nature can cause us even the worst of us to respond in the most heroic ways.

Therefore, we should promote nature as art because God's creation is able to enrich the community in the most dynamic and benevolent ways. But the value of recognizing the aesthetic interplays between physical nature and our humanity becomes even more pressing and difficult because of the next and last interrelated problem associated with the isolation of nature from common life, namely, the problem of division and emptiness.

THE PROBLEM OF DIVISION AND EMPTINESS

These two problems are grouped together because separating physical nature from everyday life engenders "class division," "elitism," and "aesthetic hunger" among the life of the organized community. By "division" I am referring to class distinctions that are promoted when physical nature is detached from common living. Nature loses its significance among us in everyday living because we perceive and describe nature, especially in urban settings, as only being found in places like state parks, nature reserves, and land owned by wealthy people. Some of us might even say consider opportunities to be with nature a luxury for the wealthy because time, opportunity, and the possession of certain resources (e.g., own a RV). But here's the concern: the seclusion of nature from common life leaves an existential vacuum whereby we are likely to seek satisfaction from art-products that are qualitatively anemic and detrimental to community and ourselves. Stated differently, the isolation of nature promotes aesthetic anemia, "emptiness," or "aesthetic hunger." Like enduring art-products that transcend time, space, and culture, when nature is isolated from the life of the organized community, we develop a hunger that translates into pursuing art-products that are both crude and of poor quality. We find the emptiness to be multifaceted.

Consider the following five consequences of nature isolation. A "superior cultural" mindset can be cultivated when certain spaces of physical nature are set apart and invested, owned, and privately owned. Once again, this false perception is that physical nature is not part of common life but belongs only to those who possess a "superior cultural status." While this posture may not be specifically directed to people, it is directed toward their interests. Thus, isolating nature from common life can promote aesthetic segregation among the lower socio-economic classes of society. Nature can be perceived as being reduced to a museum as specimens of nature are collected and exhibited. Thus, when aspects of nature set apart for private viewing or payment by the public is required, nature is isolated from the daily comings and goings of viewing. When nature is isolated from common life, artists too are affected. Since nature is not related to the collective needs of the community, art that depicts nature within the community can be marginalized or venerated (e.g., placed on a pedestal that blurs the Creator/creation distinction). As a result, individuality apart from the community emerges. They reflect this consequence by creating art-products that champions "self-expression," "independence," and "obscurity." Thus, nature and all of its apologetic and aesthetic qualities are either displaced or blurred into something that is reflective of the human condition (e.g., a celebration of the profane, sensually indulgent, and morally wicked). The isolation of art from its origin and use creates a gap between ordinary and aesthetic experience, a confusion of aesthetic values and perception. By relocating nature outside of the ordinary lives of the community, philosophies about nature find pertinent expression and development apart from the common life. Nature is put on a pedestal and can even be given "God-like" qualities that may very well dehumanize us. Division is directly linked to aesthetic hunger. When nature as art is unavailable to the community at large, hunger grows and is likely to see fulfillment in that which is poor and profane. Because we are part of and affected by our environment, aesthetic conditions worsen. This leads us to the idea of "emptiness." I suspect that the greater the isolation of nature as art from human experience, the larger the need to fill it because we were originally created in the context of physical nature. Sensibly, we can conclude that we are likely to pursue that which cheap and vulgar, artificial and counterfeit.

CONCLUSION

Nature as God's art is able to break through all sorts of barriers that divide people. The testimony of nature is a universal form of language (general revelation) from God to humanity. This seems obvious given cross-cultural appreciation for nature. Friendship and affections find completion in both the appreciation and stewardship of nature. Moreover, certain aspects of nature draw attention and enrich social gatherings and celebrations. Nature can be a catalyst to bring people together, promote sacred spaces (e.g., the beauty found at the Garden of Gethsemane and the Garden Tomb in Jerusalem), bring restoration to those who are lost in metaphysical obscurity, and be a source of all sorts of incidents and significant scenes of life. The union between people becomes a reward and a hallmark, testifying to the power of nature God created. Nature can also become a prompt of the establishment of that particular union and prod us to promote and pursue future unions. Nature can tie the past and future together as evidenced in the recognition of certain places and events. Lastly, nature has the ability to affect and infect the collective life of the community. This occurs because of the interpenetrating relationship between people and their environment. Power of nature can intensely affect our emotions, conjure ideas in our minds, dredge up to the surface what we are trying to suppress, prod our wills to greater awareness of ourselves and our relationship to our God, and bring about punctuated moments of aesthetic pleasure in a world that experiences decay, loss, and death at every turn.

Therefore, when people come across your sphere of influence, people who are confused and disconnected, perhaps it is because nature is foreign to them in their daily experience given the digital sphere in which they live. Help them reconnect with reality as it is by having them experience nature. Engage people's worldviews about the role of nature in their habituated way of seeing and doing. Teach new generations to be good stewards of nature given the fragility of life and the limited resources we possess. Be a servant leader in your community, anticipating and promoting opportunities and programs that will bring greater interaction with physical nature in your daily living.

APPENDIX TWO:

CAN YOU TELL ME HOW TO GET *OUT* OF SESAME STREET?

"Sesame Street" offers a grocery store, an apartment complex, and even a larger than life friendly bird, but never a church. Until now! The culture has met the only void on the block. Though one might not see Bert, Ernie, Grover, and Elmo sitting in the pews, it won't take very long to recognize the familiar ditties, the attractions for short attention spans, the humor, and the flashy images to perk your interest. Come with me and don't be a grouch now, you just may learn something more important than the sound of the letter "P."

In his thought-provoking 1985 work, *Amusing Ourselves to Death*, the late Neil Postman contends that the perils of television are infecting us with a growing appetite for nonsensical amusement.[451] Taken in by "dangerous nonsense," we are losing ourselves in amusement, becoming distracted, diverted, and immobilized intellectually, emotionally, and in all spheres of social and political discourse. While thirsting for the trivial, the popular, and the sensational, we have become bored with serious inquiry, analysis, argumentation, and reasoned discourse. Thus, we are losing opportunities, perhaps at an unprecedented rate given the amount of knowledge and social utilities at our digital fingertips, to make our lives count for something great. In fact, Postman writes:

> When a population becomes distracted by trivia, when cultural life is redefined as a perpetual round of entertainments, when serious public conversations becomes a form of baby-talk, when, in a short a people become an audience and their public business a vaudeville act [a variety show], then a nation finds itself at risk; culture death is a clear possibility.[452]

---

[451] Neil Postman, *Amusing Ourselves to Death: Public Discourse in the Age of Show Business*, 20th Anniversary Edition (New York: Penguin Press, 1985, 2005).
[452] Ibid., 156.

Worship as Experience

To be sure, Postman is not against technology. In fact, he argues that the solution to the dumbing down of people is not to shut down technology.[453] Instead, he brings to the forefront one fundamental principle: **how we learn is as important as what learn.** In view of the impact of the infusion of amusements in this digital world in which we now live, Postman's social commentary resonates more than ever.

Unfortunately, and perhaps due to the pervasive fallacy of reductionism, namely, focusing on one area of thought to the neglect of all others, too many churches fail to understand or willfully ignore that how we learn is as important as what we learn. Perhaps the willful ignorance is due to fixed biases by church leadership and/or congregation. But whatever the source is for ignoring this critical insight, the church needs to address their relationship to "Sesame Street" in a proactive and healthy manner.

In his analysis of television education, Postman examines the impact of shows like "Sesame Street." The goal of "Sesame Street" is obvious. He writes, "Its use of cute puppets, celebrities, catchy tunes, and rapid-fire editing was certain to give pleasure to the children and world therefore serve as adequate preparation for their entry into a fun-loving culture."[454] Yet, the very manner in which we learn from shows like "Sesame Street" is undermining the nourishing interplay that is critically needed between the educator, the student, and the setting. Considering the following:

> The learning experience is not as nourishing when you are in a private setting away (your den) and not in a place where social interaction takes place;

> No interaction with the teacher as compared to settings where interaction with the teacher takes place;

> Educational shows demand attention to images and not to the development of language;

> Watching TV is an act of choice (you do not have to turn it on) whereas attending school is a legal requirement.

---
[453] Ibid., 158.
[454] Ibid., 144.

There are no penalties if you do not watch TV versus a setting where attendance is required.

No public decorum is needed versus proper behavior at school.

Moreover, Postman observes, "Whereas in a classroom, fun is never more than a means to an end, on television it is the end in itself."[455]

Postman goes on to acutely observe three commandments that flow from the philosophy of education which television offers. The first commandment is that no prerequisites are needed. Postman states:

> Every television program must be a complete package in itself. No previous knowledge is to be required.... The learner must be allowed to enter at any point without prejudice.... In doing away with the idea of sequence in education, television undermines the idea that sequence and continuity have anything to do with thought itself.[456]

The second commandment that flows from the philosophy of education which television offers is that no perplexity is allowed. Postman explains:

> This means that there must be nothing that has to be remembered, studied, applied, or worse of all, endured. It is assumed that any information, story, or idea can be immediately accessible, since the contentment, not the growth, of the learner is paramount.[457]

Lastly, the third commandment is the greatest enemy of television-teaching, namely, the avoidance of serious exposition. He asserts:

> Arguments, discussions, reasons, refutations or any of the traditional instruments of reasoned discourse turn television into radio, or worse, third-rate printed manner. Thus, television-teaching always takes the form of story-telling, conducted through dynamic images and supported by music....[458]

---
[455] Ibid., 143.
[456] Ibid., 147.
[457] Ibid., 148-149.
[458] Idem.

As a result of these three commandments, Postman states, "The name we may properly give to an education without prerequisites, perplexity and exposition is entertainment."⁴⁵⁹

Reflecting upon insights in relation to the activities of dysfunctional, unhealthy churches, I have come to the conclusion that many of our churches suffer similar problems: No prerequisites are needed; perplexity is avoided; serious thinking is neglected.

For example, there is one type of church that seeks to entertain the masses without an intentional and effective way to assimilate them into serious inquiry, thinking, and reflection about Christian life, practice, and thought in such a way that they make their lives count for something great, namely, thinking like and living like Jesus Christ in all spheres of daily living. While the worship services may be memorable with all of its flash, sensations, and antics, they fail to qualitatively feed the whole person, intellectually, emotionally, and spiritually, in order that they may consistently habitually live out a biblical worldview. While attention may be arrested, no demand is made to actively interact in the worship service. Thus, like sitting before a TV show, the audience is in a passive state, absorbing, but not growing. Saturated with what might be good and well-meaning, this type of church has failed to offer what is best. They trivialized the time slot that was given to them and did not seize each moment, living for that which matters most. They did not take advantage to learn from the past, integrate thought and life, and use resources in such a way that lifts up what it truly means to be a committed disciple of Jesus Christ. In sum, this type of church has become "Sesame Street." Their distinctiveness and impact is lost for they have become a puppet of culture, imitating the trivialities they see elsewhere.

On the other hand, there are other unhealthy churches that fail to realize that they too are on "Sesame Street." Refusing to acknowledge the ever-changing cultural context in which they are imbedded, these churches only offer truth through mediums of the past. Unfortunately, the church's leadership fails to recognize that these mediums for which truth is proclaimed are relics, viewed as ineffective by those who walk down "Sesame Street." But they keep on playing the 8-tracks, using

---

⁴⁵⁹ Ibid., 148.

the reel-to-reel films while glorying in the past while declining or even snubbing what is before them in the present. As a result of refusing to seize the opportunity to meet people where they are, like the apostle Paul did on Mars Hill, these churches are ignored by the masses. Why? The manner in which they offer truth is uninteresting, uninviting, and disconnected from where people are. Coupled with bombastic, dogmatic, elitist, and ungracious attitudes by some of these blind churches, those who live on "Sesame Street" see no reason to step through the church doors.

While spinning their wheels in the absence of fresh creativity, the blind church's programming is all the same. No changes. No anticipation. No vision. The blind church settles for only a restatement of what they believe, expressed in the "rutted" manner of which they are familiar. Thus, championing the routine, the humdrum, they no longer demand prerequisites. See, everything is already anticipated. There is no ongoing sequence, no development, and no tension for they choose to isolate themselves from active engagement from culture that may be identified as "Sesame Street." In sum, the routine governs activity, thought, and life. As a result, *no ongoing need for prerequisites is necessary.*

Instead of engaging an ever-changing culture, which generates perplexity, the blind church on "Sesame Street" only seeks to do what has been done before. As a result of their love for familiarity, qualitative growth is stunted. Why? They are only interested in the restatement of what they have learned and in the manner in which they learned it. Consequently, *there is no perplexity because the content is all together familiar.*

Now, some people that live, move, and have their becoming in the blind church, assert themselves from a position of wanting to hear a restatement of biblical truth to a position of judging to determine whether what we have learned will be said the same way. For example, some choose to listen to the sermon to determine if it measures up to previous teaching rather than finding areas in their own lives that can be challenged unto greater spiritual maturity.

Lastly, because these churches seek to only state what they already know, there are no fresh arguments, analyses, and reasoned discourse. Excitement and passion is displaced by what is "familiar." Absent are fresh ideas and activities in reaching an ever-changing culture. The power of imagination and creative intelligence is ignored. The excitement and passion that is generated by engaging the changes that surround them are displaced. See, the blind church willfully chooses blindness by not understanding the nature and ways of "Sesame Street." Or they may know, but only go so far as to critique within their own setting but not make a life-changing difference. In other words, they do not seriously seek to meet these occupants where they are and earnestly bring them where they need to be. In sum, what the blind church offers is comfortable amusement cloaked in the routine. Therefore, what accompanies *a refusal to change is a lack of critical thinking* because it is in working out problems in the present experience that generate serious inquiries, analyses, solutions, and new realizations. We grow more from tension than comfort.

In conclusion, the irony is that while these two types of churches, that is, the church that mirrors "Sesame Street" and the church that is blind to "Sesame Street," are polarized from each other in their activities, they both suffer from the same maladies: no prerequisites, no perplexity, and no exposition.

Consider the fact that the audiences in both churches are in a passive position of learning. They sit and observe. Sadly, this passive position diminishes the potential impact they could make both inside and outside of the church. Why? Nothing is demanded from them; they are reduced to becoming a spectator rather than an active participant. Malnourishment and brittle bones are commonplace.

But these two types of churches not only lose opportunities to offer nourishing and meaningful interactions with those who walk to and fro on "Sesame Street," they also lose their effectiveness. How? Both churches fail to ask something great from us in relation to all the changes that continually occur in culture and what the God of the Bible demands from us. Because no qualitative growth finds expression, the church doors, whether it is the church that reflects "Sesame Street" or is blind to "Sesame Street," revolve with people wanting to move to another street. Or perhaps, they just choose to spend their time elsewhere, where more aesthetic, enriching, and fulfilling activities find expression.

Nevertheless, they leave the place that was originally designed to best address their greatest needs.

Refuse to live for the trivial and be immobilized by the routine. Though many in our culture have been raised on "Sesame Street," as those who belong to the Father of creativity, we can surely think of engaging ways to stretch minds, grows hearts, and deepen souls while not becoming a puppet on "Sesame Street." Although "Sesame Street" was a nice place to hang out for a while, most of us were glad for the opportunity to move on. Similarly, those who are occupied with the trivial and the mundane will relish in opportunities to dynamically grow, experience a new depth of faith, and anticipate new horizons.

NAME INDEX

Aeschylus, 33
Allen, Ronald B., 15
Allen, Woody, 192
Anderson, Jonathan, 130
Anderson, Leith, 97
Aquinas, Thomas St., 10, 195
Arendt, Hannah, 143
Aristotle, 24, 46
Arnett, Jeffrey Jensen, 105, 106
Arnson, Eric, 145, 148
Athanasius, St., 116
Audi, Robert, 13
Augustine, St., 10, 116, 195
Austin, Scott C., 4
Ayers, Mike, 4
Bach, Johann Sebastian, 33
Balmer, Randall, 126
Beardsley, Monroe C., 21
Beethoven, Ludwig van, 33
Belcher, Jim, 105, 110, 116, 117, 119, 150
Bell, Clive, 18, 31, 33
Bernstein, Richard, 13
Bolger, Ryan, 104, 150
Botticelli, Sandro, 33
Bottum, Joseph, 112, 140
Boydston, Jo Ann, 11, 16
Branaugh, Matt, 93
Brink, Jonathan, 121, 164
Brooks, David, 92
Budziszewski, J., 36, 195
Buford, Bob, 113
Bunyan, John, 52

Burke, John, 154, 156
Calvin, John, 46, 76, 173
Campbell, Colin, 146
Campbell, Keith W., 165, 166
Camus, Albert, 190
Capps, Donald, 144
Capps, John M., 144
Carroll, John, 186
Cézanne, Paul, 21
Chesterton, G. K. 15
Constantine, St., 117
Clapp, Rodney, 119
Cluck, Ted, 115
Cooper, David, 18
Crosby, Fannie, 52
Dante, Alighieri, 33
Davis, Heather, 90
Davis, Richard Brian, 11
Dawkins, Richard, 106
Derrida, Jacques, 114, 123
Dewey, John, 10, 11, 12, 13, 14, 16, 19, 21, 22, 23, 24, 25, 26, 27, 28, 29, 30, 31, 32, 33, 34, 35, 36, 37, 38, 39, 40, 41, 42, 43, 44, 45, 46, 47, 48, 49, 50, 51, 52, 53, 54, 55, 57, 66, 67, 71, 72, 74, 78, 79, 80, 81, 82, 86, 87, 88, 131, 133, 134, 136. 137, 138, 139, 140, 144, 145, 146, 152, 153, 154, 155, 156, 160, 161, 164, 165, 166, 168, 169, 171, 174, 176, 177, 183, 196
DeYoung, Kevin, 115
Dickie, George, 18
Driscoll, Mark, 113, 115, 116, 120, 124
Drucker, Peter, 102
Dutton, Denis, 33, 43, 203
Dyrness, William A., 130
Edman, Irwin, 176
Edwards, Jonathan, 10, 16, 81, 82, 140
Eliot, T. S., 33
Epstein, Jacob Sir, 33

Fish, Stanley, 123
Fletcher, Andrew, 186
Foucault, Michel, 123
Franke, John R., 107
Galli, Mark, 131
Gaut, Berys, 204
Geisler, Norman L., 199, 202
Gibbs, Eddie, 104, 149, 150
Gilbreath, Edward, 89, 91, 94, 95, 96
Gillmor, Verla, 90, 92, 96
Giotto, Di Bondone, 33
Gogh, Vincent Van, 9, 27, 134, 151
Gordon, W. Terrence, 36
Gould, Paul, 11
Grenz, Stanley J., 107, 119
Guinness, Os, 86, 94, 107
Hamilton, Michael S., 90, 106
Hart, Richard E., 19
Hauser, Kaspar, 111
Hawkins, Greg, 145, 148
Heelas, Paul, 150, 151
Hitchens, Christopher, 106
Hook, Sydney, 176
Hybels, Bill, 89, 90, 91, 95, 98, 148, 149
Hybels, Lynne, 89
Ingraffia, Brian D., 107
Ireneaus, St., 76
Jackson, Philip W., 19, 22
James, William, 144
Jesus Christ, 47, 54, 59, 82, 103, 109, 113, 117, 119, 121, 124, 125, 126, 159, 190, 191, 192, 214
Jethani, Skye, 108, 124
Johnson, Maxwell E., 118
Jones, Tony, 113, 121
Jones, W. T., 150

Justin Martyr, 117
Kallestad, Walt, 144
Kant, Immanuel, 18, 150
Kennison, Phillip, 119
Kierkegaard, Søren, 51, 179
Kimball, Dan, 113
Köstenberger, Andreas K., 120
Kreeft, Peter, 58
Kuo, David, 127
Lasch, Christopher, 111
Lewis, C. S., 10, 14, 128, 129, 190, 191, 195, 199, 202
Lightner, Robert P., 13
Lopes, Dominic McIver, 203
Lyotard, Jean-Francois, 106
MacDonald, G. Jeffrey, 147
Machen, Gresham J., 54
Marsden, George M., 82
Mauldin, Michael G., 89, 94, 98
McClaren, Brian, 113, 121, 122, 123, 125, 132
McDermott, John J., 4, 16, 19, 38, 67, 142
McLuhan, Marshall, 36, 79, 84
McKnight, Scot, 104, 108, 114, 120, 122, 123, 125, 126
Michelangelo, 33, 203
Micklethwait, John, 96, 101, 102
Miller, Rod, 187
Milton, John, 52
Mitscherlich, Alexander, 111
Mohler, Albert, 120
Moreland, J. P., 82, 83, 120
Morey, Robert A., 203
Morgan, G. Campbell, 88
Moore, Edward C., 20
Moore, G. E., 122, 199
Murphy, Nancey, 108, 119
Natoli, Joseph, 119

Narcissus, 79, 165
Neill, Alex, 186
Newton, John, 162
Norwich, Julius, John, 34
Okholm, Dennis, 119
Packer, J. I., 15
Pagitt, Doug, 110, 113, 114, 116, 120, 121
Pappas, Gregory Fernando, 4, 14, 31, 66, 146
Parkinson, Cally, 145, 148
Pascal, Blaise, 10, 15, 29, 53, 59, 189, 193, 195, 204
Paul Apostle, 47, 215
Pearcey, J. Richard, 181
Pearcey, Nancy, 60, 181, 182
Pheidas, 33
Phillips, Timothy, 119
Pierce, Charles, 20
Piero, 33
Piper, John, 15
Plato, 36, 39, 44, 45, 80, 194, 195
Pontynen, Arthur, 187
Postman, Neil, 142, 143, 211, 212, 213, 214
Putnman, David, 153
Radmacher, Earl D., 11
Randall, Hastings, 199
Reed, Eric, 89
Reid, Thomas, 10
Rembrandt, 34, 119, 128
Rollins, Peter, 122
Roof, Wade Clark, 110, 111, 150, 151
Rookmaaker, Hans, 187
Rookmaaker-Hengelaar, Marleen, 187
Rorty, Richard, 123
Ross, Allen P., 15
Roxbourge, Alan, 122
Russo-Cox, Teresa, 99

Ryrie, Charles C., 10
Sargeant, Kim Howland, 89, 101
Savile, Andrew, 186
Schaeffer, Francis A., 10, 59, 60, 194, 195
Schiller, Fredrick, 33
Seel, Benjamin, 150, 151
Shakespeare, William, 34
Shockley, Paul R., 13
Shults, LeRon, 120
Shusterman, Richard, 28, 79
Siedell, Daniel A., 130
Slater, Don, 146
Sleeper, R. W., 19
Smith, Christian, 151
Sorley, W. R., 199
Stetzer, Ed, 153
Stolnitz, Jerome, 18
Stott, John, 125
Sweet, Leonard, 111
Swinburne, Richard, 199
Symonds, William C., 90
Szersynski, Bronislaw, 150
Taylor, Charles, 105, 106, 107, 150, 151
Taylor, Daniel, 106
Temple, William, 33
Tertullian, 117
Thumma, Scott, 93, 94, 95, 102
Tolkien, J. R. R., 52
Tolstoy, Leo, 33, 36
Tozer, A. W., 7, 15
Travis, Dave, 93, 94, 102
Trueblood, Elton, 199
Trueheart, Charles, 91, 97
Turek, Frank, 202
Tusting, Karin, 151

Twenge, Jean M., 112, 165, 166, 167
Vanhoozer, Kevin J., 120
Velasquez, 33
Vialdesau, Richard, 57
Wainright, Geoffrey, 118
Walvoord, John F., 10
Ward, Karen, 159
Webber, Robert, 92, 118, 154, 156, 157, 158
Welch Ben, 4
Wells, David F., 101
Wesley, Charles, 52
Wesley, John, 116
West, David, 114
Westerfield, Karen B., 118
White, James F., 47, 55, 94, 95, 96
Wiersbe, Warren, 173
Wilde, Oscar, 128, 129
Woodhead, Linda, 150
Wooldridge, Adrian, 96, 101, 102
Wolterstorff, Nicholas, 87, 172, 183, 184
Zagzebeski, Linda, 199

REFERENCES

A. BOOKS

Alexander, Thomas M. *John Dewey's Theory of Art, Experience, and Nature: The Horizons of Feeling.* (Albany, NY: State University of New York Press, 1987).

Anderson, Douglas R., ed. *The Drama of Possibility: Experience as Philosophy of Culture.* John J. McDermott. (New York: Fordham University, 2007).

Anderson, Leith. *A Church for the 21st Century: Bringing Change to Your Church to Meet the Challenges of a Changing Society.* (Minneapolis, MN: Bethany House, 1992).

Arguing about Art: Contemporary Philosophical Debates. Edited by Alex Neill and Aaron Ridley (New York: McGraw-Hill, 1995).

Arnett, Jeffrey Jensen. *Emerging Adulthood: The Winding Road from the Late Teens through the Twenties.* (Oxford, UK: Oxford University Press, 2004).

Audi, Robert. *The Cambridge Dictionary of Philosophy. Second edition.* (Cambridge, UK: Cambridge University Press, 1995, 1999).

Balmer, Randall. *Thy Kingdom Come: How the Religious Right Distorts the Faith and Threatens America: an Evangelical's Lament.* (New York: Basic Books, 2006).

Barron, Robert. *Heaven in Stone and Glass: Experiencing the Spirituality of the Great Cathedrals.* (New York: Crossroad Publishing, 2000).

Beardsley, Monroe C. *Aesthetics: From Classical Greece to the Present.* (Tuscaloosa: The University of Alabama Press, 1966).

Bauerlein, Mark. *The Dumbest Generation: How the Digital Age Stupefies Young Americans and Jeopardizes our Future (Or, Don't Trust Anyone Under 30)* (New York: Tarcher/Penguin, 2008).

Belcher, Jim. *The Deep Church: A Third Way beyond Emerging and Traditional.* (Downers Grove, IL: InterVarsity Press, 2009).

Bell, Clive. *Art.* (London: Chatto & Windus, 1947).

_____. Third edition. (Oxford, UK: Oxford University Press, 1987).

Bernstein, Richard, ed. *On Experience, Nature, and Freedom.* (Indianapolis, IN: Bobbs-Merrill, 1960).

Boydston, Jo Ann, ed. *Guide to the Works of John Dewey.* (Carbondale, IL: Southern Illinois University Press, 1970).

Brown, Harold O. J. *The Sensate Culture: Western Civilization Between Chaos and Transformation* (Dallas: Word Publishing, 1996).

_____. *John Dewey: The Early Works: 1882-1898. Five volumes.* (Carbondale, IL: Southern Illinois University Press, 1967-72).

_____. *John Dewey: The Later Works:1925-1953. Five volumes.* (Carbondale, IL: Southern Illinois University Press, 1967-72).

_____. *John Dewey: The Middle Works: 1899-1924. Fifteen volumes.* (Carbondale, IL: Southern Illinois University Press, 1976-83).

Capps, John M., and Donald Capps. *James & Dewey on Belief and Experience.* (Urbana, IL: University of Illinois Press, 2005).

Campbell, James, and Richard E. Hart. *Experience as Philosophy: On the Work of John J. McDermott.* (New York: Fordham Press, 2006).

Campbell, Colin. *The Romantic Ethic and the Spirit of Modern Consumerism.* (Oxford, UK: Blackwell, 1987).

Capps, John M., and Donald Capps, eds. *James & Dewey on Belief and Experience.* (Urbana, IL: University of Illinois Press, 2005).

Clapp, Rodney. *Border Crossings: Christian Trespasses on Popular Culture and Public Affairs.* (Grand Rapids, MI: Brazos, 2000).

Clark, Wade Roof. *Spiritual Marketplace: Baby Boomers and the Remaking of American Religion.* (Princeton, NJ: Princeton University Press, 1999).

Cooper, David, ed. *A Companion to Aesthetics.* (Malden, MA: Riverside, 1960).

Cooper, John, ed. *Plato: Complete Works.* (Indianapolis, IN: Hackett Publishing, 1997).

Dewey, John. *Art as Experience.* (New York: The Berkley Publishing Group, 1934, 2005).

_____. *A Common Faith.* (New Haven, CT: Yale University Press, 1934).

_____. *Experience and Nature.* (New York: Dover Publications, 1958).

_____. *Theory of the Moral Life.* (New York: Holt, Reinhard and Winston, 1908, 1932, 1960).

DeYoung, Kevin, and Ted Kluck. *Why We're Not Emergent (By Two Guys Who Should Be).* (Chicago: Moody Press, 2008).

Dickie, George. *Aesthetics: An Introduction.* (Indianapolis, IN: Pegasus, 1971).

_____. *The Art Circle: A Theory of Art.* (New York: Haven: 1984).

Driscoll, Mark. *The Radical Reformission.* (Grand Rapids, MI: Zondervan, 2004).

Edwards, Jonathan. *Jonathan Edwards on Revival.* (Carlisle, PA: The Banner of Truth Trust, 1994).

Franke, John and Stanley Grenz. *Beyond Foundationalism: Shaping Theology in a Postmodern Context.* (Philadelphia: Westminster John Knox, 2000).

Gaut, Berys, and Dominic McIver Lopes. *The Routledge Companion to Aesthetics.* (New York: Routledge, 2001, 2003).

Geisler, Norman. *Baker's Encyclopedia of Christian Apologetics* (Grand Rapids, Baker, 1999).

Geisler, Norman L & Frank Turek. *I Don't Have Enough Faith to be an Atheist* (Wheaton: Crossway Publishers, 2004).

Gibbs, Eddie and Ryan Bolger. *Emerging Churches: Creating Christian Community in Postmodern Cultures.* (Grand Rapids, MI: Baker, 2005).

Gould, Paul, and Richard Brian Davis. *Four Views on Christianity and Philosophy.* (Grand Rapids: Zondervan, 2016)

Guinness, Os. *Prophetic Untimeliness: The Challenges to the Idol of Relevance.* (Grand Rapids, MI: Baker, 2006).

Grenz, Stanley J., and John R. Franke. *Beyond Foundationalism: Shaping Theology in a Postmodern Context.* (Louisville, KY: Westminster John Knox, 2001).

_____. *A Primer on Postmodernism.* (Grand Rapids, MI: Eerdmans, 1996).

_____. *Revisioning Evangelical Theology: A Fresh Approach for the 21st Century: God & the World in a Transitional Age.* (Downers Grove, IL: InterVarsity, 1992).

Hawkins, Greg L., Cally Parkinson, and Eric Arnson. *Reveal: Where Are You?* (Barrington, IL: Willow Creek Resources, 2007).

Heelas, Paul. *Spiritualities of Life: New Age Romanticism and Consumptive Capitalism.* (Oxford, UK: Blackwell, 2008).

_____. Linda Woodhead, Benjamin Seel, Bronislaw Szersynski, and Karin Trusting. *The Spiritual Revolution: Why Religion is Giving Way to Spirituality.* (Oxford, UK: Blackwell Publishing, 2005).

Hook, Sydney, ed. *John Dewey: Philosopher of Science and Freedom. A Symposium.* (New York: The Dial Press, 1950).

Hunter, James Davidson. *Evangelicalism: The Coming Generation.* (Chicago: University of Chicago Press, 1987).

_____. *To Change the World: The Irony, Tragedy, & Possibility of Christianity in the Late Modern World.* (Oxford, UK: Oxford University Press, 2010).

Hybels, Bill and Lynne. *Rediscovering Church: The Story and Vision of Willow Creek Community Church.* (Grand Rapids, MI: Zondervan, 1995).

Ingraffia, Brian D. *Postmodern Theory and Biblical Theology.* (Cambridge, UK: Cambridge University Press, 1995).

Jackson, Philip W. *John Dewey and the Lessons of Art.* (New Haven, CT: Yale University Press, 1998).

Jethani, Skye. *The Divine Commodity: Discovering a Christian Faith Beyond Consumer Christianity.* (Grand Rapids, MI: Zondervan, 2009).

Jones, W. T. *Kant and the Nineteenth Century: A History of Western Philosophy, volume 4. Second edition, revised.* (Belmont, CA: Wadsworth, 1975).

Kallestad, Walt. *Entertainment Evangelism: Taking the Church Public.* (Nashville, TN: Abingdon Press, 1996).

Kimball, Dan. *Emerging Worship: Creating Worship Gatherings for New Generations.* (El Cajon, CA: emergentYS, 2004).

Kuo, David. *Tempting Faith: An Inside Story of Political Seduction.* (New York: Free Press, 2006).

Lasch, Christopher. *The Culture of Narcissism: American Life in an Age of Diminishing Expectations.* (New York: W. W. Norton & Company, 1979).

Levinson, Jerrold. *The Oxford Handbook of Aesthetics.* (Oxford, UK: Oxford University Press, 2003).

Lewis, C. S. *God in the Dock* (Grand Rapids: Eerdmans, 1970).

_____. C.S. *Mere Christianity* (New York: Macmillan, 1952).

_____. *Mere Christianity* (San Francisco: Harper, 2008).

_____. *Surprised by Joy: The Shape of My Early Life* (New York: Harcourt, Brace, Jovanovich, 1995).

Lightner, Robert P. *God of the Bible and other Gods.* (Grand Rapids, MI: Kregel Publications, 1998).

Lyotard, Jean-François. *The Postmodern Condition: A Report on Knowledge.* (Minneapolis, MN: University of Minneapolis, 1984).

Marsden, George M. *Jonathan Edwards: A Life.* (New Haven, CT: Yale University Press, 2003).

McDermott, John J. ed. *The Philosophy of John Dewey.* (Chicago: The University of Chicago Press, 1973, 1981).

McGrath, Alister. *Evangelicalism & the Future of Christianity.* (Downers Grove, IL: InterVarsity Press, 1995).

_____. *The Twilight of Atheism: The Rise and Fall of Disbelief in the Modern World* (New York: Doubleday, 2004).

McLaren, Brian D. *A New Kind of Christian: A Tale of Two Friends on a Spiritual Journey.* (San Francisco: Jossey-Bass, 2001).

McLuhan, Marshall. *Understanding Media: The Extensions of Man.* (New York: McGraw-Hill, 1964).

_____. *Understanding Media: The Extensions of Man.* (Cambridge, MA: MIT Press, 1994).

Micklethwait, John, and Adrian Wooldridge. *God is Back: How the Global Revival of the Faith is Changing the World* (New York: Penguin Press, 2009).

Moore, Edward C. *American Pragmatism: Pierce, James, and Dewey.* (New York: Columbia University Press, 1961).

Morey, Robert A. *The New Atheism and the Erosion of Freedom* (Minneapolis: Bethany House Publishers, 1986).

Moreland, J. P. *Love God with All Your Mind: The Role of Reason in the Life of the Soul.* (Colorado Springs, CO: NavPress, 1997).

Natoli, Joseph. *A Primer to Postmodernity.* (Oxford, UK: Blackwell, 1997).

Murphy, Nancey. *Anglo-American Postmodernity: Philosophical Perspectives on Science, Religion, and Ethics.* (Boulder, CO: Westview Press, 1997).

Norwich, John Julius. *Great Architecture of the World.* (New York: Random House, 1975, 2001).

Oden, Thomas, C. *Agenda for Theology.* (New York: Harper & Row, 1979).

Pagitt, Doug. *Spiritual Formation.* (Grand Rapids, MI: Zondervan, 2003).

Pappas, Gregory Fernando. *John Dewey's Ethics: Democracy as Experience.* (Bloomington, IN: Indiana University Press, 2008).

Pearcey, Nancy *Finding Truth: 5 Principles for Unmasking Atheism, Secularism, and Other God Substitutes.* Colorado Springs, CO: David C. Cook Publishing, 2015).

_____. *Saving Leonardo: A Call to Resist the Secular Assault on Mind, Morals, and Meaning* (Nashville: B&H Publishing, 2010).

Philips, Timothy, and Dennis Okholm, eds. *Christian Apologetics in the Postmodern World.* (Downers Grove, IL: InterVarsity, 1995).

Pinnock, Clark. *Tracking the Maze: Finding Our Way through Modern Theology from an Evangelical Perspective.* (San Francisco: Harper and Row, 1990).

Pontynen, Arthur and Rod Miller. *Western Culture at the American Crossroads: Conflicts Over the Nature of Science and Reason* (Wilmington, DE: ISI Books, 2011).

Postman, Neil. *Amusing Ourselves to Death: Public Discourse in the Age of Show Business*. 20th anniversary edition. (New York: Penguin Press, 1985, 2005).

_____. *Technopoly: The Surrender of Culture to Technology*. (New York: Vintage Books, 1993).

Pritchard, G. A. *Willow Creek Seeker Services: Evaluating a New Way of Doing Church*. (Grand Rapids, MI: Baker, 1996).

Radmacher, Earl D. *The Nature of the Church: A Biblical and Historical Study*. (Chicago: Moody Press, 1972).

Rollins, Peter. *How (Not) to Speak of God*. (Brewster, MA: Paraclete Press, 2006).

Rookmaaker, Hans. *The Complete Works of Hans Rookmaker*, edited by Marleen Hengelaar-Rookmaaker, 5 volumes (Pinquant Publishing, 2002).

Routledge Companion to Aesthetics, edited by Berys Gaut and Dominic McIver Lopes (New York: Routledge, 2001).

Sargeant, Kimon Howland. *Seeker Churches: Promoting Traditional Religion in a Nontraditional Way*. (New York: Rutgers University Press, 2002).

Schaeffer, Francis A. *The Complete Works of Francis A. Schaeffer*, second edition, five volumes (Wheaton: Crossway, 1982).

Schaeffer, Francis A. *The Complete Works of Francis A. Schaeffer: A Christian Worldview*, five volumes, Second edition (Wheaton: Crossway, 1985).

Schaeffer, Francis A. *True Spirituality*. (Carol Stream, IL: Tyndale House Publishers, 1971, 2011).

Slater, Don. *Consumer Culture and Modernity*. (Cambridge, UK: Polity Press, 1997).

Sleeper, R. W. *The Necessity of Pragmatism: John Dewey's Conception of Philosophy*. (Urbana, IL: University of Illinois Press, 1986, 2001).

Smith, Christian. *Soul Searching: The Religious and Spiritual Lives of American Teenagers*. (Oxford, UK: Oxford University Press, 2009).

Smith, James K. A. *Desiring the Kingdom: Worship, Worldview, and Cultural Formation* (Grand Rapids, Baker, 2009).

Stetzer, Ed, and David Putman. *Breaking the missional Code: Your Church Can Become a Missionary in Your Community*. (Nashville, TN: Broadman & Holman, 2006).

Stolnitz, Jerome. *Aesthetics and the Philosophy of Art Criticism.* (Boston: Riverside, 1960).

Sweet, Leonard. *Post-Modern Pilgrims: First Century Passion for the 21st Century World.* (Nashville, TN: Broadman & Holman Publishers, 2000).

Taylor, Charles. *A Secular Age.* (Cambridge, MA: Belknap Press, 2007).

Taylor, Daniel. *The Myth of Certainty: The Reflective Christian and the Risk of Commitment.* (Grand Rapids, MI: Zondervan, 1992).

Taylor, Mark. *Erring, A Postmodern A/Theology.* (Chicago: University of Chicago Press, 1984).

Temple, William. *Nature, Man, and God.* (New York: Macmillan, 1956).

Thumma, Scott and Dave Travis. *Beyond Megachurch Myths: What We Can Learn from America's Largest Churches.* (San Francisco: Jossey-Bass, 2007).

Twenge, Jean. *Generation Me: Why Today's Young Americans Are More Confident, Assertive, Entitled-and More Miserable than Ever Before.* (New York: Free Press, 2007).

_____, and Keith Campbell W. *The Narcissism Epidemic: Living in the Age of Entitlement.* (New York: Free Press, 2009).

Vanhoozer, Kevin J. *Is There a Meaning in this Text? The Bible, The Reader, and the Morality of Literary Knowledge.* (Grand Rapids, MI: Zondervan, 1998).

Vialdesau, Richard. *Theology and the Arts: Encountering God through Music, Art, and Rhetoric.* (New York: Paulist Press, 2000).

Wainright, Geoffrey, and Karen B. Westerfield, eds. *The Oxford History of Christian Worship.* (Oxford, UK: Oxford University Press, 2006).

Webber, Robert E. *Ancient-Future Worship: Proclaiming and Enacting God's Narrative.* (Grand Rapids, MI: BakerBooks, 2008).

_____ ed. *Listening to the Beliefs of the Emerging Churches: Five Perspectives.* (Grand Rapids, MI: Zondervan, 2007).

Wells, David F. *Above All Earthly Pow'rs: Christ in a Postmodern World.* (Grand Rapids, MI: 2005).

West, David. *An Introduction to Continental Philosophy.* (Cambridge, UK: Polity Press, 1996).

White, James F. *Introduction to Christian Worship.* Third edition, revised and expanded. (Nashville, TN: Abingdon Press, 1980, 2000).

Wolterstorff, Nicholas. *Art in Action.* (Grand Rapids, MI: Eerdmans, 1980).

Woods, Robert E. *Placing Aesthetics: Reflections on the Philosophic Traditions.* (Athens, OH: Ohio University Press, 1999).

B. ONLINE RESOURCES

Brink, Jonathan. "A Time To Deconstruct," Emergent Village Webblog (July 18, 2010) at www.emergentvillage.com. http://www.emergentvillage.com/weblog/brink-reconstruct. Retrieval Date: July 20, 2010.

Davis, Heather. "Daniel Subwoofers Handle the Low-End for Willow Creek Church," The Briefing Room, April 14, 2009<www.blogsvconline.com/2009/04/14/danley-subwoofers-handle-the-low-end-for-willow-creek-church/>. Retrieval date: 1 June 2010.

Swinburne, Richard. "Argument from Design." www.orthodoxy.org. Accessed 10/15/2017. http://www.orthodoxytoday.org/articles2/SwineburnDesign.php.

C. PERIODICALS

Bottum, Joseph. "Christians and Postmoderns." *First Things* no. 201 (March 2010): 43-47.

Branaugh, Matt. "Willow Creek's 'Huge Shift.'" *Christianity Today* (June 2008): 13.

Brooks, David. "The National Creed." *The New York Times* (30 December 2003): 21.

Carson, Donald A. "The Challenges of Contemporary Pluralism." *Southern Baptist Journal of Theology* 1 no. 2 (Summer 1997): 5-37.

Gelder, Van C. "Postmodernism as an Emerging Worldview." *Calvin Theological Journal* 26 (1991): 38-51.

Gilbreath, Edward. "The Birth of a Megachurch." *Christianity Today* (July, 18 1994): 23.

Gillmor, Verla. "Community Is Their Middle Name." *Christianity Today* (November 13, 2000): 48-55.

_____. "The Next 25 Years." *Christianity Today* (November 13, 2000): 54.

Ground, Vernon C. "The Truth about Truth." *Journal of the Evangelical Theological Society* 38 (June 1995): 219-29.

Hamilton, Michael S. "Willow Creek's Place in History." *Christianity Today* (13 November 2000): 62-68.

Kostenberger, Andreas. "'What is Truth?' Pilate's Question in Its Johannine and Larger Biblical Context." *Journal of the Evangelical Theological Society* 48/1 (March 2005): 33-62.

MacDonald, G. Jeffrey. "Congregations Gone Wild." *The New York Times* Op-Editorial (8 August 2010): WK9.

Mars Hill Interview. "Calling, Postmodernism, and Chastened Liberals: A Conversation with Os Guinness." *Mars Hill Review*, no. 8 (Summer 1997): 69-82.

Mauldin, Michael and Edward Gilbreath, "Selling Out the House of God?: Billy Hybels answers critics of the seeker-sensitive movement." *Christianity Today* (18 July 1994): 20-25.

"Mega-Mirror: Mega Churches are not the answer or the problem." *Christianity Today Editorial* (August 2009): 20.

McKnight, Scot. "Five Streams of the Emerging Church." *Christianity Today* (February 2007): 34-39.

_____. "The Ironic Faith of Emergents." *Christianity Today* (September 2000): 62-63.

_____. "McLaren Emerging." *Christianity Today* **(September 2008)**: 58-66.

McQuilkin, Robertson and Bradford Mullen. "The Impact of Postmodern Thinking on Evangelical Hermeneutics." *Journal of the Evangelical Theological Society* 40 (March 1997): 69-82.

Mohler Albert R. "What is Truth? Truth and Contemporary Culture." *Journal of the Evangelical Theological Society* 48/1 (March 2005): 63-75

Moreland, J. P. "Truth, Contemporary Philosophy, and the Postmodern Turn." *Journal of the Evangelical Theological Society* 48/1 (March 2005): 77-88.

Olson, Roger E. "The Future of Evangelical Theology." *Christianity Today* 42:2 (February 9, 1998): 40-50.

_____. "Postconservative Evangelicals Greet the Postmodern Age." *Christian Century* 112.15 (May 3, 1995): 480-489.

Reed, Eric. "Church: Willow Creek Readies for Megagrowth." *Christianity Today* (24 April 2000): 21.

Shusterman, Richard. "Entertainment: A Question for Aesthetics." *British Journal of Aesthetics* 44:3 (2003): 289-307.

Symonds, William C. "Marketing." *Stanford Business* (February 2009): 16-19.

Trueheart, Charles. "Welcome to the Next Generation." *Atlantic Monthly* (August 1996): 47-58.

Vanhoozer, Kevin J. "Lost in Interpretation? Truth, Scripture, and Hermeneutics." *Journal of the Evangelical Theological Society* 48/1 (March 2005): 89-114.

D. SECONDARY SOURCES

Anderson, Ray S. *An Emergent Theology for Emerging Churches* (Downers Grove, IL: InterVarsity Press, 2006).

Andreaopoulos, Andreas. *Art as Theology: From the Postmodern to the Medieval.* (London: Equinox, 2006).

Aquinas, Thomas. *The Cardinal Virtues: Prudence, Justice, Fortitude, and Temperance.* (Trans. and ed. by Richard J. Regan. Indianapolis, IN: Hackett Publishing, 2005).

Armstrong, John H., ed. *The Coming Evangelical Crisis: Current Challenges to the Authority of Scripture.* (Chicago: Moody, Press, 1996).

Balthasar, Hans Urs von. *The Glory of the Lord: A Theological Aesthetics. Volume 1, Seeing the Form.* (Trans. E. Leiva-Merikakis. San Francisco: Ignatius Press, 1982).

_____. *The Glory of the Lord. Volume 2, Studies in Theological Style: Clerical Styles.* (Trans. A. Louth, F. McDonagh, and B. McNeil. San Francisco: Ignatius Press, 1984).

_____. *The Glory of the Lord. Volume 3, Studies in Theological Style: Lay Styles.* (Trans. A. Louth, J. Saward, M. Simon, and R. Williams. San Francisco: Ignatius Press, 1986).

_____. *The Glory of the Lord. Volume 4, The Realm of Metaphysics in Antiquity.* (Trans. B. McNeil, A Louth, J. Saward, R. Williams, and O. Davies. San Francisco: Ignatius Press, 1989).

_____. *The Glory of the Lord. Volume 5, The Realm of Metaphysics in the Modern Age.* (Trans. O. Davies, A. Louth, B. McNiel, J. Saward, and R. Williams. San Francisco: Ignatius Press, 1991).

_____. *The Glory of the Lord. Volume 6, Theology: The Old Covenant.* (Trans. B. McNeil and E. Leiva-Merikakis. San Francisco: Ignatius Press, 1991).

_____. *The Glory of the Lord. Volume 7, Theology: The New Covenant.* (Trans. B. McNeil. San Francisco: Ignatius Press, 1989).

Barzun, Jacques. *From Dawn to Decadence: 1500 to the Present. 500 Years of Western Cultural Life*. (New York: HarperCollins, 2000).

Beardsley, Monroe. *Aesthetics: Problems in the Philosophy of Criticism. Second edition*. (Indianapolis, IN: Hackett Publishing, 1958, 1981).

Begbie, Jeremy S., ed. *Incarnation Through the Arts* (Grand Rapids: Baker, 2001).

_____. *Music, Modernity, and God: Essays in Listening* (New York: Oxford University Press, 2013, 2015).

_____. *Resounding Truth: Christian Wisdom in the World of Music* (Grand Rapids: Baker, 2007).

_____. *Voicing Creation's Praise: Towards a Theology of the Arts*. (Edinburgh: T&T Clark, 1991).

Blewitt, John S. J., ed. *John Dewey. His Thought and Influence*. (New York: Fordham University Press, 1960).

Bustard, Ned. *It was Good–Making Art to the Glory of God*. (Baltimore, MD: Square Halo Books, 2000).

Blaising, Craig. A., and Darrell Bock, eds. *Progressive Dispensationalism*. (Wheaton, IL: Victory Books, 1993).

Brown, Frank Burch. *Good Taste, Bad Taste, and Christian Taste: Aesthetics in Religious Life*. (Oxford, UK: Oxford University Press, 2000).

_____. *Inclusive Yet Discerning: Navigating Worship Artfully*. (Grand Rapids, MI: Eerdmans, 2009).

_____. *Religious Aesthetics: A Theological Study of Making and Meaning*. (Princeton, NJ: Princeton University Press, 1989).

Brown, Harold O. J. *The Sensate Culture: Western Civilization between Chaos and Transformation*. (Dallas, TX: Word Publishing, 1996).

Campbell, Heidi, A. and Stephen Garner. *Networked Theology: Negotiating Faith in Digital Culture*. (Grand Rapids: Baker, 2016).

Carson, Donald A. *Becoming Conversant with the Emerging Church: Understanding a Movement and Its Implications*. (Grand Rapids, MI: Zondervan, 2005).

_____. *Christ and Culture Revisited*. (Grand Rapids, MI: Eerdmans, 2008).

Cooper, David. *A Companion to Aesthetics. Blackwell Companions to Philosophy*. (Malden, MA: Blackwell, 1992, 1995).

Crouch, Andy. *Culture Making: Recovering our Creative Calling* (Downers Grove, IL: InterVarsity Press, 2008).

Davidson, Joe Ann. *Toward a Theology of Beauty: A Biblical Perspective.* (Lanham, MD: University Press of America, 2008).

Davies, Stephen. *The Philosophy of Art.* (Malden, MA: Blackwell, 2006).

Dean, William D. *Coming to A Theology of Beauty.* (Philadelphia: The Westminster Press, 1972).

Derrida, Jacques. *Of Grammatology.* (Baltimore, MD: John Hopkins University Press, 1988).

_____. *Speech and Phenomena.* (Evanston, IL: Northwestern University Press, 1973).

_____. *Writing and Difference.* (Chicago: University of Chicago Press, 1981).

_____. *Theory of the Moral Life.* (New York: Holt, Reinhard and Winston, 1908, 1932, 1960).

Dewey, John. *How We Think.* (Mineola, NY: Dover Publications, 1997).

_____. *The Public and its Problems.* (Athens: Ohio University Press, 1927, 1954).

Dillenberger, John. *A Theology of Artistic Sensibilities: The Visual Arts and the Church.* (New York: Crossroad, 1986).

Dockery, David S, ed. *The Challenge of Postmodernism: An Evangelical Engagement.* (Wheaton, IL: Victor Books, 1995).

Dyrness, William A. *A Primer on Christian Worship: Where We've Been, Where We are, Where We Can Go.* (Grand Rapids: Eerdmans, 2009).

_____. *Reformed Theology and Visual Culture: The Protestant Imagination from Calvin to Edwards.* (New York: Cambridge University Press, 2004).

_____. *Senses of the Soul: Arts and the Visual in Christian Worship.* (Eugene, OR: Cascade Books, 2008).

_____. *The Earth's is God's: A Theology of American Culture.* (Eugene, OR: Wipf and Stock, 1997, 2004).

_____. *Visual Faith: Art, Theology, and Worship in Dialogue.* (Grand Rapids: Baker, 2001).

Eco, Umberto. *The Aesthetics of Thomas Aquinas.* Trans. H. Bredin. (Cambridge, MA: Harvard University Press, 1988).

_____. *Art and Beauty in the Middle Ages.* Trans. H. Bredin. (New Haven, CT: Yale University Press, 1986).

Edwards, Jonathan. *The Religious Affections*. (Carlisle, PA: The Banner of Truth Trust, 1986).

Eldridge, Michael. *Transforming Experience: John Dewey's Cultural Instrumentalism*. (Nashville, TN: Vanderbilt University Press, 1998).

Elwell, Walter A., ed. *Evangelical Dictionary of Theology*. (Grand Rapids, MI: Baker Books, 1984).

Erickson, Millard. *Evangelical Interpretation: Perspectives on Hermeneutical Issues*. (Grand Rapids, MI: Baker Books, 1993).

_____. *Evangelical Left: Encountering Postconservative Evangelical Theology*. (Grand Rapids, MI: Baker Books, 1997).

_____. Gadamer, Hans-George. *Truth and Method*. Second edition. (New York: The Continuum Publishing, Co., 1998).

Eusden, John Dykstra and John H. Westerhoff III. *Sensing Beauty: Aesthetics, the Human Spirit, and the Church*. (Cleveland, OH: United Church Press, 1998).

Farley, Edward. *Faith and Beauty: A Theological Aesthetic*. (Burlington, VT: Ashgate, 2001).

Flew, Antony. *A Dictionary of Philosophy*. Revised second edition. (New York: St. Martin's Press, 1979).

Flower, Elizabeth and Murray Murphey. *A History of Philosophy in America*. 2 volumes. (New York: Capricorn, 1977).

Forte, Bruno. *The Portal of Beauty: Towards a Theology in Aesthetics*. (Grand Rapids, MI: Eerdmans, 2008).

Gaebelein, Frank E., ed. *The Christian, The Arts, and Truth: Regaining the Vision of Greatness*. (Portland, OR: Multnomah Press, 1985).

Gilbert, Katharine, and Helmut Kuhn. *A History of Aesthetics*. Revised edition. (New York: Dover, 1972).

Gillespie, Michael Allen. *The Theological Origins of Modernity*. (Chicago: University of Chicago Press, 2008).

Guinness, Os. *Dining with the Devil: The Megachurch Movement Flirts with Modernity*. (Grand Rapids, MI: Baker, 1993).

Grenz, Stanley, and Roger E. Olson. *20th Century Theology: God & the World in a Transitional Age*. (Downers Grove, IL: InterVarsity, 1992).

Hart, David Bentley. *The Beauty of the Infinite: The Aesthetics of Christian Truth*. (Grand Rapids, MI: Eerdmans, 2003).

Hazelton, Roger. *A Theological Approach to Art.* (Nashville, TN: Abingdon Press, 1967).

Herbert, David. *Religion and Civil Society: Rethinking Public Religion in the Contemporary World.* (Burlington, VA: Ashgate, 2003).

Hickman, Larry A. *Reading Dewey: Interpretations for a Postmodern Generation.* (Bloomington, IN: Indiana University Press, 1998).

Hildebrand, David. *Dewey: A Beginner's Guide.* (Oxford, UK: Oneworld, 2008).

Hofstadter, Albert, and Richard Kuhns. *Philosophies of Art & Beauty: Selected Readings in Aesthetics from Plato to Heidegger.* (Chicago: University of Chicago Press, 1964).

Hook, Sydney. *John Dewey: An Intellectual Portrait.* (New York: The John Day Company, 1939).

James, William. *Pragmatism.* (Cambridge, MA: Harvard University Press, 1907, 1978).

Jay, Martin. *Songs of Experience: Modern Americans and the European Variations on a Universal Theme.* (Berkeley, CA: University of California Press, 2005).

Jensen, Robin. M. *The Substance of Things Seen: Art, Faith, and the Christian Community.* (Grand Rapids, MI: Eerdmans, 2004).

Jensen, Robin M., and Kimberly J. Vrudny. *Visual Theology: Forming and Transforming the Community through the Arts.* (Collegeville, MN: Liturgical Press, 2009).

Kreeft, Peter. *Christianity for Modern Pagans: Pascal's Pensées.* (San Francisco: Ignatius Press, 1993).

Kroeber A. L. and C. Kluckhohn, *Culture: Critical Review of Concepts and Definitions.* (New York: Random House, 1952).

Kuklick, Bruce. *Churchmen and Philosophers: From Jonathan Edwards to John Dewey.* (New Haven: Yale University Press, 1985).

Kuo, David. *Tempting Faith: An Inside Story of Political Seduction.* (New York: Free Press, 2006).

Kuspit, Donald. *The End of Art.* (Cambridge, UK: Cambridge University Press, 2004).

Laeuchli, Samuel. *Religion and Art in Conflict: Introduction to a Cross-Disciplinary Task.* (Philadelphia: Fortress Press, 1980).

Lubbock, Jules. *Storytelling in Christian Art from Giotto to Donatello.* (New Haven, CT: Yale University Press, 2006).

Maleuvre, Didier. *The Religion of Reality: Inquiry into the Self, Art, and Transcendence.* (Washington: The Catholic University of America Press, 2006).

Martin, James Alfred Jr. *Beauty and Holiness: The Dialogue Between Aesthetics and Religion.* (Princeton, NJ: Princeton University Press, 1990).

Martland, Thomas R. *Religion as Art: An Interpretation.* (Albany, NY: State of New York Press, 1981).

McDermott, John J. *The Culture of Experience: Philosophical Essays in the American Grain.* (New York: New York University Press, 1976).

Morgan, David. *The Sacred Gaze: Religious Visual Culture in Theory and Practice.* (Berkeley, CA: University of California Press, 2005).

Mothersill, Mary. *Beauty Restored.* (Oxford: Clarendon Press, 1984, 1986).

Murray, Peter, and Linda Murray. *A Dictionary of Christian Art.* (Oxford, UK: Oxford University Press, 1996).

Navone, John. *Enjoying God's Beauty.* (Collegeville, MN: The Liturgical Press, 1999).

Nieburh, Richard H. *Christ and Culture.* (New York: Harper Torchbooks, 1951).

Olson, David T. *The American Church in Crisis.* (Grand Rapids, MI: Zondervan, 2008).

Pearcey, Nancy. *Saving Leonardo: A Call to Resist the Secular Assault on Mind, Morals, and Meaning.* (Nashville: B&H Publishing, 2010).

_____. *Total Truth: Liberating Christianity from Its Cultural Captivity.* (Wheaton, IL: Crossway, 2004).

Plate, Brent S. *Religion, Art, and Visual Culture: A Cross-Cultural Reader.* (New York: Palgrave, 2002).

Porterfield, Amanda. *The Transformation of American Religion: The Story of a Late Twentieth-Century Awakening.* (Oxford, UK: Oxford University Press, 2001).

Prall, D. W. *Aesthetic Analysis.* (New York: Thomas Y Crowell Publishing, 1936, 1964).

Putnam, Ruth Anna. *The Cambridge Companion to William James.* (Cambridge, UK: Cambridge University Press, 1997).

Rader, Melvin. *A Modern Book of Esthetics. Fourth edition.* (New York: Holt, Rinehart, and Winston, Inc., 1935, 1952, 1960, 1973).

Rainer, Thom. *Effective Evangelistic Churches: Successful Churches Reveal What Works and What Doesn't*. (Nashville, TN: Broadman & Holman, 1996).

Ramm, Bernard. *The Devil, Seven Wormwoods, and God*. (Waco, TX: Word Books, 1977).

Ratner, Sidney, ed. *The Philosopher of the Common Man: Essays in Honor of John Dewey to Celebrate His Eightieth Birthday*. (New York: G. P. Putnam's Sons, 1940).

Rice, Daniel F. *Reinhold Niebuhr and John Dewey: An American Odyssey*. (Albany, NY: State University of New York Press, 1993).

Richter, Peyton, ed. *Perspectives in Aesthetics: Plato to Camus*. (New York: The Odyssey Press, 1967).

Robinson, David C. *God's Grandeur: The Arts and Imagination in Theology. College Theology Society Annual Volume 52*. (Maryknoll, NY: Orbis Books, 1970).

Rockefeller, Steven C. *John Dewey: Religious Faith and Democratic Humanism*. (New York: Columbian University Press, 1991).

Rookmaaker, Hans R. *Modern Art and the Death of a Culture*. (Wheaton, IL: Crossway, 1994).

Rorty, Richard. *Consequences of Pragmatism*. (Minneapolis, MN: University of Minnesota Press, 1982).

_____. *Philosophy and the Mirror of Nature*. (Princeton, NJ: Princeton University Press, 1979).

Ryken, Leland. *The Liberated Imagination: Thinking Christianly About the Arts*. (Wheaton, IL: Harold Shaw Publishers, 1989).

Scheffler, Israel. *Four Pragmatists: A Critical Introduction to Peirce, James, Mead, and Dewey*. (London: Routledge, 1974).

Sherry, Patrick. *Spirit and Beauty: An Introduction to Theological Aesthetics. Second edition*. (London: SCM Press, 1992, 2002).

Shook, John R. *Dewey's Empirical Theory of Knowledge and Reality*. (Nashville, TN: Vanderbilt University Press, 2000).

_____, and Joseph Margolis. *A Companion to Pragmatism*. (Malden, MA: Blackwell, 2009).

Shusterman, Richard. *Performing Live: Aesthetic Alternatives for the Ends of Art*. (Ithica, NY: Cornell University Press, 2000).

_____. *Pragmatic Aesthetics: Living Beauty, Rethinking Art. Second edition*. (Lanham, MD: Rowman & Littlefield Publishers, 2000).

_____. *Surface and Depth: Dialectics of Criticism and Culture.* (Ithaca, NY: Cornell University Press, 2002).

Siedell, Daniel A. *God in the Gallery: A Christian Embrace of Modern Art.* (Grand Rapids, MI: Baker, 2008).

Sweet, Leonard. *The Gospel According to Starbucks.* (Colorado Springs, CO: Waterbrook Press, 2007).

Tamme, Sister Anne Mary. *A Critique of John Dewey's Theory of Fine Art in the Light of the Principles of Thomism. Philosophical Studies, volume 175. Dissertation.* (Washington, D.C: The Catholic University of America Press, 1956).

Tatarakiewicz, Wladyslaw. *History of Aesthetics. Three volumes. Edited by J. Harrell.* (New York: Continuum International Publishing Group, 2005).

Taylor, Richard. *How to Read a Church: A Guide to Symbols and Images in Churches and Cathedrals.* (Mahwah, NJ: HiddenSpring, 2003).

Thiessen, Elsbeth Gesa. *Theological Aesthetics: A Reader.* (Grand Rapids, MI: Eerdmans, 2005).

Treier, Daniel, J., Mark Husbands, and Roger Lundin. *The Beauty of God: Theology and the Arts.* (Downers Grove, IL: InterVarsity, 2007).

Turner, Steve. *Imagine: A Vision for Christians in the Arts.* (Downers Grove, IL: InterVarsity, 2001).

Torgerson, Mark A. *An Architecture of Immanence: Architecture for Worship and Ministry Today.* (Grand Rapids, MI: Eerdmans, 2007).

Van Der Leeuw, Gerardus. *Sacred and Profane Beauty: The Holy in Art.* (Nashville: Abingdon Press, 1963).

Vialdesau, Richard. *Theological Aesthetics: God in Imagination, Beauty, and Art.* (New York: Oxford University Press, 1999).

Van Dyk, Leanne, ed. *A More Profound Alleluia: Theology and Worship in Harmony.* (Grand Rapids, MI: Eerdmans, 2005).

Vanhoozer, Kevin J., ed. *Everyday Theology: How to Read Cultural Texts and Interpret Trends.* (Grand Rapids: Baker, 2007).

Walvoord, John F., ed. *Truth for Today: Bibliotheca Sacra Reader.* (Chicago: Moody Press, 1963).

Wells, David F. *No Place for Truth or Whatever Happened to Evangelical Theology.* (Grand Rapids, MI: Eerdmans, 1993).

White, James F. *A Brief History of Christian Worship.* (Nashville, TN: Abingdon Press, 1993).

_____. *Documents of Christian Worship: Descriptive and Interpretive Sources.* (Louisville, KY: Westminister/John Knox Press, 1992).

Yates, Wilson. *The Arts in Theological Education: New Possibilities for Integration.* (Atlanta, GA: Scholar's Press, 1987).

E.   UNPUBLISHED SOURCES

Shockley, Paul R. "The cognitive sense of illumination in view of postmodern implications." Th.M. Thesis. Dallas Theological Seminary (May 1999).

_____. "How to Bridge the Culture Gap: How John Dewey's Aesthetics May Benefit the Local Church." Ph.diss, Texas A&M University, 2010.

CPSIA information can be obtained
at www.ICGtesting.com
Printed in the USA
LVOW13s0356080618
580020LV00003B/5/P